BALLAD
— OF A —
SOBER
MAN

BALLAD

— OF A —

SOBER MAN

An ER Doctor's
Journey of Recovery

J.D. REMY, M.D.

Published by AnnElise Publications

Edited and designed by Girl Friday Productions
www.girlfridayproductions.com

Design: Paul Barrett
Project management: Alexander Rigby
Image credits: Pixel-Shot/Shutterstock, ShalenaOlena/Shutterstock

ISBN (paperback): 978-1-7354813-0-2
ISBN (ebook): 978-1-7354813-1-9

To my children, who dwell in my heart forever.

CONTENTS

Came to believe that a Power greater than
ourselves could restore us to sanity.
                    —Step Two of the Twelve Steps
                        of Alcoholics Anonymous

PREFACE

Creating a written account of the most difficult and transformative five years of my life was not nearly as much of an artistic challenge as it was a visceral one. The words detailing my days in rehab, flashbacks of scenes with my children, and descriptions of old and new relationships seemed to flow out of my fingers and onto the laptop screen with relative ease. Ironically, it was the rereading and editing of the passages a second and third time that really smacked me down, emotionally speaking. Far too often over those twelve months, while typing away, I would, midsentence, explode into tears or a fit of rage, or otherwise simply melt down into a soggy heap.

The innocent and unsuspecting laptop got shoved violently across the kitchen counter, slammed shut, thrown, or simply covered in saltwater as my mess of a face rested on the keyboard in a state of absolute emotional exhaustion. I have come to recognize that not only were the past experiences vital to my long-term recovery, but so was the very act of recounting them and putting them in a black-and-white, tangible form. The process of developing this book was, undeniably, a portkey in my recovery journey.

At age fifty, I found myself living alone for the first time ever. In September of 2017, a whopping ten months sober, I closed on a house in which I would be the sole human resident (I would adopt my dog Skipper from the pound a week later). Beginning with my childhood years and straight through my higher education, there had always been others cohabitating with me. Courtship and marriage followed quickly after medical school, and from there it was off to the races with career and family. On November 3, 2016, my world caved in around me; on that single day I lost my home, marriage, career, children . . . and almost my life. It was, beyond any doubt, my absolute bottom in every way imaginable. As my mother would convey to me over the phone two days later while I was in my hospital bed, "You are broken, deep in a ravine, and have a mountain to climb."

And climb I did—one baby step, one AA meeting, one job, one relationship, and *one day* at a time.

Recovery from the nightmare of active alcoholism and drug use is very much a rebirth. We emerge kicking, screaming, and terrified into a cold environment, far too glaring and harsh for our oversensitive central nervous systems. We slowly learn how to adjust our senses without the protective, but faulty, shield of euphoria-producing chemicals. Having regularly used alcohol to suppress the emotions I never permitted myself to process and develop, I was forced, in sobriety, to adapt; I had to learn the skills and coping mechanisms needed to handle life situations in a healthy, adult manner. During my drinking years I was certainly capable of dressing myself, showing up, passing exams, attending events, and generally acting civil in my social and professional life; in reality, any decent actor could have managed that. Meanwhile I was, in all respects, emotionally stunted, my development as a human being frozen in time by my self-spun alcoholic cocoon. I trapped myself in a multide-cade stage of spiritual suspended animation.

The day alcohol ceased to flow through my veins, I was completely dysfunctional, an invalid. Much like a spinal trauma victim, I forced myself to relearn how to move, walk, and feel without the "aid" of alcohol. Gaining proficiency in simple tasks took me only a few days or weeks; other tasks will take a lifetime. Some impairments were quickly fixed, some continue to be a work in progress, and still others will remain permanent disabilities that I must learn to accept and work around.

Successfully getting sober is much like successfully getting wealthy—it's slow and methodical, and it requires patience. It is a blessing that alcoholics and addicts never have to do it alone. My recovery required a letting go of my ego-driven independence and trumped-up sense of self-importance; I col-lapsed, figuratively, off my pedestal and into the arms of a car-ing crowd, allowing myself to be held up by the glorious mosh pit of my sober network. I had to, as Tyler Durden exclaimed in the movie *Fight Club*, "Just. Let. Go."

I had been provided with the gift of desperation. As par-adoxical as that sounds, I have found it to hold true. Only through extreme emotional and physical conditions have I been able to overcome my disease, get stronger, and start to evolve. I needed to learn to feel and process previously incon-ceivable and intolerable amounts of anguish and pain to spur my spiritual development and propel myself into a new para-digm of living. Profound grief, rather than making us wither, has the uncanny capacity to expand us, introducing new door-ways in our minds, leading to previously unexplored passages. Facing fears, embracing the *now*, ditching the overindulgence of self, reaching out *for* and *to* help, and staying vulnerable have been the cornerstones to my recovery, modalities that I continue to work with today and every day. Sometimes I feel like the recovery version of the superhero in *Deadpool*, only without Ryan Reynolds's sassiness.

The Alcoholics Anonymous culture is full of seemingly paradoxical sayings—"success through surrender," "giving it away to keep it," and "receiving strength by accepting powerlessness," just to name a few. They didn't make sense to me either at first, but over time and with practice—and a lot of help—these concepts have become clearer to me. As with any skill, progress always seems to come in the form of two steps forward, one step back. I still frequently panic, feel rage, get impulsive or passive-aggressive, indulge in self-pity, or generally get pissed off. To quote the nineties band Bush: "Everything zen. I don't think so." Still, every moment must be a stand-alone experience, taken with a healthy dose of acceptance and patience.

I almost titled this book *Letters to Hannah* since so much of the pain in my recovery seems to involve the loss of my relationships with my children. To underscore the degree of pain and grief that served as the foundation for my recovery successes, I was fully prepared to insert various selections of the hundreds of emails I sent to them over the years. In the end, I decided that even though Hannah, Robert, and Toby were instrumental in my healing, they were only one part (albeit a large chunk) of so many vital experiences that factored in.

I wrote these pages while I learned how to live an alcohol- and chemical-free life. Strangely enough, ditching the vodka (my drug of choice) was the "easy" part. It was maturing in sobriety that required massive effort. With the ever-present help from the Twelve Steps of Alcoholics Anonymous, sponsors, therapists, family, and friends, I was able to successfully navigate between my own personal Scylla and Charybdis to this moment. Sirens' songs were resisted, and my cyclops was smote. Alas, even while I wrestled with the challenges described in these pages, a new mammoth one presented itself:

I found myself facing, as a rehabilitated emergency physician, the biggest pandemic our planet has seen in over a century.

Within these chapters, you may recognize phases of growth, drawing parallels to the challenges that every baby, toddler, child, and teen goes through in "leveling up" to the next change of life. There could have been no other way; there were no shortcuts. My doors of perception have been flung open, and as I step through, I do so carefully, methodically, and fully aware, all the while holding your hand. I feel truly humbled and grateful . . . one day at a time.

Please note: some names have been changed to protect privacy.

CHAPTER 1

WITH A WHIMPER

I watched from my cot through bleary, stinging eyes while Bathrobe Tommy paced back and forth, reciting scripture in front of the room's only window. He spoke loudly when reading directly from his well-worn Bible, transitioning to more of a whisper when he had a given passage memorized. It was no concern of mine, of course; my so-called roommate could do whatever the fuck he felt like doing. As he shuffled across cracked linoleum in bunny slippers, his MO seemed to be to read to himself, or God, or the nailed-down nightstand, or to whomever would listen:

> And Jacob was left alone. And a man wrestled with him until the breaking of the day. When the man saw that he did not prevail against Jacob, he touched his hip socket, and Jacob's hip was put out of joint as he wrestled with him. . . . Then he said, "Your name shall

no longer be called Jacob, but Israel, for you
have striven with God and with men, and have
prevailed."

I lay there at the far end of my echo tunnel, hearing him
drone on with verse after verse of Deuteronomy, Numbers,
Revelation, whatever. My flimsy hospital gown was as thin as
the single bed sheet provided me, and I felt the chill of antiseptic air. The shade, meant to block out the outside world,
managed to have a perfectly placed tear in the fabric, letting
in a single beam of light from an outside streetlamp that hit
my eyes through the night as I attempted sleep. Sleep: ha, that
was a joke. My dreams or visions or hallucinations or whatever
they were would build momentum and explode in a fury out
of my head all night long, like a shaken-up bottle of soda. They
would reach a crescendo and bubble over, reset, give me a brief
respite, and start up all over again.

Wayne checked on us. Again. It seemed as if every med
tech on the lockdown unit of the Penuel Psychiatric Inpatient
Center was named Wayne. Each was half orderly, half security
guard, and they would monitor the halls, occasionally peeking into the patient rooms. If somebody got loud or disruptive, or if a fight broke out, they were on the scene in seconds,
attempting to control the mayhem. Occasionally, I would see
a Wayne snoozing in one of the lounge chairs set up at strate-
gic points along the hallway. I knew this because in between
my head's fizzy vision cycles, I would rise up and quietly coast
the corridor, carefully choosing when to say hello. Too many
hellos and you were eyed with suspicion, too few and you were
seen as antisocial, something that could be reported to the
morning staff. I really didn't need the publicity; I was trying to
keep my head down and get out of this hallucination as soon as
humanly possible.

Freedom of movement on the lockdown unit was limited, so I walked within its confines in my laceless running shoes until the common area opened up for the morning at six. This was my day's exercise—up and down the hallways several times, around a corner to the locked unit doors, and then back to the nurses' station. It was a far cry from the rolling hills of western Virginia I had been accustomed to, but it would have to do.

▲▲▲▲▲

I was able to cope reasonably well because, of course, none of this was real. It was some grand vision, some twisted fairy tale from which I would soon awaken, have a coffee, and go on an actual run in the morning air with my actual dog, Tiberius. As I made my way into the now open recreation room and found a seat, I was only vaguely aware of my surroundings. A stout, middle-aged woman wearing a purple terry-cloth bathrobe and a 1987 makeup style sat down next to me, extolling the virtues of taking a break from her role as CEO of a large multinational company to spend time on the unit "away from the executive sycophants." Across the lounge from us, a gigantic disheveled woman, wedged into her bariatric wheelchair, sat screaming at a TV tuned to the network morning shows. I heard my name called out and rose to receive my breakfast tray from Morning Wayne. I brought it to the large center table and sat down with my plate of reconstituted eggs. This was morning number two for me, and I quickly realized the only things that stank worse than the breakfasts were my coresidents. I was in a nightmare, of that there was no doubt, and I was waiting for my bladder to wake me for a dream-stopping bathroom break.

I also quickly recognized medication time, because at eight o'clock on the dot, the other inpatients abandoned their breakfasts and congregated around the pharmacy window in the hall, like pigeons to some discarded bread. I personally had no interest in taking a little paper cup of pills. *Help me, Randle McMurphy.* Yet I knew if I didn't get in line, I might be flagged as "uncooperative." I stood next to a serious-looking man who bore an uncanny resemblance to George Costanza, the overweight, balding best friend in *Seinfeld.* Although when he spoke to me, or rather at me with his hand on his forehead most of the time, his tone and demeanor were slow and relaxed, his volume almost a whisper. He stated he was an engineer for an architectural firm and had checked himself in, just as the delusional CEO woman had, to take a break from his life and to mellow out. The contrast was not lost on me. If George Costanza ever took tranquilizers and antidepressants, he would be this guy.

He described to me the difference between a voluntary admission and a "voluntold" one. The voluntary residents of this lockdown unit, and there were a few, were not under any formal temporary detaining order and were free to come and go, free to discharge themselves and return to the outside environment that had landed them in the psychiatric ward in the first place. Those here under voluntold conditions, like me, were technically free to skip out at any time against medical advice, but a shitstorm of negative consequences would rain down on them afterward if they did so. Even though I felt like I did not belong, discharging myself would most likely result in the end of my professional license, my health, and my life.

Fortunately for me, it was all a wacky dream from which the inevitability of a new morning or a full bladder would soon rescue me.

It just so happened that I had been admitted on Friday night; from my years working at a hospital as an emergency physician, I fully understood the implications of that timing. Nothing would be happening with me, clinically speaking, until Monday. It was Sunday. Even though psychiatrists existed

24-7 in the medical world, they were still part of a system that largely operated within banker's hours, with an on-call doc a page away for emergencies. It didn't require a doctor to open a med window and serve meal trays. The TV was the main source of entertainment; Saturdays and Sundays were the quiet days, when we were safely contained and kept alive while the majority of medical professionals had their weekends (except ER and inpatient docs). New weekend admits were seen by the psychiatrist Monday morning. Fisticuffs between patients could be handled by the Waynes, or if a patient got particularly violent, the emergency room. There was plenty of staff around to feed us or clean up when somebody shit on the floor.

So proceeded my first weekend on the *other side* of the locked door. I was able to occupy my time with old favorites like Monopoly, Battleship, and Yahtzee. I had to be careful about how I played with the other residents. I was too smart for them. Get too aggressive or win too much against the wrong inmate, and shouting would almost certainly ensue. The midmorning activities coordinator came in to engage us in a game of charades. Perhaps that's when I cracked my first authentic smile. I vaguely recall a young woman with an advanced body mass index attempting to act out a scene from *The Lord of the Rings*. At first I wasn't sure if she was trying to pretend to be an orc or a supersized Gollum. Next, an overmedicated, frail man was tasked with *Weekend at Bernie's*; this was pretty easy for him. I found myself both grotesquely amused and impressed with my imagination, here in my dream state.

There was always television. Endless, endless television. The first TV hour in the morning was largely dedicated to the news junkies in the crowd, as well as sports and weather. Several residents sat motionless, transfixed by the screen all day long. For the rest of us, a random movie would hold our attention until a meal presented itself, a fight broke out, or the med window opened.

Watching the movie *The Blind Side* with Sandra Bullock, I surprised myself with how I was able to predict each part with such vivid recall. I had only seen this movie once, years before. How did I store this film in my subconscious so completely? I even cried at Ms. Bullock's performance in the final scene. As all of this was a figment of my mind, I thought, *Damn, Dr. Remy, you have so much locked-up intelligence, to dream a seven-year-old movie so thoroughly. If only everybody knew: the ER doc in the loony bin can remember an Academy Award–winning performance with incredible mental precision.*

So many of the daily routines we take for granted in the "real world" are not necessarily standard in a mental health psychiatric unit. If I wanted to shave, I had to request an aide to sign out a razor at the nurses' station and accompany me to the bathroom to observe, lest I use the sharp edge to commit an act of violence against myself or someone else. There was a zero-tolerance policy for shiny objects with sharp edges in the asylum.

That second morning, I did shave, and I returned the razor thinking I was finished, only to realize I had missed a small spot on my chin. Wayne scowled in annoyance when we had to go through the whole process of going to the nurses' station, signing out the razor kit, and returning to the bathroom to finish the job. The situation was even worse for flossing. Since the dental floss came on spools, and nothing with which we could potentially hang ourselves was permitted on the unit, dental hygiene was verboten. Even in this ugly, drawn-out alcoholic nightmare, I could not envision a scenario where a person could conceivably asphyxiate himself or someone else with dental floss. Shoelaces . . . maybe.

▲▲▲▲▲

Time seems to distort in REM sleep. When you're asleep, minutes can feel like days.

In those first two days, I probably spent more time studying the ceiling tiles in my dream room than anything else. I tried repeatedly to force my brain into a consciousness reboot. *Wake up, Joe, please wake up. Go for your morning run. Make the kids' breakfast before school—the toast you cut into strips that they love so much, with the melted margarine in a cup on the side for dipping. Kiss your wife when she emerges from the bedroom all sleepy eyed. Get to your shift on time in the emergency room.*

Bathrobe Tommy, all six feet plus of him, shuffled in the corner, Bible in hand, offering up a few passages out loud. Lying there, surrounded by bare walls painted a pale mustard, I watched as the November evening's dusk faded and the piercing rays of that damn streetlamp snuck through the rip in the shade to reach my left eyeball.

Ironically, it was nighttime when I felt most awake, most in touch with myself, with the moment. My tremor seemed to come out strongly after midnight. *Could these scenes I am acting out be real?* I had thus far declined my PRN Librium at the medication window—mainly because I felt some need to suffer a little bit in this dream, experience the sensation of a pickled brain drying out, so that just maybe I could do the same in the real world. Memories materialized of sneaking to my basement back home and popping several Valiums from my hidden stash. I suspect refusing a tranquilizer was one standing order that the on-call psychiatrist didn't care about; since it was offered "as needed," I had the right to decline. Some of my coresidents were not so lucky, although I don't suspect they saw it that way, considering how they swarmed like hungry carp to that magical window when it opened. This was a little world where the highlights of the day for its citizens were the medication window and mealtimes, and I was having little of either. So there I would lie, supine on my creaky cot, trembling and waiting for the palpitations, sweats, and racing thoughts to pass, listening to Tommy's Bible recitations:

> For you have been born again, not of perish-
> able seed, but of imperishable, through the liv-
> ing and enduring word of God.

The thumping in my chest was like the business end of a boxing glove pounding my sternum. I thought it was going to knock me off the cot. Perspiration pooled under my arms and along my lower back and then dried up just as quickly, causing me to shiver. My hands were like those of a Parkinson's patient. The compilation of all these sensations felt like an extreme version of influenza combined with a bad acid trip. It all felt, well, like withdrawal. Very, very real withdrawal.

▲▲▲▲▲

Monday morning after "awakening," I endured a tepid trickle shower, donned my only set of clothes—gray drawstring sweatpants and a brown cotton T-shirt, freshly laundered by Overnight Wayne—and slipped into my laceless running shoes for my third morning hallway walk. When the day-shift crew showed up, I observed the shift change sign-out: the semistructured ritual of an off-going night crew getting the daylight staff up to speed on the unit. I had viewed this all weekend in abbreviated form, and I'd had to remind myself that I was not part of the process, I was not on staff, and there-fore I had nothing to report. *Toto, I don't think we're in Kansas anymore.* On Monday morning, as expected, things were a bit livelier and more detailed because, after all, the denizens of the real world were getting caffeinated and back to work after a weekend with their families.

Reality was starting to infiltrate; I was waking up to the fact that this all might really be happening. My dream-excuse denial was starting to melt into the shocking awareness of my circumstances. Watching that shift change was a wake-up call. I was not at home about to emerge from some convoluted nightmare to have my coffee and run with my dog. I was an inpatient in a psychiatric facility about to experience the workday routine of a Monday.

No. I decided that I needed to be on the other side of the fence, the proper side for Dr. Remy—emergency physician, saver of countless lives, leader of medical mission trips to Haiti—loved and respected by all. I had to reassert myself as the important doctor in control that I was. After the staff's morning huddle, I mingled with the aides, offering to help them take vital signs and providing input and commentary when I overheard medical conversations. My recommendations were met with blank and dismissive stares. I grew upset; my ego was having a tantrum. *Doesn't anyone around here know who the fuck I am?*

When my blood pressure was taken and found to be significantly elevated, I intellectualized to the young aide and offered her my diagnosis: alcohol withdrawal and mild DTs ("delirium tremens" according to the medical texts); my inhibitory neurotransmitters were offline and my excitatory pathways were surging, and my CIWA score was probably in the double digits. For my shared insights, all I received in return was an empty, robotic smile.

▲▲▲▲▲

The unit's activity director was a petite woman in her twenties who seemed to be entering her third trimester of pregnancy. Fresh faced and youthful appearing, she kept a friendly but detached demeanor while attempting to engage the group in

bingo, charades, or whichever activity she deemed appropriate for the afternoon. Some residents were enthused, others
indifferent, and still others milled about in the background,
clearly "checked out." I participated in the games with feigned
interest, as I knew it was advantageous to lay the groundwork
for that afternoon's patient reviews. It would be noted and discussed behind their closed meeting-room door that I played
well with others. Hallucination or not, I was getting the fuck
out of here as fast as possible. I observed her, realizing she was
just the type I dated in medical school (minus the pregnancy
part). I contemplated engaging in side conversation with her,
maybe flirting, letting her know about my background and the
MD behind my name, but opted against it. I wondered if she
was faking as much enthusiasm about working here as I was
about her being here.

That evening it was my turn to use the ward's shared
patient telephone for my permitted fifteen-minute call (all cell
phones were confiscated at check-in). Lights had been turned
down, as they were nightly, and I sat with the phone at my end
of the hallway, away from the center of activity, to contact my
family. At almost seventy-two hours into my time on the unit,
my tremor had graduated to visible shaking, to the point where
holding the receiver steady against my ear took effort. I had
declined the after-dinner Librium dose, which was a mistake,
as I knew the long-acting tranquilizer would have steadied
my shakes and my racing brain, as well as stopped the boxing
glove in my chest.

I dialed my home number. I had to tell my wife that this
was just not doable anymore. Staying here was a mix-up and
not what I needed. I had to get back to my job, my family, and
my life. She had a brother who lived on this side of Virginia,
not too far from where I thought I was. I could easily use my
manipulative wiles to slip past the locked unit doors and find
my way outside. I could make my way to a predetermined

meeting point—maybe at some mall parking lot, maybe a clearing in the woods. She and I could arrange it all. I could stay in the shadows and run—after all, I had the shoes (without laces, though, which could be a problem).

Since I had neither money nor any form of identification in my possession, maybe I would have to hitchhike. But as a really smart dude, I could conjure up some workaround; plus it wasn't that cold outside. If I could only escape out of this madness, I could find a rally point and lie low, where my brother-in-law—who had no knowledge of any of this, and was lukewarm on me to begin with—could leave his wife and new baby, in the middle of the night, and come find me. Rescue me. Take me back to the loving arms of my wife and my children and my life from only a few days prior. And then I could resume my daily routine as dad, husband, ER doc . . . and be rid of this nightmare. It all was a well-crafted plan and made plenty of sense. *Awesome plan, dude . . . while you're at it, why don't you conjure up a mute Indian chief to lift a marble water fountain and heave it through the social room window? I mean, who the fuck do you think you're kidding, Joe?*

And I was the sane one here.

▲▲▲▲▲

Three nights earlier, in the darkness of midnight, I had been unceremoniously dumped at the doorstep of the Penuel Psychiatric Inpatient Center after an extended ride in the back of an ambulance wearing only my gray drawstring sweatpants and brown cotton T-shirt. I had no wallet, no form of ID, and no hope of returning to where I had come from. There had been no grand send-off—no hugs and kisses from a supportive wife and children, no tears of hope, no "Now go get well; we'll come visit and are praying for you!" That simply didn't exist. In my oblivious state, I thought I could have saved the medical transport fees and driven myself (and then I would have had an escape vehicle). Maybe I could have just been discharged home from my hometown hospital, where I had spent the previous night, and then checked into Penuel the next day with my family at my side. The doctors should have let me go home first; after all, I knew what I was doing. I'd helped patients in similar situations for years, decades even. I should have been more insistent and pushed for my way; they would have listened to me, and the situation should have . . . should be . . . should, should, *should*.

I was led by Overnight Wayne into the facility through the after-hours entrance, where I heard the sharp metallic click of the front door locking behind me. It was clear that these doors could unlock from the inside only if the night security guard at the desk made it so. I glanced out the entrance window and my medical chariot had vanished. The ambulance—the last vestige of my old life—was now gone and the outside dark was absolute. I was entering into a new dimension, my own personal Alice-style rabbit hole, where a tall black man in a white linen uniform and matching shoes led me through a dimly lit lobby abutting the lockdown unit. *I'm late! I'm late! For a very important date!* The next set of doors—those to the inner sanctum—heavy, gray, and windowless, opened for us, and we walked through. These latched behind us with something that was not a click, but more of an authoritative thunk. The lit keypad I noticed on the wall clinched it. Ain't no waltzing out of this joint. I was led to a side room, a small changing area no larger than eight feet square, more of a brushed-stainless-steel box, where I was liberated of my small overnight bag and asked to undress for a full body search. My clothes were examined and my shoelaces were taken; a disturbing memory bubbled to the surface of my mind. I remembered a time many years prior, when, as a young doctor, I raced from the ER up to the psych ward of my hometown hospital to respond to a "code blue"—hospital vernacular for cardiac arrest. Our attempted resuscitation of a mental health patient who had managed to hang himself by the neck on a door hinge using his own contraband shoelaces did not end well. It may have been a different hospital, but I was entering *that* place now. I was entering the *shoelace-free zone*.

Once I was gowned and out of the changing room, I was brought to the nurses' station, where I stood under the fluorescent lights. The changing room door behind me locked shut. *I swear to God this place is a series of fucking one-way locks.* I inspected my surroundings more closely. The work area was a circular array of counters and desks, computers and filing cabinets. Glowing white hallways radiated out in every direction. I was assigned a room at the far end of one of them.

▲▲▲▲▲

The nightmare was paralyzing in a way no other nightmare had ever been. Glaring images flashed for a few seconds and then were replaced by others in such rapid-fire succession that there was no time to register what was actually going on. My children laughing, my room at my hometown hospital, scattered empty plastic vodka bottles, my dog. . . . The scenes increased in pace and intensity until my physical body spasmed under the thin bed sheet. My eyes, half-aware, opened, and the beam from the streetlamp outside the window tickled my brain. It was not a friendly tickle, but one of those harsh, digging tickles one receives from a mean-spirited playmate. Bolting upright in bed, I glanced over at Bathrobe Tommy; he was facing away from me in a fetal position, breathing deeply. Thank God he did not snore—or would it really have mattered?

As bad as the nightmares were that third night, lying awake and keeping still on my cot was beyond me. I got up to pee and looked out into the hallway. A few doors down, Wayne was snoring in his lounge chair on wheels. He had covered himself up with a blanket and appeared as comfortable as anyone who worked hospital night duty could be. I walked by, barefoot, and glanced at the nurses' station. More snoozy attendants. If I only had my trusty nightstand bottle . . . a few gulps of that firewater always got me another couple of hours' shut-eye.

The social room was dark. Moving along, I stared unbelievingly at the well-secured exit door; I just stood there, in my sweatpants and plain brown T-shirt. (Not wanting to lose myself completely, after the first night I stopped wearing the standard-issue hospital gown.) All was quiet on the ward.

I made my way back down the hallway, glancing through the windows at the frozen hands on the activity room clock-face. Four minutes had passed since I last checked. *Woo-hoo.* I went back to my room. I found Tommy awake and sitting up in bed, book in hand, whispering passages from Genesis.

Let there be light.

▲▲▲▲▲

The next afternoon, day four, I was unable to focus on anything except mathematics, and went into personal accounting mode. During afternoon activity, instead of participating in "I Spy," I took a paper towel and crayon and, sitting at the activities table among the games of Monopoly and Chutes and Ladders, made an accounting of my household's liquid assets from memory, line by line. I calculated the number of years I could be unemployed (I was resigned to the reality that I would never be allowed to practice medicine again) and still have enough money put away for my family to survive. I scribbled numbers, creating subtotals in the margins—cash in the safe deposit box, my whole-life policy, the rainy-day fund. I had gold and silver coins and other hard assets. I felt like I might actually be awake, that *shit was getting real.*

I took a disturbing comfort in the knowledge that the end result of decades of professional sweat and toil could sustain us all until a strategy for regular income could be worked out. Initially I could be at home, and hopefully my wife could work, and perhaps I could eventually find a job, maybe in a lab or as an online medical consultant, and we could live simply until my family received the life insurance payout after my anticipated death. Thank God I had been religious about monthly contributions into the kids' college funds.

CEO Sissy waddled over, plopped herself beside me, and offered her expertise in corporate finance. She was still in her nightgown with half a sandwich in her hand; she reeked from the combination of peanut butter and unwashed armpits. I became paranoid. What was her angle? Was that other dude looking over my shoulder? I decided I had better destroy my tabulations. I tore up the paper, but not before imprinting the bottom-line numbers in my head so I could divulge them to my wife when she arrived with the rescue team.

Daytime hours on the ward were beyond monotonous. There were only so many times I could watch the news clips, go to my room, or hear the same conversations played out over and over again among some of the long-term residents. I tried to bide my time by having "intellectual" conversations with the staff, losing myself in movies (impossible), and listening to Tommy's Bible recitals. I repeatedly calculated the hours, still in double-digits, since my last alcoholic beverage. I would check myself, holding my hands out horizontally in front of me, to see if my tremors were subsiding or if I was going into full-blown DTs. I had the capacity to do this; I was, after all, the smartest doctor in the crazy house.

On that fourth day, I acquiesced to the Librium offer. The tremors and racing thoughts had come to dominate almost every moment, but those were not the symptoms that ultimately changed my mind. In the wee hours of that morning, long after I recognized that falling asleep was futile, while I stared at my bedroom ceiling, I observed out of my peripheral vision a large insect—about the size of a woman's hand— scuttle up the wall, then vanish.

A few minutes later, another hand-sized scuttling critter . . . visual hallucinations. *Fuck.* I was just under five days sober, and right on schedule for DTs. This was the last thing I needed—a clinical setback to keep me stuck longer in this godforsaken place. It was Tuesday morning, the day the head honchos would hold rounds and ultimately make decisions about me. They could not know about this. I had to look normal, relaxed, asymptomatic. I needed an Oscar-winning performance today, and a benzodiazepine tranquilizer would help me keep it together to dance for them. That morning I lined up at the med window with the other fruitcakes and graciously accepted my Librium. Ken Kesey's Mr. McMurphy would have been soooo disappointed.

▲▲▲▲▲

The clinical team panel consisted of the lead psychiatrist, a psychiatric social worker, a psychiatry resident, the lead unit nurse, a medical student, and the case manager. After being summoned in from the hallway, I entered the crowded room and sat opposite the gang at a dull wooden table.

Here we go. It's showtime, baby.

Dr. Sanjay was a distinguished-appearing, gray-haired man of Pakistani descent who very much looked his part in a blazer and tie. His glasses were balanced on the tip of his nose as he paged through the binder containing my chart. The interview began.

I introduced myself and proceeded with the usual name, rank, and serial number. After this, I was asked essentially to tell my "story." This would be the very first of many recountings of the series of unfortunate events that had ultimately led my ass into the chair in which I sat, paying homage before the mental health tribunal. In this first run-through of the intimate details, I spoke slowly, carefully, and truthfully, through the brain of an alcoholic who needed an Oscar-winning performance. The Librium was doing its job, and I was steady and controlled, but far from polished. Their subtle facial expressions suggested I got the important messages across. Even in my impaired state of consciousness I was, after all, still Joseph David Remy, MD—veteran of the emergency room battlefield, commander of rescue squads, and leader of Haiti missions; when motivated, I could sell snow to an Eskimo. Yes, even in my diminished stature on a mental ward, I felt confident I could convince the panel that I was truly one of them and deserved to be on their side of the table. Someday I would learn about my character defects, but this was not that day, and some of my most severe flaws were on display—ego, pride, narcissism, and manipulation.

I waxed poetic before the team for one primary purpose—to get myself an honorable discharge from that loony bin ASAP and get the hell home. Leaving AMA, or against medical advice, I had realized at that point, was not a viable option; I needed to jump through the proper hoops with precision in order to keep my file neat and tidy. Winning over the mental health panel was the means to that end. When Dr. Sanjay recommended to the team his short-term plan—immediate release from Penuel and transfer to the professionals' residential treatment program across campus, I felt relief in my partial victory.

I'd like to thank the Academy . . .

▲▲▲▲▲

Later that afternoon, during a round of Battleship with Mellow George, a staff member came over to inform me that, because of procedural and processing issues, it could be another "day or two" before my transfer. *Fan-fucking-tastic. I get to wander around this fishbowl among the schizoaffective and bipolars even longer,* I thought. More *Judge Judy* and reruns of *Full House.* More smelly meal trays. More group games with some postadolescent activities director who didn't know (or care) about shit. More sleepless nights with the lamppost light and Bathrobe Tommy.

▲▲▲▲▲

That evening, I put my call time to good use and contacted my investment company to liquidate assets and have the funds transferred to the marital joint checking account. I was surprised how transferring one's own money around can be a significant challenge when attempted from a landline, with no forms of ID, no internet access, and absolutely nothing to prove to some low-level call center rep on the other end of the line that I actually was who I said I was. I'm not sure I would have believed me—liquidating stocks while sitting on the floor in the hallway of a locked sanitorium. Thank God I remembered my passwords, date of birth, and social security number.

I may have been a self-absorbed, selfish, arrogant prick in other aspects of my previous existence, but buffering my family with a substantial financial cushion through the years with rainy-day money had always been a priority, and now it was fucking pouring. I had taken out loans for my higher education, coming out of medical school in mammoth six-figure debt, and was obsessed with paying it off as quickly as possible and building the household's nest egg while I was capable of doing so, in case I flamed out and became unhirable. With the transfer of assets done, my wife could run the house and pay bills for a few months if need be, while I was doing whatever I was doing. I hung up the phone, sighed with relief, and proceeded to the med window, open for evening business, the line stretching down the hall.

I quickly learned the dos and don'ts of the medication line. Avoid the mad rush to line up fifteen minutes before the window opens and the subsequent jostling for position; hold back and give way for the most annoying patients (CEO Sissy, for example) to line up, so as not to get caught in endless conversation; expect certain patients to engage in long, heated conversations with the nurse dispensing at the window; when it's your turn, swallow the pills and step aside before the residents behind you lose their shit over the delay. Medication time at the *funny farm* was serious business and any negative patient interactions were magnified. Personally, I would have been just as happy to avoid the line altogether—the best chairs in the activities room were briefly available during that time. Unfortunately my tremor and racing thoughts would rapidly worsen if I passed up my pills. Perhaps the Librium was my first taste of *acceptance*.

▲▲▲▲▲

After dinner, midway through a round of Boggle, I was pulled away by the nurse manager into one of the smaller interview rooms. Apparently Dr. Sanjay and his management team had made the decision that I was safely out of DT danger, and they were hastening my release from the unit and transfer to the residential recovery treatment center. Arrangements were being made for the next day. During her disclosure, a petite, wiry, and hip-looking young man with shoulder-length, dark-brown hair and Native American features came in and introduced himself as Tony, a representative of the treatment center. He proceeded to give me the overview on my upcoming stay at the "East Coast's premier alcohol and addiction recovery center." I felt as if I were getting a life insurance pitch by an overexuberant salesman. I thought to myself, *Really, dude? What fucking choice do I have?* At this point I had abandoned my plans to escape into the forest. During the previous day's call home, my wife told me, "You need to stay as long as it takes—two months, six months, *whatever.*" I felt like a shivering, naked Alaskan tourist getting the hard sell from a parka salesman.

▲▲▲▲▲

My final night on the ward, as I dozed intermittently on my cot, I noticed a distinct lack of spoken Bible passages. I looked over; Tommy was silent but restless in his bed, constantly shifting under his sheet. After another moment, I heard him groan and watched him hang his head over the bed and proceed to vomit loudly and copiously onto the floor. This was followed up with dry retching, and I jumped out of bed, ran to the bathroom, and fetched the wastepaper basket. I was far too late. He had managed to spew chunks of his partially digested dinner all across his side of the room. I went into the hall and called the monitor (Wayne was off that night) and went back into the bathroom for a washrag. I warmed it under the sink tap and brought it over to Tommy. He was sitting motionless on the clean side of the bed. While the monitor cleaned up the floor, I tended to Tommy, washing his face, helping him into a fresh undershirt, and sitting him in the corner chair while a nurse stripped and remade his bed. The smell of the room was horrid, reminding me of the busy nights in the ER during the local university's homecoming weekend. I asked Tommy how he felt, and he told me he was better, and we tucked his six-foot skeleton frame back into bed. I lay down in my own.

After several minutes, just as I was convinced that I heard his breathing pattern become more regular, Tommy sat bolt upright again. Fortunately, I'd had the foresight to place a mop bucket, which we'd lined with a trash bag, next to the head of his bed. I had prepared myself for the eventuality of another sleepless night. I sat next to him, tilting the bucket as he emptied the remnants of his stomach contents into the pail. When he finished for the moment, I swapped out the dirty liner with a fresh one (a task relegated to me because I was the roommate), laid Tommy back in his bed (again), pulled up his bedsheet, and replaced the washrag over his forehead. I went back down the hall to the nurses' station to inquire who the on-call physician was who would attend to this matter and was told by the sleepy, annoyed-looking nurse aide that they would call if there was a problem. If there was a problem? A seventy-five-year-old man, on numerous psychotropic meds, with multiple episodes of vomiting likely to continue, and nobody was being called? The emergency physician in me was restless and disturbed.

I turned back toward our hallway and thanked the monitor, now comfortably nestled back in his hallway sofa chair. Upon entering our room, I saw Tommy was supine in bed, washrag intact. Although it was dark, I could see that he was not asleep. Something was askew here, not right. His Bible, usually in his hands even as he slept, was instead on the floor, open and face down. I went over and picked it up. It was slightly larger than a deck of cards, worn and flexible, the bound leather amazingly soft. I placed it next to him in bed, where it belonged, and asked him how he was feeling, and received a simple response. "I'm OK, thank you for your kindness." These were the first words I ever heard Tommy utter that were not scripture.

Unfortunately for everyone involved, the story of the night did not end there. Tommy dry heaved in his bucket another half dozen times overnight. All his stomach contents had long been evacuated, but the anguished stuttering sounds of an old vomiting man tore through the nighttime silence. After each occurrence, I would get up, check the bucket, help him lie back down, and refresh the washcloth on his head. I sat next to him and picked up his Bible. I opened it and read to him.

> So do not fear, for I am with you; do not be dismayed, for I am your God. I will strengthen you and help you; I will uphold you with my righteous right hand.

A new sense of purpose came over me. As I comforted my roommate and began to wake up to my new reality, I had, for a few moments that night, stepped outside my own insanity, ego-driven fear, and self-pity. Morning light came, and as expected, the outside lamppost switched off. Night was finished.

Unfortunately, Tommy's illness wasn't. It only moved south, as expected. He spent the remainder of the morning in our bathroom releasing voluminous diarrhea. Given his age and the degree of estimated volume losses and underlying cachexia, I figured a metabolic derangement and possible kidney insult was in the cards, expressing as much, doctor-style, to the morning staff, who on cue summarily ignored my pleas for medical assistance.

▲▲▲▲▲

It was after breakfast on the day I was to be discharged from the inpatient psychiatric unit and transferred over to the residential rehab facility. While still feeling as though my skin was crawling with fire ants, I felt, and was visibly, less tremulous. I sat in the activities room at the meal table, making small talk with Mellow George. To look at this guy on the street, one would never know he carried a psychiatric diagnosis (but frankly, couldn't the same be said of many, myself included?). I contemplated all the people I knew in my life or crossed paths with on a daily basis who, at least in my opinion, could use a similar program of mental health readjustment.

Vital-signs rounds were performed during the breakfast hour. Normally I wouldn't think twice about my blood pressure being taken; I always had great results at my doctor visits, which I attributed to my obsessive exercise routine and maritally-imposed plant-based diet. However, my readings since arrival had been steadily climbing. The previous evening, I had requested a blood pressure and it was measured at 170/100. Acute hypertension of alcohol withdrawal, I surmised, could potentially prevent my discharge and keep me locked in here another day or two; this was something that I desperately needed to avoid. I had approached the nurses' station several times that morning in an attempt to justify and explain away my pressure readings so as to get the results dismissed by the decision makers. When the time for vital signs arrived, I sat in the chair and the nurse aide pressed the button on the side of the machine, inflating the automatic cuff around my left arm. *Doesn't anyone around here know how to take a goddamn manual blood pressure?*

175/105. *Crap.*

I marched up to the nurses' station and demanded a "proper" set of vitals, explaining that these kinds of blood pressures could easily keep me stuck in Cuckoo's Nest Land longer than necessary. *Maybe this is their plan,* I obsessed. They knew I was a doctor and paying customer, and they might use any pretense they needed to keep me here. Maybe I was never leaving, and I would end up like CEO Sissy or Bathrobe Tommy, destined to live out my days as mayor of Crazytown . . . or at least on its city council.

Breakfast ended with my tray untouched, and when the med window opened I made sure to step up as the first customer. A simple solution for the blood pressure issue had come to me. The nurse handed me my Librium in its paper sherbet cup, and I popped the pill in, chewed it thoroughly to release the bitter powder out of its gelatin casing to coat my mouth, and swallowed it with a healthy gulp of water. I then went to my room to lie down. The stench of Tommy's intestinal illness was wafting from the bathroom. Nevertheless, I was able to close my eyes and let the anxiolytic do its job. Racing thoughts melted and I felt my heart rate slowing, my frustrations abating. After an undetermined amount of time, I floated back to the activities room and convinced the impressionable young aide to repeat my blood pressure, which then read 160/95. Getting my face up close to hers and looking into her eyes with intensity and authority, I "asked" her if she would be documenting this new reading in my record, and she nodded timidly. I had used this Jedi mind trick in the past at my own hospital to get patients discharged. *These aren't the droids you're looking for.* Satisfied with my actions, I praised the aide, faced my cold eggs and soggy toast, and ate.

▲▲▲▲▲

Just before the day's first activity with the pregnant activities director, I was once again called out by the unit manager and informed I would be discharged after lunch. *Halle-fucking-lujah.* Of course, until it happened . . . until I was physically walking out past the locked doors with my signed discharge order and my baggie of possessions, I was suspicious, and for good reason. Too often these processes fell through, usually due to some oversight or administrative snafu. I played nice with my "peers" during the games hour, taking on the role of good patient, not giving anyone in any position of so-called authority an excuse to keep me locked away here.

▲▲▲▲▲

About midway through a particularly engaging session of charades, while Sissy acted out *Driving Miss Daisy*, Tommy made one of his rare social appearances. Early on I had sized up my roommate as a garden-variety schizophrenic, likely heavily medicated. I had come to learn he had been on the ward as long as anyone could remember, without a place to be discharged to. He was routinely given a pass from any daily group activities. He became somewhat of a mascot to the staff, and no patient I had spoken to actually recalled any time they had been here without Tommy around. He apparently had no family (at least none who took responsibility for him), no home, and no motivation to leave. As a result, he was a legitimate placement problem for the case managers at the institution. I surmised he had been on the unit no less than several months. In an atypical maneuver for him, he made eye contact and approached me, and before I could establish my personal space shield, he grabbed me and gave me a giant bear hug.

"Thank you and God bless you."

It was clear to me that this was his gesture of gratitude for helping him while he was sick overnight. I actually initially appreciated the hug until it morphed into more of a tight embrace, dragging on uncomfortably long. He was a full head taller than me, so the side of my face was planted in the front of his unwashed neck. Transmission of the GI bug was of some concern. I gave him the old "pat on the back, then push away" finished signal, which he wasn't receiving; I finally had to firmly dissect myself off. He remained in front of me, smiling ear to ear, still far too close, and so I moved from my spot sitting on the windowsill edge over to a nearby folding chair. I was impressed that he was vertical and ambulatory at all that morning. He seemed to have bounced back from the pukes and shits quite nicely.

His second gratitude hug caught me by surprise. I had been engaged in dialogue with Mellow George, who was going to be leaving the ward to return to his family, his job, and his life. George was relaxing to be around and the closest thing to a new friend I had in the place. He was a "regular" guy who said he knew his disease well enough to know that he needed an inpatient tune-up when he sensed impending decompensation, and I believed him. We were exchanging email information when I was blindsided by Tommy.

His vomit-stained robe pressed against my right shoulder blade as his scaly, sinewy arms wrapped themselves around my torso. I received another "God bless you," this time whispered inches from my ear. This side hug was probably more disturbing to me than his initial assault, and I had to literally rise from the bench and wiggle around 180 degrees in order to kindly, but assertively, push Tommy away. I felt like the female cat in a Pepé Le Pew cartoon.

"Really Tommy, it was an honor just to help you. Look, Sondra is doing card tricks." I used the time-honored "distract-the-child" maneuver. He went on speaking to me, oblivious to what I said. I freed myself and backed away, but he pursued. The slow-motion chase was on.

Attempt at embrace number three closely followed number two. I had moved to the other side of the room with Tommy staggering close behind. I was reminded of many episodes of *The Walking Dead*, where a character would be pursued by a single slow-moving zombie. *I have to impale his head with something sharp.* Knowing what was coming, I positioned myself near the front door of the room next to Dayshift Wayne. He had picked up on Tommy's behavior with the third assault and decided to intervene. Just as Tommy came near with raised arms, he and another aide grabbed him by each arm and firmly guided him to a chair while I explained to my soon-to-be ex-roommate, in terms I thought he could understand, that his thanks were accepted, and we were even. I pulled the Bible out of his robe pocket and, before he would become alarmed, placed it in his hands. I then did an about-face and departed the room.

▲▲▲▲▲

Having passed my vital-sign test, finished my breakfast, and completed my goodbyes, I went back to the room to "pack." It was a pretty straightforward chore, as I was still wearing all the clothes I possessed. I made my bed, did a sweep of the room before final checkout, and decided to lie down for a few minutes. I was apparently more fatigued than I realized, or maybe Librium was building up in my system, because for some time I managed to doze off into a dreamless haze. *Was that screaming coming from the activities room?* I noticed the sunbeam through the window had changed angles, so I figured at least an hour had passed.

Rising up, I slipped into my shoes and slung my bag, containing my toothbrush and comb, over my shoulder and exited the room to go hang out at the nurses' station until checkout time. *There won't be incidental charges, since I didn't open the minibar or order any porn movies.* I could see, in a cubby on a back counter, the more important half of my worldly possessions—my phone and recharger. Ward policy was no cell phones until formally discharged, so I didn't ask.

Since the counter was opposite the large window looking into the activities room, I was able to see something else: Dayshift Wayne and another monitor were prying Tommy off a distressed-looking CEO Sissy. Apparently, in my absence, he had transferred his intense love and gratitude to some of the other patients.

"Joseph, it's time for your discharge interview."

Although release from a behavioral health ward was a new experience for me (but not on my personal bucket list), it was obviously routine monotony for the staff. I was led into a small, sparse room containing nothing but two plastic chairs and a folding table, where I filled out some forms inquiring about my stay, like I was leaving the Grand Hyatt. A unit representative, a meek-looking, pale woman who appeared to be in her midthirties, sat opposite me and asked my "intentions" once released.

Intentions? Really? I am going to run across the fucking road naked, climb the flagpole, and sing "Don't Worry, Be Happy."

I signed my release papers, was led out of the room, and was asked to wait once more at the nurses' station for the representative of the residential treatment center in charge of my intake.

I passively observed the comings and goings of a busy Tuesday afternoon. Patients were checking in. A distraught-appearing, disheveled, heavily tattooed thirtysomething white male in handcuffs appeared with two law enforcement escorts. Farther down the hall, a longtime resident of the ward was pleading her case to a monitor about how her medications must have been somehow switched that morning. The gigantic woman was sitting in her wheelchair in the activities room, watching a daytime talk show, oblivious to her surroundings. White coats were busily scurrying in and out of side antechambers.

I heard a wretched howl. Looking across the hall and through the viewing window of the activities room, I saw Tommy on the floor on his back, pinned by Afternoon Wayne and a security guard, his sinewy arms and legs flailing. It looked like a tag-team wrestling cage match. His physical demonstrations of love had clearly crossed a boundary; he had apparently hugged one person too many. I reckoned my previous night's show of sympathy to an old, sick mental health patient had triggered this disproportionate and uncontrollable response in his dysfunctional brain, resulting in the shit show that was unfolding before my eyes. He had broken from his Bible routine and turned himself outward, to the extreme, without the benefit of any social filter or understanding whatsoever. Although the sounds in the room were somewhat muffled (the door had been shut presumably so he could avoid escape), I could hear his shrieks of panic as the monitors flipped him and held him facedown while the attending nurse spiked his left ass cheek with what was no doubt either a heavy tranquilizer or an antipsychotic, probably both.

He remained aware long enough for us to fleetingly lock eyes. Then he spoke to me directly.

> And they shall look unto the earth; and behold trouble and darkness, dimness of anguish; and they shall be driven to darkness.

My head plunged into dark scenes. A cold basement floor ... emptiness ... men in uniforms above me ... my own vomit. *Where are these images coming from?*

I did this to Tommy. What did I do to this simple old man with no family and no place to go, who spent his days with his nose in his Bible and almost never left his room? Was I culpable in his impending transfer to the unit on the other side of the building? The place where the more violent patients are housed? The block with the criminally insane? Did my Florence Nightingale act last night damn him to this fate? Should I have just minded my own business? Should I have been more assertive with the staff about his illness and insisted on a transfer to a local hospital ER? These questions buzzed inside my skull like angry hornets looking for escape. I realized that there was no predicting the outcome of my intervention early that morning, only possibilities. And so, while I would soon be escorted out of the building to check into a cushy rehab across campus, Tommy would be hauled off to a more severe fate, literally kicking and screaming, to the high-risk patient ward.

Tony the rep arrived to lead me off the unit and bring me to his office to process my entry into the treatment center. I was officially detoxed and discharged from the psychiatric ward. My cell phone and shoelaces were returned to me, and we were cleared for departure . . . but not before I had a chance to thank random staff members—the young vital-signs tech whom I exercised power over, the nurses at their stations, and one of the monitors. I couldn't speak to Dayshift Wayne. He was too busy "packing up" Bathrobe Tommy, who had transitioned from meltdown to medicated mode, for his transfer. We moved to the security door and were buzzed out. I braved one final glance behind me. In the activities room, CEO Sissy was facing Mellow George, talking with vigor, her arms flying about. I stepped out of the lockdown unit of the Penuel Psychiatric Inpatient Center as a former patient and alumnus for the one and only time in my life.

CHAPTER 2

RESIDENT

I sat idly in Tony's office while he performed the extensive paperwork for my transfer. We may have been sitting in the same building as the psychiatric ward, but in that chair on the other side of his desk, I already felt miles away. His office was as sparsely furnished as the patient interview rooms from lockup. Tony sat at his workstation, inputting my demographic data—the usual stuff: name, rank, serial number. Eventually his questioning led to the more pertinent mental health and alcoholism questions (my last four days had been spent talking all about these lurid details—didn't their computers communicate with each other?).

Tony's cell phone rang, and he gave me the finger-in-the-air one-minute sign while he answered the call and stepped out of his office. It may have been a procedural slipup on his part to leave me alone, but I had no real interest in snooping. I was in mental health purgatory, momentarily suspended between (pointless) treatment venues. *We are the hollow men.*

Since my phone would once again be confiscated at the next stop on the Recovery Express, I powered it up and began frantically texting. I messaged my wife, my therapist back home, and my good friend Tom: *In Williamsburg, released from psych ward, moving to residential treatment.*

I received an immediate response from my therapist, who recognized the institution where I was and responded with a "thumbs-up" emoji. I took it as a good sign that, despite the fact that she practiced on the other side of the state, she knew by name the place where I was about to spend an undisclosed number of days. OK, great, it was a reputable place, but I already knew that. With internet access for the first time in days, I checked all the usual stuff any present-day American might. Over one hundred new emails, mostly spam. *50% off sale at Sears. Amazon pre-Thanksgiving sale. Coupon for free order of waffle fries at Arby's with a purchase of any of our gourmet sandwiches.* Delete, delete. Delete. Then along came the message that my medical practice was retooling the entire emergency department schedule to account for all the shifts I had previously been assigned but would not be working. Viewing that email precipitated instantaneous chest pain with nausea, rapid breathing, sweats, and palpitations. My tremor immediately intensified. I felt the panic build. *Will I ever work a shift again? My life is over.* I may have gotten past some physical withdrawal, but the higher functions of my central nervous system—rational thought, memory, emotion—had not begun to recover. I clung to the delusion that this was all just a bad dream from which I would, hopefully, soon awaken. Couldn't Captain Kirk just appear, beam me up, and assign me to sick bay? *Dammit, Jim! I'm a doctor, not a mental patient!*

I received no response text from my wife, so I called her but got her voicemail. I called my sister in Philadelphia and she answered. I unleashed a torrent of stream-of-consciousness laments on her at breakneck pace about how my life was finished, that it was *game over* for me. Beyond confused, I had absolutely no clue about how to even walk the next step or take the next breath. *Who can I turn to? Is there any hope?* My anxiety ruled me.

▲▲▲▲▲

Tony returned and we resumed my processing. Apparently my little emotional decompensation with the email took a more physical toll on me than I initially realized. My shirt (still the only one I had) was soaked. I stared down at the yellow hospital footies I wore under my shoes. The psych ward let me keep them as a parting gift. Closing my eyes and taking a few deep breaths, I was able to regain the remnants of composure, and we wrapped up the intake process. We rose and he led me out of the office, down the hallway, and out the back door of the building into the warm eastern Virginia November sunshine.

OK, Remy, keep playing along. We stood on the back patio of the Penuel inpatient building. Laid out just beyond me was an expansive, grassy quad with crisscrossing walking paths, not unlike the kind one might see on a small college campus. The smell of fallen leaves filled my nostrils, and bright sunshine warmed my face. We began to traverse the quad toward a large, steepled academic-looking building on the far side. I felt real grass brushing under real shoes, with their real laces back in. I took in the voices—people talking, laughing. I saw them walking in pairs and groups, backpacks slung on their shoulders. Two young men were kicking around a soccer ball. People were wearing plaid shirts, jeans, denim jackets—normal human clothes.

The building with the spire, our destination, looked as distinguished as any college building could, complete with adorned front benches and a large flagpole. Off to the left were dormitories. All of this was about to become my new home. As we arrived at the front door and walked through, I could only wonder how this place could somehow miraculously cure me of my alcoholism and transform me back into a . . . *husband? Dad? Doctor? Human being?*

Was I going to be cured, and if so, would I be some hopeless, sober, unemployed basket case in the future? I was engaging in one of my daily bad habits—catastrophizing.

▲▲▲▲▲

The inside of the building looked less like an academic center and more like some stately manor home past its prime. Tony led me through a maze of narrow, carpeted corridors with uneven, creaky floorboards and around corners until we arrived at what appeared to me like a makeshift nurses' station, as if the lord of the manor had retrofitted it in the tight confines of a hallway connecting parlors. A burly, serious-looking man in navy-blue scrubs, perhaps sixty years old, with a solid gray Afro, stood behind the desk, staring. I froze.

"'Relax,' said the night man, 'we are programmed to receive.'"

On the opposite wall hung a giant whiteboard, stretching ceiling to floor. Black electrical tape created columns and rows, forming a giant table filled with random symbols in combinations of red, green, and blue. The first column contained capital letters in pairs. It must have been a status board associated with resident names, I surmised. I didn't see my initials up there . . . yet. Before I could even think to ask a question, Tony was introducing me to Avery—a young, fair-skinned, and chubby nurse with fiery red hair and a knowing grin, who would coordinate my new resident orientation. I became vaguely disoriented with sensory overload, and before I could think to ask him anything, Tony was gone. I flashed back to my private pilot training, when the flight instructor and I would be at seven thousand feet and he would have me close my eyes.

He'd proceed to put the aircraft in a highly awkward orientation, then have me open my eyes, grab the control yoke, and return to straight and level to learn how to reorient the plane. That was then. Here, I had no training. This kind of disorientation was something I had never prepared for.

Avery led me into a small side room that appeared to be a clinical exam room, but which I would soon come to know as the whiz quiz room, in honor of all the pissing in cups for drug screenings that the residents would do during their stay. I remained there for two hours while nurses examined me, drew my blood, and collected my urine. A painstakingly detailed medical history was obtained, and I was fingerprinted. I was provided with overly photocopied information about the facility and general policies and procedures. I read the description of the professionals' treatment program, which I would be enrolled in, and how the stay would range from six to seventeen weeks, depending. I was stunned. The inpatient psychiatrist back at my hometown hospital had spoken about a week to ten days' stay (which meant he was either clueless or deceptive), and just a few hours earlier, Tony had described four to six weeks. *Don't bullshit a bullshitter,* I thought to myself. I was handed a copy of the Treatment Center Policy and Procedures Manual, as well as the *Big Book of* Narcotics Anonymous. Apparently they were out of AA books that day. My orientation binder was pieced together and finalized. After I was fully processed, Avery gave me the ten-minute, fifty-cent tour of the building.

I remembered almost none of my so-called orientation. As it turned out, it wouldn't matter. The real orientation at the facility would be in the hands of the established residents.

It was five o'clock—suppertime—and just as my "tour" was drawing to a close, the halls were filling with residents coming out of the classrooms and heading to the cafeteria back across the quad, in the very same building in which I had woken up that morning. Avery introduced me to RJ, a resident of eight weeks, and he escorted me over.

RJ thus became my first "peer" in sobriety. He was a young, stylish man in his thirties, burly and impeccably dressed, and he used ample product to keep his short-cropped hair neatly styled. In real life he had a position as a senior manager at a large Virginia-based software corporation. As we exited the main building to cross the field to the cafeteria, he informed me that at no time were any residents permitted to be alone outside. I remember being glad to hear this since my orientation was very sparse and the last thing I needed was to be reprimanded on the first day for ignorance of rules. We coalesced with four others and walked as a group of six men to dinner (walking with females, I would also come to learn, was forbidden). Arriving to the cafeteria, I saw that the chow line stretched down the hallway. The rehab business must be hopping.

I was the proverbial deer in the headlights; I didn't even know what I didn't know.

The cafeteria's offerings were plentiful, but I had no appetite; I exited the serving area with a tray of various samplings I wouldn't touch, then followed RJ to a circular table of men already seated in the main dining hall. I took the last empty seat. Jokes and laughter permeated the discussions, and it was completely lost on me how these people could kid around while their asses were in rehab, while their lives were put on hold at the very least.

RJ introduced me to Dick, a professorial-looking, black-haired psychiatrist who sported thick-rimmed, dark glasses. He was a serious man of few words and very standoffish. Also in attendance was RoboKarl—an orthopedic surgeon in his fifties, nicknamed aptly due to his large, chiseled physique and broad, square jaw. After my small talk failed to break the ice with Dick despite my best attempts, I turned my attention to

RoboKarl, whom I found much more welcoming. As I pushed around the potatoes on my plate, the tiny lucid part of my brain wanted only one question answered: How long did I need to spend here until I could go home? I learned that RJ had been a resident for eight weeks, Dick seven, and RoboKarl nine. *Tony from intake told me six weeks! Liar!*

When I pushed for an explanation, Karl calmly but firmly explained, with a pointed, mentor-like demeanor, that he'd never seen nor heard of a physician discharged (honorably) from the treatment center in under ten weeks and I needed to accept this fact and move on. *Accept?! What the fuck? How much say do I get in this??*

Our little table's group chat rolled on with a continuous string of jokes, playful taunts, and laughter. I was having none of it; I was here to focus on myself and my ever-unfolding misery. I seriously questioned what was going on, how these professionals—who were all clearly *doomed*—could casually banter about their plight and each other in a jovial and seemingly carefree way. Must be the meds.

As dinner came to a conclusion, the clan rose together, stacked meal trays, and walked out into the night air. It was getting dark now, and the quad was intentionally well lit. RJ sensed my apprehension about, well, everything, and suggested I settle into my room back at "the Big House," which in the dusky light was looking more and more like a miniature version of The Shining's Overlook Hotel. He described the men in treatment as akin to a fraternity of sorts, instructing me to ask for help from my new peers as much as possible. I wasn't sure why I would need any alcoholic's or addict's help, but I nodded in faux appreciation.

Arriving back at the main building, I witnessed robust activity everywhere. Baby-faced residents were grouped in the halls loudly chatting, all three hall phones were in use, and animated conversations about roommates, upcoming activities, and class assignments were all around. I felt like I was standing in a high school corridor between classes just before the late bell sounded. Peering over at the status board, I recognized my initials written in red next to my room assignment. I scooted and dodged my way down the hall past the crowd, arriving at the entrance to my assigned room. Swinging the door open (there was no lock), I stepped into my new residential space.

My roommate, Mike, sat on his bed, quietly tending to his neatly folded pile of undershirts. He was tall, thin, and dark haired, with refined facial features. A young man in his late twenties, he sported a green polo and khaki shorts. We exchanged introductions, and I plopped my bag, binder, and books onto my bed. Yup, it was my freshman year dorm room all over again: a couple of simple low-end bed frames, cinder block walls, and two freestanding open particle-board closets for hanging clothes, complete with built-in shelves underneath. There were no drawers, which was no surprise to me—they would have made the random room inspections more difficult on the staff. Simulated-wood vinyl flooring made for easy vomit cleanup, and two garbage pails stood ready if a new resident had use for them (and the wits to find them). The only difference from college was that I was thirty years older now, and there was nobody in the room passing around beer or bongs (that I noticed).

Mike and I engaged in icebreaking conversation. He was a professional golfer on the PGA tour who apparently never passed up the mobile fairway bars without a pitstop. I seemed to have lucked out with this roommate. He appeared tidy, polite, and most important, he had one week of sobriety behind him before he ever set foot in the treatment center. From the looks of his impeccably organized closet and general appearance, I was to at least be spared any of the overnight detox drama of vomiting and screaming that was so prevalent in the Big House.

Mike was also personable and generous. During my check-in and orientation, it was made clear to me that the facility was out of their *Big Book* supply, and mine was on order. I had already been given my first reading and written assignments and was told I would need to borrow the book from another resident until a fresh shipment arrived. The over-achiever in me was eager to complete what was assigned to me as expeditiously as possible, and Mike was all too happy to offer me his spare volume. This was apparently his second admission into the treatment center, and therefore he had doubles of many required items, including the *Big Book of Alcoholics Anonymous*. Sensing some relative peace and quiet (except for hall chatter) for the first time since Implosion Day six days earlier, I stretched out on my bed and opened the book to "The Doctor's Opinion" and began to read. Mike seemed to have an extensive wardrobe for rehab, but my inventory was comparatively skimpy, still consisting of the clothes I had on, an overnight tote with one extra pair of socks, and my orienta-tion packet. There was not much to unpack.

My eagerness to complete assignment number one stemmed from my old college and med school patterned ways— get shit done rapidly in order to have the rest of the night to drink and scope out women; this was a hardwired behavior in me. Throughout my early academic career, I always kept ahead of schedule in the assignment category, favoring com-pletion of the work over actual absorption and processing of the information. I was quite adept at completing assignments as a means to an end—study to party.

There was no booze or women as an end prize here. I was to learn, as subsequent homework would come in, that playing good student was not what this place was about.

The writing in the *Big Book* was simple and antiquated, the early chapters having been authored in the 1930s; whereas I would normally knock out twenty or thirty pages effortlessly, I found doing any reading at this phase of my recovery far more challenging than I had anticipated. I would begin a paragraph only to find extraneous thoughts creeping into my conscious mind, followed by fears, followed by panic. I would look away, close my eyes, breathe, and try to pick up where I'd left off. I'd make it another paragraph or two, and the process would start once again. I recognized that much of my emotional volatility was the neurophysiology of the early stages of a wet brain drying out, and so I read only as long as I could comprehend the words before the anxiety demons infiltrated the page and my field of vision.

This is gut wrenching, I can't do this. I'm not eighteen years old anymore and I am not in Ruef Hall at Lafayette College skimming through some English 101 assignment while getting ready to head over with Warren and Andy to Theta Chi for pub night. I'm a grown-ass man with three children and a hugely important job and my brain is buzzing and stuttering like a faulty streetlamp and I can't comprehend the sentence I'm reading, nor remember the one I just finished. My brain is dead, and this is all very hopeless and futile. I'm scared. My most important asset—my brain—is offline. I'm an invalid.

After about an hour, I gave up. It was time for the detox meeting—an on-campus Alcoholics Anonymous and Narcotics Anonymous meeting for residents of the treatment center officially on "detox status." The detox designation required that a resident's activities be restricted to the Big House (leaving campus was prohibited), including attending only in-house meetings. Once transitioned to "residential status," residents were expected to team up and attend meetings in the city.

Mike and I left the room and walked together along the far end of the corridor in the main building toward the lecture hall where that evening's AA-NA meeting for detoxers and new arrivals was to be held. Cell phone–deprived youths stood in line for the wall phones, waiting their turn to contact their friends, families, dealers, pimps, whomever. It was obvious these scattered hallway portals to the external world were our only permissible means of live outside communication, and even then, they were only switched on during specific designated hours when there were breaks in the sanctioned schedule. What was also evident was that I had so much yet to learn about the place—its routines, its culture, the way I should speak and act, whom to talk to. Things had the feel of a second-rate life-in-prison movie, only with less fighting and admittedly cushier surroundings. It may have been recovery bootcamp, but it was high-dollar university-style.

I had been to AA meetings before, but sitting in a tight circle with a dozen trembling, shifting, sweating, disheveled white-chippers was a new experience. I was a member of the club and was trembling and disheveled as well. I recognized the general AA procedures, but this first gathering in the big rehab lecture hall, with its sky-blue carpet, rows of chairs, and huge *Twelve Steps* banner hanging from the front wall seemed more intimate, its participants more fragile.

RoboKarl was the meeting's leader that night, and I shared with my first group of sympathetic ears how far gone I was on the day of my "bottom," how I was completely insane the afternoon I was rolled into my own emergency department by the rescue squad.

Karl responded to my story: "Joseph, you're not the first doctor to land in his own emergency department."

I felt a twinge of comfort in this. The softness and genuine empathy in his voice seemed sincere; my tension eased at the sound of it. His rock-hard muscular exterior defied the gentleness of his comment. I was not alone here, but rather was among other smart, good-hearted, but broken people whose disease revealed itself to the world over the course of a single fateful day, week, or month. *I am* not *alone.* Suddenly, without really knowing anything about the program, I yearned to hear everybody's "shares" at the meeting—every nervous word uttered, every phrase, every non sequitur. Listening to others' stories felt better than blabbing about my own. Yes. I was not alone.

▲▲▲▲▲

We realized we were powerless.

Although at first pass Mike seemed like a nice enough guy, it was RoboKarl who made a deep initial impression on me. In a circle of folding chairs, in the dim lighting of the main lecture hall, a dozen fucked-up strangers sat in fellowship, the enormous *Twelve Steps* banner hanging behind us. Even though I could not recite a single step, it was by listening to Karl and others that I was given my initial glimpse of what the program was about. Through the haze of my delirium and agitation, a kind peer had reached out with a glass of cool water, and the ugliness of my life receded one tiny step back toward the peripheral vision of my consciousness.

After the meeting, I wandered into the residents' lounge, a large, hospitable room with a sitting area, two computer stations, a refrigerator stocked with high-calorie "nutritious" snacks, a juice fountain, cushy oversized furniture, and a huge big-screen TV mounted to the wall. It was not lost on me that it was encased in a protective Plexiglas box to protect it from damage when a resident occasionally lost his shit and became violent. I sat in a soft chair and made forgettable small talk with random faces. It was not until I looked up at the TV screen that I realized it was election night, and the talking heads on the cable networks were discussing how Hillary might redecorate the Oval Office once in the White House. I barely gave it a second look. Any enthusiasm for politics in me seemed to be extinguished along with my interest in . . . well, anything.

Anything, of course, except successfully navigating this treatment center ASAP and (pointlessly) graduating summa cum laude.

Big animated maps of America flashed in front of me, with states colored blue, red, and yellow. I recalled actually once being excited for these historic nights, rooting for candidates during what had now become my past life. I remembered twenty-four years earlier, during my medical internship, I had arrived home one evening from a long shift in the ER back to our tiny lovebirds' apartment in downtown Baltimore, where my fiancée and I excitedly watched as Bill Clinton cruised to victory on election night. She had prepared loaded nachos, which we consumed heartily as the returns came in. We were two young kids in love, defying our families, uncorrupted by life, sitting joyously on an old, beat-up, secondhand sofa in our tiny apartment high above Charles Street.

The flashback caught me by surprise, and I felt strong emotion welling up inside me. *We were so innocent. How did I screw everything up so badly?*

It had been a long day, and after a short time, I decided I'd had enough, so I bid a quiet congratulations to Hillary on her election as President of the United States and shuffled back down the hall to my room. Although it was only nine o'clock, the room was dark; Mike was doing the characteristic deep breathing of someone sound asleep. Wearing my sweatpants and T-shirt (still my only clothing), I slipped in under the sheet and cover of my bed. *Welcome, JD, to the residential treatment center, your home for months to come.* My body merged with the mattress, which consumed me.

▲▲▲▲▲

The obsession that I was still in some twisted alternate reality strongly returned overnight, although perhaps a bit less nightmarishly. A historic inn in Colonial Williamsburg, packed with alcoholics and addicts, was where the deities of my celestial temple placed me. I was floating above my bed. The door to my room opened and a flashlight beam stunned my eyes. The deep voice behind it asked me to report in five minutes to the nurses' station for vital signs. What time was it? I sat up and put on my psych-ward yellow footies and shuffled out into the hallway, moving down to the nurses' station, which glowed eerily with nighttime lighting.

I spotted the analog clock on a back wall; it read 5:15. Two nurses were standing behind a long counter, engaging in relaxed, caffeinated conversation about Donald Trump's election-night victory. One of them was sipping coffee out of a royal-blue mug that displayed the words "Chicago Cubs: 2016 World Series Champions."

Trump victory? Chicago Cubs, World Series champs? Clearly, the celestial deities of my alternate reality had a disturbed sense of humor.

After floating my way into the whiz quiz room, I sat in the phlebotomy chair, where the nurse secured the blood pressure cuff around my right arm and it immediately tightened. The digital readout displayed 150/90. I guessed my dream gods had done their research on transient hypertension. Suddenly I felt chatty and began a dialogue with my nurse. She was a stout woman, perhaps forty-five, with a prominent wine-colored birthmark on her face the size and shape of a silver dollar. *Silver dollars.* They were a trademark of mine, and I gave my children and nephew many of them over the years for birthdays, on holidays, or upon completion of another grade in school.

My floaty, dreamlike disposition was shattered by a woman's shriek from down the hallway. Peeking out the whiz quiz door, I witnessed a slender redhead girl, no more than eighteen or so, screaming and writhing facedown on the hallway carpet, toddler-style. Nurses, assisted by the security guard, firmly picked her up and "assisted" her down the hallway, feet drag-ging behind her, a trail of bilious vomit in her wake. I guessed I was no longer the newest resident of the treatment center. I flashed back to my emergency department during the times I would wrestle with unruly, intoxicated patients who would vomit or take a swing at me (usually both) and follow up with some threat on my life. That was business as usual during my working days; now, just as in the psych ward two days earlier, I was on the patient side of the clinical fence. The new recruit was escorted to her room, complete with a bedside bucket for her puking pleasure. The door was shut.

Rather than disturb my roommate (I would never get back to sleep anyway), I leaned against the station desk and jumped into the conversation with the weary staff nearing shift change. The dynamic reminded me of the zombie-like state of the ER nurses and techs in their eleventh hour as morning drew near, and how the protective filters on conversation were usu-ally lifted. The most entertaining, and revealing, discussions quite often happened among hospital staff at five thirty in the morning.

At this so-called witching hour in the emergency depart-ment, we would occasionally receive a drunken, immobilized auto wreck victim, or perhaps a lonely lady with palpitations, or maybe just a geriatric regular who would arrive by rescue squad to have his toenails trimmed. The general attitude of staff at this very strange time of day—the hour when one doesn't know whether to say good morning quite yet—was much more uninhibited. It seemed all the stresses and anxieties—like the bulk of the patient workload—were behind us, and visions of our warm beds offered closure to our fading mental states. We would reflexively start IVs, place monitor leads, obtain EKGs, or trim toenails with the same punchy, carefree attitude of those who might be having a group picnic on the Fourth of July.

Leading the conversation my first morning at the center was Wendell, a tall, wiry man who was getting on in years, with more white than black in his cropped hair and reading glasses perched on the tip of his nose; his voice reminded me of Scatman Crothers. He greeted me with all the warmth and understanding of a veteran of a substance abuse treatment facility, a man who had seen cocky guys like me on their first morning in rehab thousands of times. I introduced myself and asked him if the election results were real or if I was still dreaming, or if the whole conversation was just a setup to mess with the new kid on the block. He assured me that in fact this was all very much my reality. I really wasn't dreaming—I was actually standing in the hallway in footies, in rehab, in a city I had not yet seen, around alcoholics and addicts I'd never met, while children in Chicago slept under their "World Series Champs" posters and president-elect Trump basked in his ego over at election HQ. I wasn't dreaming; truth was stranger than fiction.

▲▲▲▲▲

7:30: Breakfast

I sat at breakfast with RJ, RoboKarl, an anesthesiologist whose name escapes me, and a couple of others enrolled in the professionals' program. I was told that men of the same program were a clan, and that we sat together, walked together, socialized together, met together. It was in the campus rulebook that residents of the center were to affiliate only with same-gender peers in the same program. Comingling with the "28-Dayers," composed largely of wayward youths, was prohibited, and fraternizing with the opposite sex was a particularly egregious offense, punishable by expulsion. Fine, easy enough. I was still resentful over having been lowballed about how long I would need to stay, God only knew why. Perhaps at the time, I was still orchestrating my own long-term schedule in my head, instead of accepting my situation. Karl, I reminded myself, had calmly reflected that no physician ever seemed to complete the program in under ten weeks. There was no going back to my old life before then. There was no going back to my old life at all.

In the first step of AA, we were supposed to accept that we were powerless over alcohol, that our lives had become unmanageable. My appetite for that concept was as nonexistent as the appetite I had for the runny eggs on my plate. Management provided us with an unlimited supply of calorie-dense food; it was apparently important to the recovering alcoholic and addict. Eggs, bacon, waffles, and muffins were plentiful, but there was no coffee, as it was deemed a mood-enhancing chemical and was therefore considered "relapsive," (a new word I would come to know and despise). So while people in the world outside campus were sipping lattes in their cars on their way to work, I was forced into caffeine withdrawal on top of alcohol and tranquilizer withdrawal. Awesome sauce.

I rose with the group, dumped my untouched plate, racked my tray, and proceeded with "my gang" out the cafeteria door and across campus to begin my first full day in recovery bootcamp.

8:15 Meditation

After breakfast, the professionals' group gathered in the smaller of the two classrooms near the back of the building. Chairs were lined up around the periphery of the room against the walls. The lights were kept off and only ambient light filtered through the shaded windows. I found a random seat and cluelessly waited; it wasn't long before I was informed by a middle-aged blonde woman beside me that sitting next to females was also verboten in this bizarre universe, and I had to relocate to a spot with the men. I moved, sitting next to a cheerful gentleman who looked to be in his fifties; he was compact, lean, and fit, and could have been the actor Ed Harris's doppelganger. We exchanged introductions as the session began. It happened to be the morning of a "tagging ceremony" for one of our own who was graduating from treatment and transitioning back to her outside life. It was a touching little sendoff in which the graduate was bathed in complimentary platitudes by her "small group"—those four to eight peers from her daily therapy circle who knew her most intimately. A dog tag inscribed with inspirational words was passed hand-to-hand as each peer reflected, finally making it to her. She spoke from the heart about her rehab, her treatment, and the friends she made in her weeks at the center. The idea, I suspected, was to inspire her while motivating the rest of us to follow the program.

After the ceremony, there was a round of announcements—the day's agenda, rideshares to AA and NA meetings that evening in Williamsburg, and info about a special evening event. There was an opportunity for newcomer questions. In these morning sessions sometimes a grievance would be aired or a problem from the previous day addressed. There were also moments for peers to express gratitude toward another person, group, or the campus community as a whole. For my first full day, it seemed like a spiritual variation on a departmental business meeting.

Several preselected members then read from the AA-sanctioned daily meditation books, such as *Twenty-Four Hours a Day*, *As Bill Sees It*, and *Daily Reflections*. I listened to the rhythmic passages, looking for some larger meaning or at least the reason as to why I was sitting there. I observed the spectrum of interest in the room—those attuned to the moment, those uninterested, those in defiance, and one or two sound asleep. I decided to attempt to be part of that first subgroup.

After the morning's readings, a portable DVD player was turned on and instrumental new-age music filled the room for some quiet meditation. I had a fleeting urge to disrobe, lie facedown, and await the arrival of my massage therapist. But I behaved, and despite my residual tremor, I initiated my novice personal relaxation techniques, letting my body settle and my mind float. Fifteen minutes later, we were instructed by that morning's meditation leader to emerge. We stood, gathered in the center of the room with the tagging ceremony recipient standing in the middle, touched her, and in unison recited the Serenity Prayer. Morning meditation adjourned and it was on to "Community," immediately followed by the nine o'clock lecture.

9:00: Community and Lecture

We professionals grouped outside the bigger, main lecture hall while the 28-Dayers remained inside and finished up their morning meditation. The Ed Harris look-alike (aka Eddie) approached and began to speak to me. A fellow physician, he told me he had overheard me talking about the Marine Corps Marathon and deduced I was still an active runner. He practiced internal medicine in Hawaii (when not receiving DUI citations for smashing up sportscars) and was himself an avid distance runner. Since doing anything solo, including running outdoors alone, was a strict no-no, we immediately recognized a mutual benefit and sparked up a hearty conversation. After a few minutes of talking, it became clear to me that this guy was quite the competitor, and not just with running. Yeah, he and I would get along just fine.

We were summoned into the lecture hall and found random vacant seats among the 28-Dayers. The next hour started off with Community, which was essentially a dialogue between residents and staff, facilitated by a designated counselor for the purposes of airing grievances, problem-solving, and answering questions, usually intended to assist the newer residents. We were reminded that walking outside or being in one's apartment alone was strictly prohibited, smoking was prohibited, conversing with the opposite sex was prohibited, and being in the patient lounge by oneself or with a member of the opposite sex was also prohibited. Every once in a while, a new rule would be handed down and tacked to the side wall. I felt like I was seated in front of Dolores Umbridge in a Hogwarts classroom. *Whatever.* Rules were by and large easy to follow for a guy like me. Just like Julia expressed to Winston Smith in *1984,* keep the little rules so you can break the big ones.

During Community, the Big Man himself, CEO of the facility, "Dr. Dan," would randomly appear with his "I'm the Boss" coffee mug and make a show of removing a resident from the program. Humiliation and expulsion from treatment were usually the end result of some sort of egregious infraction such as insubordination, fighting, drug use, or sex with another resident. Made an example of in front of the entire audience, the rule breaker would be instructed to "pack your shit and leave." We were told these incidents were meant to protect the rest of us from being exposed to bad behaviors, which could lead to our own relapse. As I saw it, this was no more than an intimidation tactic to keep us scared and in line. It seemed to work, because for the most part, violations of campus law were infrequent. The cardinal sins of fighting and fucking were kept to a minimum.

As we sat together in nine o'clock lecture, Eddie instructed me how to fill out a "reflection sheet"—a form we completed for every class, therapy session, or activity attended on campus.

We were essentially asked to write down some facts about the event and our thoughts on what we learned from it. There were numerous spaces to fill out as well as some larger boxes to detail how the particular time benefited the resident. It was obvious to me that these were done for the purpose of submitting them to insurance companies so the facility could be paid by the session. Every time I sat down in a new place over the course of a day, one was required, and the previous day's stack of reflection sheets was turned in at a small group session later that morning.

The morning lectures were attended together by the entire campus—professionals and the 28-Dayers. Each day offered different designated subjects. General topics such as "Dealing with Triggers" or "Shame versus Guilt" were offered by individual counselors, visiting speakers, or Dan the Big Man himself. We sat through talks on "Nutrition in Recovery" on Tuesdays and "Spirituality" on Sundays, and we had alumni speaker lectures (one of my favorites) on Thursdays. These were given by graduates of the center who would tell their stories of recovery and share their experiences about recovery life on the outside, friendships, job matters, and family and intimate relationships. Often, after a detailed recounting of their descent into chemical dependency, the speakers recalled their experiences at the center while they were residents, followed by anecdotes about their clean and sober afterlife. Some of them painted pictures of tough sledding after their discharge from rehab—rejection, divorce, unemployment, jail. I shuddered. More often than not, however, they were success stories, *clawed-my-way-back* stories.

10:00: Small Group

If one boiled down a day in recovery bootcamp to its vital
core, it would be the two-hour segment known as small group
therapy. "The meat and taters of the day" was how one older
peer, Jeff, a businessman who wore a house arrest anklet,
would come to describe it. This was the time every day when
we patients gathered in our designated counselors' offices for
the slow process of deconstruction, exploring as a group each
individual's essential makeup, and the character flaws that
led us to drink and use. Why did we drink and drug? What
made us tick and behave the way we did? Newcomers spoke
of themselves and their backgrounds and the events of their
lives that led to their admission to treatment; more senior residents would reflect on daily experiences in recovery and how
they were attaining personal growth and, ideally, long-term
sobriety. These were the sessions where difficult assignments
were presented—essays on how we became active abusers and
worksheets outlining elements of necessary personal change.
There was usually a round-robin check-in where each par-
ticipant would convey how he felt physically, spiritually, and
emotionally; if there was a "burning desire," a euphemism for
some immediate personal mini-crisis, the group collective
processed it and provided feedback and support. If there was
a conflict between two group members—which happened frequently, given that we lived together 24-7—we engaged in supportive conflict resolution.

It was that first week in small group that I was introduced
to Barry, our group counselor and my designated patient
advocate. He had the demeanor of a disciplined pit bull; he
was friendly but firm and would always keep the conversation
moving forward. He possessed the clinical ability to draw out
the difficult secrets we were reluctant to share. He had a small
frame, a shaved head, and piercing blue eyes that bored through

our defenses as he leaned back in his desk chair asking pointed questions meant to get us to open up. We sat in a tight circle in his cramped office with the lights low, reluctantly revealing facts about ourselves ranging from uncomfortable to outright agonizing. Rather than personally respond to a revelation, he instead would allow other group members to jump in, one at a time, permitting a thought, feeling, or concept to materialize and be evaluated and processed to maturity by our little gang. He was able to mix in just the right amount of levity when the groupthink darkened and to lay down boundaries when an exchange became too heated. I would learn over the weeks and months to appreciate Barry's gift for handling a group of ego-driven alcoholic and addict professionals.

Each day, we would check in, share a concern, express a burning desire, or complete a course assignment. The assigned projects, built into the curriculum to be completed slowly and methodically over the course of our treatment stay, were designed to help us face our disease—how we got here, what inner workings and character defects we needed to recognize, and how we were to stay "sober" rather than "abstinent" (a critical clinical distinction). Our first assignment, the "crisis statement," was a short introductory profile about ourselves, read aloud in group, focusing on the months leading up to our landing in the treatment center.

The next assignment, "first step," was a testimony on how unmanageable our lives had become and about our complete loss of control as summarized in the first of the Twelve Steps of AA.

This was a crucial early assignment. It is repeated frequently in twelve-step meetings that without the mastery of Step One, the addict or alcoholic cannot advance in the program. Examples and anecdotes about the crazy behaviors we engaged in to access alcohol and drugs and then hide our addictions from the world were spewed into the middle of the room for group participants to hear, digest, respond to, and process for feedback.

It felt like a giant confessional where the degree of vulnerability we permitted ourselves correlated directly with healing and success. This unfiltered exposure and feedback from Barry and the group underscored that this illness was not something that could be overcome by will or individual strategy, but required an absolute letting go of the ego-self and falling backward into the arms of the group. Talk about a challenge for a bunch of self-absorbed egomaniacs like myself. Others would empathize, relate to the dark, painful stories, and offer support through related personal accounts and empathetic responses.

Our stories seemed to have far more similarities than differences. When the assignee was perceived to be hiding something, the group sensed this and called the member out. As we were continuously reminded, we were only as sick as our secrets.

▲▲▲▲▲

It was in small group where I first met the man who would become my roommate through the entirety of my stay at the center. Matthew darkly and quietly sat in a corner chair for my first small group session. He was a short, bald, and stocky nurse with a long-term narcotics addiction who described his bottom as having "a trapdoor." That first day in group therapy, he maintained a look on his face that was a cross between sad puppy dog and repentant mass murderer. He espoused to the group how "fucked up" he was. He scared some of the group members, me included.

"I'm so fucked up . . . so fucked up." Authentic tears streamed down his face.

Apparently, Matthew, prior to my arrival, had done a stint in the psych ward *after* he arrived in residential treatment. He was transferred there by Barry after he revealed in small group some violent ideations directed toward his peers. I was hesitant to learn exactly what, but I got the impression it was something truly unsettling, since he was sent to the ward at Penuel with the more violent residents, the place where Bathrobe Tommy landed on the day I was released. Matthew shared extensively, dominating the session, and his words at first pass seemed genuine and heartfelt. He was an intense person and peppered his shares with a significant amount of profanity. His intensity and authenticity drew me in.

Was this the true objective of small group? To get its participants to break down and blabber on about how badly screwed up they were? Or was this particular dude just batshit crazy? I sat quietly that first day and observed as group members jumped in to question, comment on, or relate to Matthew's reflections. Apparently, my first day in small group was also his first session since returning from the mental health unit.

As attention turned to me, I introduced myself as I would if I were beginning a classroom lecture or an academic discussion with fresh-faced medical interns. I kept my bio professional and businesslike, which I quickly learned was quite transparent, and not what Barry or the group was interested in. They wanted the real stuff: the pain, the crazy alcoholic Joseph to step up to the plate and throw out some emotional red meat for the gang to chew on. Having just shown up, I was nowhere ready to let strangers into my vault. As far as I was concerned, my opening statement was meant for introductions and basic factual information about how my drinking triggered a series of events that landed me in treatment, no more.

Small group ended, as it apparently always did, with a group embrace and the Serenity Prayer. I was huddled up tight with my new siblings, complete strangers to whom I would eventually be forced to bare my soul, reciting the prayer loudly and emphatically.

As far as I was concerned, there was a lot I could change and very little I couldn't; therefore, in my mind, serenity was not nearly as important as courage. Courage to get through this all at the top of my class, with no demerits, and move on to restore my life to the way it used to be, the way it needed to be once more.

This was going to be a few months unlike anything I had ever experienced before, that was for damn sure. The session ended, the door opened, and we broke for lunch.

12:00 Lunch

I walked across the quad to the cafeteria, books and binder under my arm, with Eddie, RJ, and some of the other guys. Eddie, who happened to be in my small group, and I once again sparked up a conversation about running, races we had participated in, and our exercise plans while guests at the center. There was an agreement with a local YMCA to let campus residents who were off detox status and in good standing use the facilities. Naturally, we were not allowed to go alone, so we utilized the buddy system during free time (before eight thirty in the morning or after five o'clock at night) on alternating days with the women. I really didn't see the early morning workouts as a problem, since back home, Tiberius and I went on daily runs in the early morning darkness (even during my heaviest drinking days). Eddie, RoboKarl, and a few others were as methodical about their fitness routines as I was. Since I was going to be stuck to a lecture hall chair all day, every day, I decided I may as well start the day getting some excess energy out on a gym treadmill.

The male professionals generally took up the same two lunch tables each day in the dining hall. I sat quietly that first full afternoon and watched, amused, as another one of my peers, Monte the optometrist, consumed two burgers, three milks, and several pieces of pie while continuously spewing forth crude and offensive jokes. Monte was a big man with a buzz cut and a face with huge features; he was large in personality and the life of the party. He enjoyed loudly farting while exclaiming who in the cafeteria he'd like to have sex with, how, and where. Thus, he became known among the peers as Dirty Monte. Like many groups, we had ourselves a mascot.

1:00 Afternoon Lecture

The after-lunch schedule varied depending on the day. In *Big Book* Study we read assigned chapters aloud and discussed the passages Bill Wilson and his cowriters so carefully and methodically crafted. Some days we had art class, complete with construction paper and crayons, and created mandalas or Zen circle art; volunteers would then share the meaning of their drawings with the class. Big Man Dan usually gave his lecture on Tuesdays. One dared not miss this. On Big Man Tuesdays, we all made sure to get to class on time, sit at attention, and God forbid, not doze off (I often ate a light lunch or skipped eating completely to prevent an after-meal coma).

The time with the CEO had to be the most stressful hour of my week, and I was certainly not alone. Dan was a tall, imposing man in his sixties with sharp features, a midwestern accent, cowboy boots, and a cold stare. He had the power to toss a resident out of the program on a moody whim, as I had witnessed several times. His lectures were admittedly informative and interesting, but also served as an excuse to finger specific residents for open ridicule. His MO seemed to be education through intimidation. He would speak on topics such as shame, ego, self-pity, or arrogance, targeting one of us—usually a newer member of the program—to be made an

example of. He obviously received inside information on each
resident in his morning conferences with the counselors, their
so-called "flash rounds," and would use this information to
verbally dismember us, exploiting one or more of us to person-
ify some personality trait that led to our chemical dependen-
cies. This strategy had its intended effect—we were unnerved
but became enlightened nevertheless.

My turn for waterboarding was no different. The topic was
arrogance. I had no doubt that during that morning's flash
rounds, the Big Man made a mental note of some counselor's
early observations of me. The lecture started benignly enough.
I was "randomly" chosen to answer a question or reveal some
general information about myself to the class; I was a relatively
new face, after all. But shortly after the dialogue was established, the interaction turned confrontational and unsettling.
After I shared parts of my backstory, the Big Man tightened
the screws, using me as an example of why arrogance is a character defect that plagues alcoholics and allows them to justify
their drinking.

"Joe, I understand you are an arrogant son of a bitch."

No words came out.

"You sit there, with your MD label, trumpeting your sense
of self-importance and stressors on your shirtsleeve for all to
see, so you can justify your drinking as your right, hiding and
deceiving your loving family, all the while destroying yourself
and those who love you. Your self-pity and sense of entitlement
are disgusting."

I remained frozen.

I was being called not only arrogant, but deceitful and
manipulative as well. I shrank in my chair as the entire class—
thankfully—avoided eye contact. I remember how he referred
to my eyes "as brown as [he'd] ever seen"—an allusion to the
concept that I was so full of shit that it was reflected in the
color of my irises. I sat and "accepted" his description of me;

what choice did I have? This man had the power to boot me off campus on the spot. I was uncomfortable and upset, partially because I felt humiliated and small, and partially because, well, Big Dan's comments about me were spot on. I had lived a life of arrogance, manipulation, and deceit, and within twenty-four hours of my arrival, he knew it, my peers learned it, and I, for the first time in my life, had to publicly face it.

2:00–4:00 Activity

The late afternoon schedule varied widely. We were able to sign up for elective classes individualized to our specific needs. Classes such as Tobacco Sobriety, Grieving Sober, and Music in Recovery were options. If the weather was nice on weekends, we were led on "mindfulness walks" or played "recovery volleyball." Nathaniel, one of the counselors, also gave engaging sessions on Relapse in Recovery.

I truly enjoyed Nate's lectures. A boyish-looking Latino man, he brought a certain natural flow and comfort to the room. He spoke among us, not at us. He lectured on the critical topic of recognizing relapse triggers from a position of experience with his subject, while engaging us at sea level. He had us attentive and understanding, yet still comfortable enough to joke around a bit. We would share in the room freely, expose our feelings, and allow ourselves to be vulnerable. I always departed Nate's lectures feeling a little more comfortable in what I was doing. His emphasis was getting me to recognize my environmental and emotional triggers to drink, such as having excessive pride over a job well done, victimizing myself, entitlement, or even walking into a casino. Opening my eyes to see the full spectrum of external or internal cues that could lead to relapse was an invaluable lesson, and one that I still retain today.

I had enrolled in Music in Recovery. This session was run by Jacob, the lead counselor at the center. We would suggest to him songs with which we had some emotional connection, and he would find them on YouTube. The lyrics would flash across the TV screen on the wall. After the song ended, the person who chose the music would share its meaning in their addiction or recovery, and the rest of us would chime in. We sat in Gratitude Hall, listening to songs for an hour. For the most part, I found it very relaxing.

Among the songs chosen during my first class was Steve Winwood's "Can't Find My Way Home," one of my all-time favorites. There I sat on my first day at the center, everything was new; I was living in a different universe from my home world, just days out from my hospitalization. My tremor was still prominent, and I was still apt to palpitations and rapid mood swings.

As I heard the melody and lyrics, my tremor intensified, and I lost it.

Sitting there in my classroom chair with the lights off, watching "Little Stevie Winwood," now in his golden years, sing those words and play acoustic guitar while sitting on a hearth was overwhelming. The mist in my eyes became a rain-fall, and I began to cry loudly. Where was I? Who was I? Where were my loved ones, my wife, my beautiful innocent children? Where was I going? The stream of tears became a torrent. My sobbing became uncomfortable, uncontrollable. I let go and emotion poured out; the dam burst. I was far from home, alone and lost. Nobody was coming for me. I was alone in rehab, *and this might not be a nightmare after all.* Self-pity be damned.

I stepped outside myself and let the waterfall run out. Don't resist the pain, an old therapist had once told me. The exercise of mindfulness required that we feel the pain to its fullest, experience it, and let the thunderstorm pass naturally. I couldn't have stopped that emotional freight train even if I had wanted to. I suppose what I felt at that moment, sitting in the dark with a musical memory playing, was a combination of self-pity, nostalgia, and a spasm of neurochemicals desperately looking for a new balance in a pickled brain beginning to dry out. As the song ended, the moment passed, the tears dried, and I "returned" to the room.

The other songs aired during that session didn't have the same trigger for me; either that or I was tapped out for the moment. I regained composure, thankful that nobody present in the room made a big deal of it. Apparently my reaction was not unique, and the counselors left us to our own processing devices without interfering.

We had a few minutes between Music in Recovery's completion and the coining ceremony, so I stopped back in my room to drop off my books. Upon entering, I saw that my roommate's bed had been stripped bare and his closet emptied. There was no evidence of his presence whatsoever. Peeking back at the door, where there had been two names posted, now there was only mine. It didn't take much deductive reasoning to understand what had happened.

The first question I asked myself, standing in the doorway of my now lonely-looking room, was what exactly went down. As I would come to learn, when a resident vanished from the center, any speculation over it was just that; openly discussing it with others was discouraged. Mike the golf pro roommate was gone, poof. Not only that, but nobody I could stop in the hall, at the nurses' station, or within the professionals' group would speak of it. People who disappeared in this manner not only were gone from the center, but seemingly never existed in the first place. I was living the rehab version of George Orwell's *1984*.

A handful of people did, however, speak in whispered rumors. We were human after all, subject to all the juicy, gossipy speculation that infested our lives before and after our time on the campus. Apparently after lunch Mike had been seen sitting in class with bloody, scraped-up knuckles around the same time someone else had reported a broken mirror in the Big House men's room. He later would admit to punching it in a fit of rage, shattering it, and had been told to leave treatment. Violence or sex always got us kicked out, and he'd engaged in the former.

I glanced down at my nightstand. A telephone calling card sat atop a folded sheet of paper with my name on it. He knew he was leaving and had left it behind for me. We had known each other not even twenty-four hours, and he had provided me a *Big Book*, two shirts, some early advice, and as a final act in his brief stay, free long-distance calling. As a mental thank-you in return, I prayed his injury didn't affect his golf swing.

Two weeks later, I learned of Mike's suicide.

▲▲▲▲▲

Just before dinner, the entire campus gathered in the main lecture hall for the coining ceremony of a graduating resident. I sat between Eddie and Monte. As it was explained to me, there would be two "coinees" that day—one from the 28-Dayer group, and one from our own professionals group. The ceremonies followed an identical sequence—the graduate would sit up front along with his main counselor and closest recovery buddy, and hear all about himself from each. The community would listen as we heard about what a "hot mess" the graduate was upon arrival at the center, the character defects recognized in the peer groups early on, and the progress made. Finally, there was well-wishing and offers of hope for the future. The graduate would then address his counselor, friend, small group, and the community at large, in that order.

Words at a coining ceremony generally consisted of gratitude and appreciation as well as advice for those of us still in treatment. While there was the customary bit of rambling as happens whenever anyone makes a speech, there were also some nicely worded sentiments from each coinee. I listened. How many weeks would it be until I sat up there, and more important, how long would it feel like? Would Big Dan snare me on some infraction and toss me out on my ass? As the second ceremony wrapped up, we gathered around the two grads, formed a web of contact, and recited the Serenity Prayer. We adjourned and broke for dinner.

I walked in quiet reflection across the quad with the dozen or so in my men's group; it was early enough in November that at five o'clock, the sun was still above the horizon. I had so many questions. My male peers seemed only too happy to answer.

One of my first learned lessons was how to *ask for help*. I always prided myself on my independence; everything I ever attained in life I felt I did myself, with my own hard work. I was taught at the center that I could not beat this disease alone— it, quite literally, was going to take a village (sorry about the election, Hillary). First lesson of recovery: use your village. Ask for help. Rely on your peers. It sounded easy, but in reality, for a guy like me with ego-driven motivations, who was accustomed to being in a position of some power and running my own show, it would take a significant retooling of my thought patterns.

Second lesson of recovery: learn the rules. On the recovery campus, most rules were unwritten and needed to be passed along verbally. It forced us to follow lesson number one. This was intentional on the part of the counselors or built into the culture of the center. In either case, it was *listen and obey* or lose. Here I was. *Learn the rules.*

I sat in the dining hall with Eddie, Matthew, and Dick, and stared at my plate. While on the psych ward, I had barely eaten. Hell, while I was there it had been an effort just to breathe. I

picked around the edges of my veggie burger and fries. I was
still trying to be a good little vegan for my wife, although in
reality I never truly had been. I always had tried, even to the
point of convincing myself that I would keep to it at home and
eat anything else when out of the house. It was another one
of my little deceit patterns. *Keep the little rules, break the big
ones.* I espoused veganism, lived it in front of the family, but
snuck in a slice of pizza or some mac and cheese at the hospital and guzzled vodka in my basement. In the end, during
my heavy benders, I ate large amounts of whatever I found in
front of me. My alcoholic diet perfectly symbolized, especially
near the end, how I had been living my overall life—a clean,
righteous appearance above ground obscuring stealthy, subterranean, self-destructive behaviors.

Eddie and I planned our anticipated running routine. He,
like I, craved exercise on a daily basis. Call it habit, call it a process addiction (like gambling or internet porn, but healthier),
we mapped out our morning runs on the program-approved
off-campus foot paths. Once I came off detox status, I would be
permitted to leave the property with one or more male peers—
for exercise, trips to the supermarket, and AA meetings. There
was a pretty two-mile walking trail through some woods just
off campus where residents could walk or run at the start or
end of each day.

Eddie underscored his great cardio condition from the
way he talked about his life in Hawaii and his various marathon race times. He seemed to maintain his strong competi-
tive spirit, even in rehab. His enthusiasm would serve us both
well in the weeks to come. We would run hard before morning
meditation and then sit more comfortably in lectures all day,
learning about how our disease had screwed up our brains and
bodies.

Back in the Big House, where I was housed until I was off
detox status and could move into the apartments, I waited in

line to use the hall phone, Mike's calling card in hand. I was still wearing the only set of bottoms I had—gray sweatpants. Fortunately, the couple of T-shirts Mike had donated to me before his untimely departure served me well. (I still had to wash out my underwear those first few nights before RJ lent me ten dollars and made a Walmart run for me.) Inked and pierced twentysomething women were lounging in the hall chatting, laughing. A desperate-looking kid of eighteen or so was trying to plead his case about whatever to the nursing staff. Through a wall somewhere, I heard heavy vomiting interspersed with sobbing. People walked up and down the narrow corridor, stopping to look at the community bulletin board, or otherwise sat against the wall cross-legged with eyes closed. The three wall-mounted house phones, once turned on each evening by management, were in continuous use. When it was my turn, I entered my calling card number and dialed my wife. The call went straight to voicemail. "I love you and hope the kids are well and safe. I'll try you again tomorrow."

The detox meeting that evening was intimate and not entirely uncomfortable. It was led by two residents in the professionals' group (as detox meetings always were). Our numbers from the previous evening had visibly shrunk. I suspected that a few people had gotten expelled or went AWOL; a few others had come off detox status and found meetings in town. That second night's meeting was Narcotics Anonymous–based, but the order and feeling of it were largely the same as AA—Serenity Prayer, individual shares, and readings out of the *Big Book of NA*. I was a self-declared alcoholic, and I did not consider myself a narcotics addict, despite the fact that I had stashed Valium in secret places in my basement to use whenever I wanted to have a dry period without drinking, when I felt the need to give my liver a break—"hepatic holidays," if you will. I often did this for a few weeks just before an annual blood draw, so my liver function panel would be normal for my unsuspecting family doctor.

We newbies sat in our little circle and talked about how many hours it had been since we had last used drugs or drank. The arrivals fresh off the boat shared the series of unfortunate events that had brought them into the room. We shared how many relapses we'd had; we shared about how "unfair" life was. Sometimes I focused on the person speaking, sometimes my mind drifted. I was not yet fully accepting this strange new reality, this bizarre universe. Somewhere on the other side of Virginia, I was performing my nightly routine of tucking each child into bed, starting with my youngest. Little Toby was asking me to let him read yet one more chapter of *Captain Underpants*. Robert was hugging me goodnight, telling me I was the best daddy ever. Hannah was recounting her day's dramatic events as an eighth grader. That's where I *really* was, where I *had to be*. Not sitting in some circle with drunks and addicts, two hundred miles away.

The meeting ended and I walked back to my dorm room. I sat on my bed and found myself completely alone for the first time in almost a week, certainly better off than *last time*. I opened the *Big Book* and picked up where I had left off the previous night—"Chapter One: Bill's Story." I labored through the antique prose of the 1930s as I read about Bill's gradual descent into alcoholic hell. Despite it being eighty years old, his story resonated with me. He was a highly successful and intelligent man; his bottom sounded absolutely agonizing. Was this where I was? Had I hit bottom, as I was "supposed" to do in order to discover true recovery? I reflected on the pages but soon felt my lids closing, and I extinguished the overhead light. I was alone in the dark . . . again. Six days earlier, I had been alone in the dark, shivering and sweating in my basement bed, half a fifth of vodka in me, scenes of Dad's funeral flashing in my brain. I had screamed over and over out loud into the dark.

I hadn't cared whether I was alive or dead. I had drunk-dialed every close contact I could find in my cell phone, leaving voice-mails about how I was alone in the dark. I had zero hope. Alone, like a scene described for children in *Oh, the Places You'll Go!* by Dr. Seuss, a book I read to Robert at bedtime every night for months.

Through the walls, I heard a girl's scream again. Her demons were attacking her, torturing her. At that very moment, mine were less intense, only poking at me with difficult memories. I attempted to settle my mind with a share I remembered from the meeting: to be grateful I am sober today. If nothing else, today I did not take a drink, and that would have to do. My first full day at the center had come to a close not with a bang, but with a whimper.

CHAPTER 3

TRANSITIONS

During the several weeks since I had first arrived at the treatment center, many new patients had arrived, and other residents had departed. Most had "graduated" successfully, but there was a handful of others who had been asked to leave. ("Pack your shit and go.") Our numbers in the professionals' program had shrunk from a high of around twenty-eight women and men down to about fifteen. This apparently came as little surprise to the staff, as we were in the midst of the holiday season, when the census apparently ebbed only to surge again immediately after New Year's Day. For those of us spending Christmas week on campus, this was advantageous, as we were able to receive more individual attention from our therapists and had more space to spread out in the lecture halls and therapy rooms.

On the flip side, fewer of us meant it was more difficult to get rides into town for meetings. Of the half dozen men remaining, only two had vehicles on campus, and space filled up fast.

The alternative to a resident's car was the shuttle, which was mainly reserved for the 28-Dayers. It was generally frowned upon for the professionals to ride to a meeting in this fashion, given the potential for us to commingle (it was still lost on me why talking to the men in the other program was forbidden). Fewer of us also meant I had to get along reasonably well with the remaining men around; alienating one or two could make for a long, difficult day.

After those first few overnights in the Big House, I was cleared off detox status and moved into the residential apartments—comfortable group dwellings abutting the quad and only fifty yards away from the main building. The units were small but efficient, each containing two bedrooms for four residents, a kitchen, and common area with a TV for lounging (and meeting). We also were blessed with a coffee maker (apparently Big Dan, who paraded around each morning with his oversized "I'm the Boss" coffee mug, looked the other way when it came to caffeine consumption). All things considered, the spaces were quite livable, and downright luxurious compared to my accommodations that first week. If I ignored the middle-of-the-night spot security checks, complete with flashlights in the face, it almost felt like college living.

My initial designated housemates included Matthew from small group, as well as two very personable and neat residents from the other program. (Apparently, the center could break its own rule about mixing programs in living quarters when occupancy dwindled. We were simply advised not to actually talk to our 28-Dayer cohabitants.) My housemates were all quiet and tidy, making the mornings and evenings spent in the apartment quite pleasant.

Matthew, my roommate for the entirety of my stay, and I got to know each other very well, and we got along nicely (for the most part) under the artificial, imposed circumstances. Although nursing was his chosen profession, he was actually a jack-of-all-trades; he had worked as a restaurant chef and electrician. He was also a big motorcycle enthusiast. His willingness to talk in depth on recovery topics and reach out to those around him balanced out with his occasional moody eruptions, which at times could get a bit scary. What I appreciated most, however, was his courtesy in the evenings to quietly prepare for and get in bed long after I had turned in. I gave him equal consideration in the mornings when I got up to meet Eddie for a predawn run or trip to the YMCA. In that regard, Matthew and I had a relationship of mutual respect.

Over the ensuing weeks in treatment, my sober network of friends grew. Eddie and Matthew had become my closest sobriety pals early on; RoboKarl, Dirty Monte, and RJ were ever-present and willing providers of support and advice. As new residents entered the professionals' program, my circle expanded.

It was right around Thanksgiving that Emily arrived. I was feeling despondent about not being with my family during the holiday and had been wallowing in a perpetual state of self-pity. A platinum-haired, attractive plastic surgeon from Charlottesville, she opened up immediately in small group, crying openly in her first session with us. This was not an uncommon phenomenon—with the sudden, radical environmental change combined with chemical withdrawal, we were all primed for emotional outpourings in our first few days at the center. In another universe, I would have regarded her as the knockout blonde of the gang, but in this clinical environment, and as screwed up as I was, she was just another fucked-up member of the crazy club.

We were all hot messes; Emily was no different than the rest of us, and her tears fell heavy in those early sessions. I found myself drawn to her vulnerability (and maybe her looks), and we began a quick recovery friendship from very early on, despite the restrictions on male-female fraternization.

I was able to "legally" communicate with Emily in small group, and share stories of hospital life, doctor-patient interactions, and personal relationships. Her circumstances were somewhat different from mine, but we had enough in common professionally and geographically that we immediately formed an early bond outside Barry's office. There seemed to be an unspoken acceptable distance a member of the center could get from a peer of the opposite sex before violation alarms sounded, and Emily and I respected those boundaries. Before and after classes and group session, we shared our backgrounds and stories with one another; at meetings, we were able to relate to each other's experiences in active chemical dependency. It was only a few days into her rehab when we found ourselves sitting together at an AA meeting in town. I used the off-campus opportunity to safely chat (flirt?).

"Great job in group today. You really know how to share emotion like a seasoned pro."

The dried, smeared mascara gave her the appearance of a baseball shortstop, except one who was way hotter than any I ever saw at Yankee Stadium. "Uh, thanks. It all kind of falls out when you lose so much in your life in a single day."

Now why does that sound so familiar?

I found that making connections with a female, with her alternative views and angles on relationships, addiction, and other life issues, enhanced my recovery; the feeling seemed mutual.

▲▲▲▲▲

It was December 28, 2016, seven weeks into my stay at the center and my fiftieth birthday. The contrast with my other zero-year birthdays could not have been more extreme. When I turned thirty, my wife threw a catered party at our new house on the hill overlooking the lights of the city, with many friends and family in attendance. My career had been launched, I had "arrived," and there was much to celebrate. For my fortieth, she surprised me with a week in Tampa at New York Yankees fantasy camp, a dream come true for me. She was pregnant at the time with our third child and, even so, was willing to send me off to play baseball in Florida with my childhood heroes.

The day I turned a half-century old could not have been more different. That morning, I arose from bed, made some coffee, and threw on my warm running clothes. Eddie and I had a well-established exercise routine by this point, and that morning we'd planned a four-mile trail run. I left the apartment, met Eddie at his, and the two of us headed over to the Big House to sign ourselves out to leave campus. I remember having a bit more pep in my pace that morning, which was fortunate, since Eddie was a swift runner, and despite regular exercise, I had managed to gain a few pounds over the holiday season.

The trail was quiet and dark, and the run relaxing. The early morning temperature was in the mid-thirties, and I had come to appreciate the calm, wooded surroundings. After we returned and signed back in, I showered, dressed, and performed my morning devotions—a silent prayer, readings out of *Twenty-Four Hours a Day* and the *Big Book of AA*. By that time my roommates were stirring, and we headed over as a group to breakfast. Mornings were generally the most comfortable part of the day for me, and the four of us sat in silence as I ate my breakfast of eggs, toast, and juice. A few 28-Dayers filed in, violating the quiet peace with their adolescent banter.

Back in the main building after breakfast, some of us headed over to the medication window; others sat in the lounge, filling out the previous day's reflection sheets or waiting their turn at the computer. I chose to hang out at the nurses' station and speak with Wendell and Caroline, two of my favorite staff members. There was something I found very comfortable about them; since my first intense days, I had settled down into my daily rituals, and those two were a pleasant part. We talked about recovery, politics, and campus happenings. I actually looked forward to the days I was summoned for a random drug screen, so I could hang out in the whiz quiz room with the morning staff a little longer. I'd review the resident board to see who was new, who was gone, who was on restriction, and who had changed rooms. While the staff could not speak about other patients, I knew enough about the system by then to figure out who had been granted honorable discharges and who'd simply vanished. I generally was not surprised by either.

Immediately after morning meditation, the group sang me a happy birthday song—the first of several I would receive that day. It felt nice; I had mentioned my birthday to Emily and Kathy (a new resident and the only artist among the professionals), and they had apparently passed it along to the rest of our peers. I found myself selfishly desiring some validation throughout the day, without too much fanfare. I appreciated the sentiments from my kindred spirits, but what I truly looked forward to was the telephone call I was promised from back home. My wife had emailed me to expect a lunchtime call from the children. I hadn't seen or heard from them since my arrival, and I was full of expectation and hope.

After lunch, I made my way back to the apartment with Matthew. At twelve thirty the telephone rang, and I picked it up, put my ear to the receiver, and heard the tiny voice of my youngest son, Toby. He offered me birthday greetings, and like a nine-year-old often does, quickly launched into a stream-of-consciousness rundown of his day. It was Christmas week and the kids were out of school. I got to hear all about playdates, the dogs, the cat, and disappointment at the lack of snow back home. I basked in his soothing voice. I was starving for my children's love, and he provided much-needed relief. He could have read from the dictionary and I would have been happy. My middle child, Robert, then came on, and his voice sounded tentative; his demeanor was more subdued, very reserved. Nevertheless, I detected warmth in his voice, and absorbed myself in dialogue with him. My daughter never came to the phone. The hollowness I felt in my chest at Hannah's refusal to speak to me was not quite balanced by the gratitude I felt in connecting with the boys.

That evening before dinner Emily and Kathy gave me a birthday present. They had been to Walmart, and presented me with a bag of Starburst candies, which I immediately opened at the nurses' station and shared with everyone around. The bright moments in my recovery, I came to recognize, were coming in small single-serving packages, and I tried to savor them individually, avoiding "outside thought interference." A song, a handshake of congratulations, a bag of candy, or my child's voice—these were all reasons to celebrate the moment, in the now. Routinely staying present was not easy, but when I could achieve it, I felt reprieve. Staying out of my own head and away from what I *should be doing and getting* felt like a getaway minivacation.

After dinner, I had my weekly face-to-face with my sponsor in the main lecture hall. We first met at a twelve-step meeting in town. I had been at the center barely a week and was still trembling and heavily medicated. Our counselors had required us to get an off-campus sponsor within our first week of arrival. That weekend, we filed into the large church-basement social hall and I scouted the room. I spotted a group of gray-haired, relaxed-looking men sitting and chatting at a far table. They appeared to be AA veterans (how I knew this, I do not know). I approached. It was a very simple process. I walked up to Doug, introduced myself, asked, and he immediately said yes. As it turned out, Doug—tall, midsixties but in good physical condition, with well-kept silver hair and a distinguished "professor's beard" to match—was a regular temporary sponsor for us professionals at the center. Sober thirty-five years, he was a legitimate rags-to-riches story, very personable and obviously comfortable in his own skin. With our first conversation, we immediately clicked. He came to the center every Monday after dinner to help me work the steps.

Our first meetup involved an informal conversation about our backgrounds and how we got to our respective places in life. Starting with meeting number two, it was all business. Sponsors are more recovery personal trainers than friends. I spent hours with Doug learning the Twelve Steps of Alcoholics Anonymous, doing reading assignments, and putting pen to paper. He guided me through my fourth step, and I wrote out my first-ever moral inventory—an accounting of all my self-centered resentments and fears. With his gentle guidance, I permitted myself to feel the pain of my sins and the relief of admitting them; this process woke me up to the fact that this rehab shit was getting ever more real. Doug sometimes nurtured, sometimes advised, but always forced me to face my character defects and how they factored strongly into my interactions with humanity. This was what a good sponsor did—got the sponsee to reflect on, and take responsibility for, his own transgressions, which were often self-justified through the endless game of blame, deflection, and making excuses. Drinking or drugging was but a mere symptom of a much larger disease. Deconstruct myself successfully with the help of a sponsor, friends, and a Higher Power of my choosing, and long-term recovery was not so formidable. With Doug to guide me, there was hope. I was drowning in a sea of self-pity and self-centered fears, and he showed me how to let go of those encumbrances, untie the rope around my ankle connected to the cinder block, and swim—or at least tread water. Recovery to me seemed to boil down to three basic principles:

1. Trust God
2. Clean House
3. Help Others

▲▲▲▲▲

I rounded out my birthday with a guys' road trip. A group of us decided to get out of town for the evening (yet stay within the permitted twenty-mile radius of the campus) and attend a Christmas week "speaker meeting" at a beautiful church beside the James River. As we stepped inside the adorned sanctuary, the mood seemed festive, and there were plenty of desserts made available to the attendees.

After filling a plate with cookies and brownies, I sat next to the new guy, Chuck, who had been admitted to the center the day before and was, not surprisingly, a hot mess. A cardiologist by training and admitted alcoholic and cocaine addict, Chuck drank and drugged himself out of his medical practice and was facing felony charges back home. As I chewed on a snickerdoodle, he shared with me his month-old story of being heavily intoxicated while driving the streets of Charlottesville, looking for an acceptable place to park and put a bullet in his skull. He found a quiet side street with a parking spot (lucky, since finding legal parking in Charlottesville can be *such* a nightmare), pulled out his handgun, placed it against his head, and pulled the trigger. Fortunately for him, in his extreme drunken stupor, he managed to miss his brain, the bullet merely grazing his eye socket. The projectile continued on, shattering the driver's side window as it departed his vehicle and struck a building. Unknown to him at the time, he had parked in a school zone, and the building hit was an elementary school. I almost choked on my first bite of brownie. Automatic felony charges ensued, and after a stint in the trauma center, he was transferred to the treatment center while the DA pursued a conviction. Chuck, technically speaking, had fired a gun at children. Now he was sitting next to my ass in a meeting, listening to a speaker who seemed even more batshit crazy than either one of us.

As with Emily and others, I bonded well with Chuck, who happened to live geographically close to my home. Like me, his mood wavered between melancholy and despondent. This wasn't his first go-around in treatment; he seemed well schooled in AA doctrine. During his first stretch of sobriety, he served as the medical director of Virginia's Health Practitioners' Monitoring Program for impaired medical providers—a rigorous program designed for physicians and nurses maintaining long-term recovery as they returned safely to practice. After his relapse, he was asked to resign the position (go figure). He sobered up and enrolled in the very program he had once managed . . . until he relapsed a second time, threatened the lives of his medical partners, and discharged a firearm in a school zone.

Our first evening together, we sat side by side as the speaker droned on about his drinking years, epic fall, bottom, and recovery. Speaker meetings, I found, followed a standard template. After opening prayers and readings, the speaker would launch into colorful descriptions of early life crises, usually crescendoing into a heavy chemical abuse pattern and a near-death experience. This was followed by the discovery of a new way of living through AA (or NA, or both). I drew the parallels in my personal history, with details changing but themes remaining the same. Through hearing others' accounts, I learned that there was nothing particularly unique about my story. This disease afflicted others just as it had me. We were more alike than different, a concept I found both disturbing and comforting. Misery loves company, and for the first time in my life, I was happy not to be special.

▲▲▲▲▲

More time passed in rehab, 2016 became 2017, and my comprehension of the depth and breadth of this illness, and what
I was up against, improved. Like learning any new discipline
or field of study, I began to understand just how much I didn't
know. I stayed attentive in class, opened up emotionally with
peers, worked with my sponsor, and listened intently to others;
I absorbed share after share in meetings. All of these experiences were slowly enhancing my grasp of this godforsaken
illness. Residents continued to graduate in coining-out ceremonies; others were expelled for various infractions, or simply
left on their own. New arrivals replaced graduates, and I had
the opportunity to see with newbies the same early-day patterns I remembered enduring—panic, confusion, emotional
explosions, open resentments, and blame. I repeatedly relived
my earliest days through watching the newbies and empathiz-
ing. I received my thirty- and sixty-day chips while still a resident at the treatment center.

Eddie eventually departed to return to his life in Hawaii.
RoboKarl released himself after twelve weeks, fighting with
the counselors near the end about his discharge date. After
failing a drug screen, he had been told he needed to stay longer,
and he declined. Through it all, housemates came and went,
except Matthew. He remained my roommate and primary
source of peer support throughout my entire ten weeks, short
of a few days. The friendship Emily and I forged grew stronger
as we continued to work on ourselves and support one another
through our mutual family and professional woes.

When the end of my time on campus grew near (we were
only informed of our approved discharge a few days before
release), I began to feel a mix of accomplishment and panic.
Seventy days without a drink was nowhere close to a record for
me, but at least with my newly developed coping tools and a

deeper approach to the problem, I stood a fighting chance out in the world. I wavered between the excitement of moving on and apprehension over leaving the nest.

One of my greatest fears was my destination after discharge, which was unknown. My wife had made it clear that I was not welcome back home in my current state, that she and the children had no interest in pursuing a relationship with me at the time. This scared the living shit out of me; had I not been in such a protective clinical environment, I quite possibly may have relapsed. My family was my life and expected primary source of support, and I felt completely abandoned. Given the situation, counselor Barry told me that I could not safely return to a hostile environment and should instead seek out a "sober living house" to live in after my discharge. It would be a place I could continue to strengthen my recovery while the rest of my life would return to some semblance of normalcy (whatever that was).

In my last week at the center I completed my "defenses" assignment. This particular project involved an intense deconstruction and final self-analysis with plenty of group input. I sat in the middle of the classroom surrounded on three sides by my peers. A sheet of blank white poster paper was tacked to the front wall; on it were drawn two large concentric circles. A peer volunteered to do the writing in various colored markers. In the innermost space, the "hole in the doughnut," I verbally listed my core character defects—fear, insecurity, sadness, inferiority, arrogance, entitlement, and others. Surrounding this list, in the next ring out, my peers shouted out my defenses (the coping strategies I used to protect my core shortcomings), which they had observed while living alongside me. My defenses included pride, intellectualizing, deflecting, blaming, humor, sarcasm, passive-aggressiveness, and withdrawal.

The key to this exercise was that, while the core defects were mine to list, the defenses had to be behaviors observed by the group at large—those who had roomed with me, been in therapy with me, and socialized with me. If I learned to recognize them, I could get past them and confront my inner deficiencies, lessening my need to drink over them. The poster would be filled in for all to see, but for me to absorb. As with others who'd endured this assignment, my group was spot-on accurate.

On the outside of the doughnut along the rim, my addictions were written—both chemical and behavioral (process addictions). The counselors encouraged that not only my main dependency be listed, but also any mood-altering substance I had ever used in my life to escape. While alcohol was my substance of choice, marijuana (college) and Valium were written up. Gambling, exercise, and firearms were listed as process addictions.

In the remaining space, along the edges of the poster, the group listed my positive qualities—kind, loving, compassionate, giving, sensitive, good dad, intelligent . . . and sober. Every resident who completed the defenses assignment finished this way. We were all very uncomfortable having our strengths listed—for me, even more so than the inside lists. When we finished, there was a round of applause, and the poster was rolled up and handed to me.

The long-dreaded defenses assignment was behind me.

▲▲▲▲▲

Three days later, I was discharged from the treatment center, having successfully completed ten weeks of the professionals' program. I had nice tagging and coining ceremonies, and my *Big Book of Alcoholics Anonymous* was signed by everyone in my professionals' group. Barry gave me a wonderful send-off at coining. My final speech to the campus community was well received, but in my opinion, very forgettable, which was just fine with me. Eddie and Matthew had departed a few days before me but had left their contact information. Emily, Chuck, and I made vague plans to meet up in Charlottesville, which was to be my next stop on the recovery train.

It was a clear but blustery day in mid-January. My suitcase and a box full of books—neither of which I possessed in early November—sat alongside me in the front lobby of the center as I awaited my rental car. This was the area where residents said their final goodbyes to staff and friends as their loved ones arrived to transport them, newly clean and sober, to their new futures. For me, this would not be the case; I was driving alone to a city I had never lived in, to a halfway house where I knew only one resident. I held my cell phone for the first time in over two months, unenthusiastically scrolling through unanswered texts from old friends and hospital contacts who likely wondered if I had fallen off the earth.

As I waited for the rental car company to come get me, I reflected on and processed the insanity of the moment. Reflect and process—wasn't that what the center trained me to do every chance it had? I still didn't have my wallet, so I used my health savings account debit card, sent to me early on, to make the car reservation. That, my driver's license, and about $200 in cash my mother had loaned me were all I had in my pocket. I did have my graduation chip and dog tag. My ceremonial send-offs had been comforting, but now I was headed out the door. "Door to door," as my counselors had advised. Barry helped me secure a room at the Oxford (halfway) House in Charlottesville.

There would be no going home; in addition to not being welcome, I was told that for someone in the delicate early stage of recovery, living in a hostile environment was highly relapsive. Seeing my wife and beautiful children, even as a sober and better man, could trigger relapse if they had no interest in receiving me, let alone being supportive in my recovery. Holy shit.

I wondered quietly who among my peers would also be told that the home they had come from, where their spouse and children lived—the one place in the world where there had been the most love—was now "hostile." Like my sponsor encouraged me, I tried not to stew too much. Rather, I would "tenth step" it—admit my role in the situation and address the character defects that helped create the problem in the first place.

But surely they will come visit me, email me, offer me hope and encouragement? This is a family disease, right?

My chariot arrived. My debit card was accepted, and after a side trip to drop off the driver, I headed due west on I-64. I put in a call to Doug and he wished me well. As he was temporary, I would need to find a new sponsor at my next destination. I played the radio as I drove, recalling scenes from my time at the center, trying to stay away from the bad thoughts, the ones that reminded me I was jobless and without a family, the fear that nobody would ever see me if I diverted to some liquor store just off the highway. I tried to not even think about one week into the future, let alone the upcoming year ahead of me.

As the miles passed, I continued to reflect on the preceding seventy-five days. I had arrived at a psychiatric ward alone and in the dark, in the back of an ambulance with my only possessions the clothes on my back. Now I was departing with not much more. Or was I? I was seventy-five days sober. I had been detoxed by doctors, decommissioned as a professional, and deconstructed by counselors. I was introduced to the basic principles of the *Big Book of AA*. I was alive. Nathaniel had taught me how to make a gratitude list; Barry and Doug had trained me how to overcome ego and self-pity.

The topography of I-64 transitioned from flat to hilly. I was approaching the Piedmont and my new home in

Charlottesville. Just beyond were the Blue Ridge Mountains and the Shenandoah Valley, the place I had called home my entire adult life. It was where my family and job were, or used to be, but I would be reaching my next stop well before there. Would I ever make it all the way back? Was I a new man? A sober man? Yes, on that particular day I was, and my program taught me this was all that mattered.

CHAPTER 4

NEW TO THE TEAM

I did my best to mimic Paul's routine. He may have been a simple man, but he had an aptitude and stamina for this sort of work. He spoke very little, and we often went an entire hour without a single verbal exchange. He was a sixty-five-year-old, stout, gray, nose-to-the-grindstone workhorse. I stood close to observe, but not so close that we invaded each other's personal space. I was taken back to memories of my after-school warehouse job in high school, remembering how much fun I had stocking shelves and horsing around with the other guys for $3.35 an hour. This work was not much different, except minimum wage had increased somewhat in the last thirty-two years, and I wasn't enjoying myself nearly as much.

Requirements for the position were basic. Stock shelves, I could do that; my OCDish mind quickly took to it. In addition, I remembered the technique to rapidly and efficiently break down cardboard boxes, a skill acquired at age twelve while working in my stepdad's deli in New York. I certainly knew how to smile and say hello to customers. Many classy ladies strolled the aisles; yes, I most certainly could be very nice to them. I could escort them to the Greek yogurt, salsa, or almond milk. Everything had its place in the back storehouse and out in the aisles, and I took pride in memorizing each item's specific location. The manager still had me occasionally shadowing Paul, who was assigned to orient me in my first days as a stock boy. Even though I had been hired on at the Kroger supermarket only a week earlier, I already felt like I was getting the hang of it.

My assigned hand truck that particular morning was piled high with boxed merchandise. Management decided that although I was technically still on orientation, I could be of some additional help working on my own. Paul recognized I had half a brain and sent me to stock canned goods, cereal, and salad dressing in the nearby aisles. The resistance of the heavy load wasn't too much of a challenge as I wheeled my cases to a centrally located but out-of-the-way spot so the morning shoppers could skirt by with their shopping carts. Little blue-haired old ladies, university students, and professors populated the store that morning. From somewhere above, a subdued Muzak version of the Talking Heads' "Burning Down the House" filled the air. *How perfect,* I thought.

I finished lining up bottles of Newman's Own salad dressing on their shelf and cracked open my next box—Rice Chex. This was one of the few "mainstream" items we kept in the pantry back home—in my real home, my true home, not in the basement room in which I was currently sleeping. *And the place I will return to, eventually.* I did as Paul had instructed and stocked the new boxes behind what was already shelved, sliding the cereal with the older expiration dates up to the front. When I finished, it looked pretty good—nice and neat for the discriminating shopper's eye. I straightened up the adjacent shelving, righting the items knocked over by careless shoppers, a technique I had learned from my training as "conditioning" the shelves. This was a routine practiced by every stock clerk in the supermarket continuously through the day, even while other tasks were performed. It kept the rows aesthetically appealing. After a few minutes, the shelf looked super good, almost perfect. It was 8:57 a.m., and I had made a nice neat row of household name brands. I wheeled the flattened cardboard to the back warehouse, where the baler compressed them into tight packages for recycling. This was accomplishment number four of the day.

Accomplishments number one, two, and three were basic but vital, consisting of (1) waking up sober and staying that way, (2) getting in a predawn run, and (3) clocking in on time at work. The job hadn't been all that difficult to get. Shortly after my arrival from the treatment center to the Oxford Halfway House for Men in Recovery, I had been informed that unless on full disability, residents were required to be either in school or working. So I went online (the house was equipped with a computer and Wi-Fi, subsidized by Region Ten of the Community Services Board) and soon found an opening for a stock clerk with Kroger. The interview was a breeze—almost fun—and I was hired. After a few hours of online corporate training and orientation (policies, proper stocking technique, handling spills in the aisle, reporting theft, etc.), I was handed my work shirt and official name badge with the attached orientee ribbon (*Hi! I'm new to the team!*). Voilà . . . I was employed.

Every morning I clocked in at eight o'clock and went into the back to load up my hand truck (I made sure to get the good one, the one that rolled most smoothly) with cases of peanut butter, sardines, dog food, or toilet paper, and proceeded to the main shopping floor to unload. Boxes were emptied, the cardboard was flattened and loaded up for disposal, the next pile of stock was retrieved from the back, and the process was repeated. The work was very Zen. I became quite adept at my job duties and usually had my share of the merchandise stocked and the shelves conditioned well in advance of clock-out. I was given thirty minutes for lunch and a fifteen-minute break, but rarely took it. With the leftover time I would address the "loose merchandise," and for the rest of my shift, I "filled the holes" in the shelves. Being seen idle was not a good idea, lest the boss notice and put me in the freezer unloading the trucks of frozen food, an assignment I didn't much care for.

The work was all so orderly, so nice and neat, and so simple. I learned to appreciate simple. Every so often a University of Virginia mom would approach and ask where the quinoa or dark chocolate was located, and I would take extra care to walk her to the exact spot, discuss the product options and nutritional content, and offer her additional assistance.

My supervisor, Billy, took notice of the fact that I had some knowledge of nutrition, as well as a flair with the customers, and early on I was reassigned to stock and maintain the "natural foods" section of the store. I enjoyed it—many of the products I handled were items we had back at home . . . my real home. *Where my wholesome, vegan wife keeps a cupboard of wholesome, vegan foods. At least, I* think *she's still my wife.* I sported my company shirt—a nice, navy, wrinkle-free polyester blend with a collar and the company logo above a breast pocket. My name badge was displayed on the left side, per policy; the *Hi! I'm new to the team!* tack-on ribbon would remain on it for the first thirty days.

This was my recovery job. It was, I learned, supposed to reacquaint me with humility and gratitude, two emotions that were ostensibly so vital to my early success in the program. At first it took a significant amount of morning prayer and meditation for acceptance of my situation to gain traction. Here I was, a board-certified emergency physician of twenty-two years, working as a stock clerk and taking orders from supervisors half my age.

Is this really what my recovery requires? Is this what I must do? This is more than humility; it is sheer humiliation. I am supposed to listen to my sponsor and accept my situation and address my egoic ways. Does that really mean playing stock clerk? Must I be reduced to working a position meant for teenagers and social security recipients?

The first couple of weeks were volatile—sadness and panic blew through me like summer storm cells multiple times a day. I handled these emotions the way my sponsor and I discussed—reciting the Serenity Prayer, turning things over with the Acceptance Prayer, and recognizing that this was, essentially, early-stage treatment for my chronic condition. Healing hurt, but I was moving in a positive direction. Occasionally I would find a quiet spot for some quick breathing exercises; I would remind myself I was not defined by the job I did but by who I was as a human being. I made $8.85 an hour, lived in a recovery house, and had zero contact with those whom I held dearest in my heart. I reminded myself that the situation was all temporary, lest I go insane, or worse—relapse.

This was my early sobriety.

▲▲▲▲▲

Several weeks into my employment, I returned to the house after work to find Bardy, one of my housemates, waiting for me. He was a baby-faced, quick-witted young man who managed to drink himself out of college despite the fact that both his parents were executive administrators on campus. We had met in rehab, and when we discovered our mutual geographic destination, quickly became acquaintances. Bardy was scheduled to leave the treatment center a week before me and had discovered the Oxford House in Charlottesville as a place we could both settle in as residents. While I was off stocking supermarket shelves, he was renting out moving vans and managing a Putt-Putt golf center. In the evenings he, like my other housemates, generally kept to himself in his room, playing video games and swiping around on Tinder. Occasionally we would sit together in the common room, with or without the others, and discuss the locations of the better AA meetings in town, our jobs, his dating life, or whatever else came to mind. He kept the conversation very lighthearted, and I usually felt pretty good when he was around. He was house president and took the role seriously, chairing our weekly meetings.

That particular afternoon, the moment I walked into the house and saw the look on his face, I knew something was off. Bardy usually made eye contact when he spoke—a trait I appreciated, since I was never very good at it—but this time he was looking at the floor and shuffling side to side. He glanced at me briefly and told me something came to the house by courier and I'd better sit down. Before he had finished the sentence, I *knew* the contents of the thick manila envelope sitting on the coffee table in the TV room. It was now only a matter of opening it up and setting eyes to paper. The day before, I had logged into my bank's website to see if my paycheck had cleared, only to find the entire joint checking account emptied out, the balance showing near zero. That should have been my final confirmation, but I chose to ignore the clue, still fighting the reality.

Deep down, I knew. From the moment of my arrival at the Oxford House, I knew it was coming. She had asked that I not stop by home—not even to pick up clothes or personal items; they would be delivered by friends—and said that my presence in the house was not welcome. Emails went unanswered; my phone calls were ignored. A week earlier, while attending a meeting, I received a surprise phone call from Hannah, who asked me to leave her alone for a year to give her space and "time to heal," as she described it. My daughter wanted no contact with her father for a full twelve months. Toby's occasional phone calls to me had virtually dried up; Robert never called at all.

The previous Sunday morning, about a month into my time in Charlottesville, I had awoken from a dream in which my children and I were playing together at a local park. We were laughing, chasing each other around, acting silly, and hugging. I awoke sweating, with palpitations and shakes—my housemates would have thought I was detoxing. I immediately emailed my wife that morning and begged her for communication with the children. What I received instead was a telephone call from her, in which she read a prewritten note to me explaining why she was divorcing me. So that was it. After twenty-three years, my marriage was unofficially over. The call ended abruptly, and I immediately dialed Doug, my old sponsor, and he talked me off the ledge; yet I remained in denial.

So there I sat later that week, in the common room of the halfway house, still wearing my work shirt and name tag (*Hi! I'm new to the team!*), the large manila envelope on my lap. Breathing deep, I removed the contents and thumbed through the pages. There really was no point in torturing myself and reading every word. I skimmed the highlights. I was a named defendant. I was a bad husband. I was a dangerous and scary father. The document went on to describe, in frightening detail, the "reasons" why I no longer deserved a marriage, why I no longer deserved fatherhood, and why I no longer deserved to exist on this planet. My breathing stopped; I felt no heartbeat. Page after official page detailed horrifying allegations of my behavior, things I may have done or never did, embellished in wording that could only have been crafted by a seasoned divorce attorney and translated into legalese to appear as damning as possible. Any reader would have thought I was deserving of the death penalty. I sat for an unknown amount of time, frozen in the chair. My mind unlocked just long enough to remember the emergency procedures that the program had instilled in me:

1. Breathe.
2. Recite the Serenity Prayer.
3. Repeat the Serenity Prayer.
4. Remind myself I'm a good person with a bad disease.
5. Remember I have today.
6. Call my sponsor.

I placed the document back in the envelope and reached for my phone. It felt like a brick in my hands as I dialed Murphy, my new sponsor. He didn't answer, so I left a voicemail. Then I began texting—closest friends and family first, followed by some newer friends from the program. Murphy called me back, and as all good sponsors do, referred me to teachings out of the *Big Book* to help settle my mind, which by this point was ablaze. I was assigned the task of reciting the Acceptance Prayer. We hung up, and I opened the book and read. I seemed to find the passages I needed, and the fires in my head started to extinguish.

7. Find a meeting.

That was easy. It was pushing six o'clock and my preferred Charlottesville gathering of sober drunks was only a mile away and was starting within the hour. I would go and hang out at the coffee maker with the early birds.

Langston emerged from his bedroom. He was a thin, good-looking guy in his early forties who worked as a sous chef. Like me, alcohol was his nemesis. We had met on my first day at the house, and I found him to be quite cordial and easy to talk to. I badly needed to share, yet it was still too soon to leave for the meeting; the church in which it was held was likely still locked. He went to the kitchen for a soda, but before he could return to his bedroom, I blurted out my acute distress and he diverted, sitting down opposite me on the sofa to offer a sympathetic ear. As he sat attentively I conveyed the events of the previous few days with the culmination of the arrival of the manila envelope, my anxious and desperate tone evident. He sat with me for half an hour and offered me the support of a brother in recovery, letting me spew emotion all over the room while being a good listener. He then offered advice, letting me know I was not alone with this or any other problem, and spoke of his own divorce only two years prior. Having the direct human connection, even with an almost-stranger, stabilized me for the moment. Then, just as my sponsor had done, he told me to find a good lawyer.

The next day I was off work, and the task du jour was securing legal representation. It so happened that Emily, with whom I continued to stay in regular contact, was able to send me to her ex-husband, an attorney in town whose firm handled divorce cases. By noon that day, he and I were meeting over his lunch hour as an emergency add-on. I found myself in a surprisingly focused but brief moment of clarity as we discussed my case. I felt fortunate, in a sense, as this man had once been married to Emily and likely understood addiction and alcoholism, at least from an outsider's perspective. After taking my essential information and referring me to one of his partners to handle my case, he ended with the comment, "Well, at least now she can't prevent you from seeing your children."

Little did either one of us realize how wrong he was.

▲▲▲▲▲

I drove back to the halfway house in a haze of confusion and remorse. A divorce had been thrust upon me, and that was an inescapable fact. I'd had virtually no contact with my wife while I was in rehab, nor had she made any overtures to take me back home. Face-to-face conversations, attempts to amicably discuss separation and come to terms directly, and working out some sort of arrangement with the children were not even on the agenda. There was none of that, only the cold service of a legal document to my ramshackle place of residence. After twenty-three years of marriage, it was that cut-and-dried. Our entire relationship was about to be marched through the harsh realm of the legal system for lawyers to shred and all the world to see. I asked myself how the hell I was going to stay sober through it all. Somehow I made it back to my room in one piece.

▲▲▲▲▲

Over the ensuing weeks, I met frequently with Mr. Barney Q. Hitschmeiser, my very own divorce attorney. I was still living in denial, hoping I could somehow salvage an amicable separation through direct dialogue, but my phone calls back home were blocked and emails responded to with extreme hostility, when they were answered at all. We would sit in his office and Barney would discuss strategies, go over facts, and lay out his overall game plan with me. I was instructed by friends and others who had been through the same process to listen to and do everything my lawyer said and asked of me. Acceptance was the centerpiece of my fledgling recovery skills, and I knew it would be a gut-wrenching process to have to defend myself against the woman I had loved and was married to for my entire adult life. Even though she came at me guns blazing, I wondered if I possessed the intestinal fortitude to effectively fight back. It was made clear in the separation decree that she had no intention of negotiating any shared custody of the children, that she was filing for total parental custody in the final divorce. This would be a nonstarter for me, and I promised myself that I would find the strength to fight, with every fiber of my being, any attempts to remove the children from my life completely.

The entire process was wretched, nauseating, and mind numbing. Retaining my sanity, let alone my sobriety, through it was going to require a complete and absolute immersion into my recovery program through all channels and by any means necessary. I was at emotional DEFCON 1. In addition to literally "living in the rooms" of Alcoholics Anonymous (multiple meetings a day), I was going to require continuous contact with my sponsor, my therapist, and my expanding network of sober friends. If I felt like I was fighting for my life, it was because I was. There was simply no way I was going to get through this alone. The only way I was going to survive was by taking a few proverbial deep breaths and leaping faithfully into the recovery mosh pit. The craving for a drink clawed furiously and continuously in my gut. That little alcoholic voice in my head sprang to life, megaphone in hand.

You fucking loser, if you keep down this path it's game over for you. Look at you—a respected physician reduced to living in a damp cellar, stocking grocery shelves, and sitting in a room with other underemployed, poorly dressed, divorced losers. I am your only friend, and I am telling you that a drink is your only relief, your only salvation. What has sobriety done for you thus far? Your world has become a canyon of shit even deeper than when you were drinking. When you and I were buds, I could take you away from all this, even for a little while. She took complete advantage of you, harpooning you when you were down, at your weakest and most vulnerable. If you let her, she will suck away everything you ever worked so hard for and will destroy you. She took the "in sickness and in health" vow and shit all over it. You busted your ass for years under extreme conditions, building a life and socking away cash for her while she sat around planning her bike rides and triathlon training. Did she ever, even once, express the gratitude you so much deserve? What lies is she telling your children about you? What false memories is she programming into their developing brains? How distorted is the reality they will be forced to live?

Take your assets, your retirement savings, and anything else not bolted down, and set up a bank account overseas where she can't get to you. Tap out all the equity in the house and convert it to cash. Get your ass to Guatemala where you and your money will be safe. Find a nice beach house with nubile young servants and enjoy yourself. You deserve that, not this suffering your so-called program has smacked you upside the head with. Fuck that. Fuck her. Fuck them all.

And don't forget to bring me, so you can feel good all day.

▲▲▲▲▲

I had to remember my lifelines both inside and outside AA. Having new friends was great, but time-tested old buddies who knew me in my former life and who witnessed my downfall were going to be instrumental. Tom, my lifelong friend and emergency room colleague, and I stayed in regular contact, and he provided badly needed logistical support. One rainy afternoon that February he arrived for a visit and brought with him suitcases of my clothing and other necessities. I led him into the house and introduced him around to my housemates. We carried my belongings down to the basement, and he saw where I slept. Rainwater was leaking through the exposed cinder blocks around the filthy high cellar window, and the water made trickling sounds as it flowed down the wall.

"This is my room." I could tell he was having trouble responding.

"It's a room," was all he could muster, averting his eyes.

▲▲▲▲▲

About a week later I was home from work when I received a phone call from my old medical school friend and roommate Darryl in Pennsylvania, and he offered to come visit me. I had kept in touch with him and his wife, Judy, through the years, and like many longtime friends, we could resume conversations after long absences as if we saw each other daily. We made plans for dinner and to go to the UVA-Duke basketball game. Darryl was a guy's guy and always the catalyst for fun at gatherings without being (too) obnoxious. He was an intelligent, accomplished man of poorly disguised high morals and a heart of gold who worked in emergency medicine. Sometime after my implosion and stint in rehab, he had apparently spent hours on the telephone patiently listening to my wife.

He arrived in the late afternoon and took me out to dinner, where we ate a high-end meal (his treat) while I filled him in on the details of my present life—although he knew all the basics about the ugly reality. At John Paul Jones Arena, we sat in the nosebleed seats as the Cavaliers and Blue Devils went at each other, while Duke's Coach K paced and angrily shouted at the referees (I'm not sure why, since every call went Duke's way). Conversation at the game stayed lighthearted and guy-oriented, and I was thankful. That night, my friend slept on the floor of my basement room, refusing to take my bed. This was the kind of friend, the kind of support, I had *outside AA*. How could I go wrong? Before I fell asleep, I dropped a line to my alcoholic voice.

Hey alcoholic voice—fuck you. *You only brought me and my family misery and constant sorrow, dressed up in an alcoholic buzz.* My *money? Guatemala? No, asshole. I am going to do this the right way, no matter how much it initially hurts. I am going to keep stepping in the right direction for the good of all. I will stock shelves and sleep in a moldy room and sit daily with my peers in recovery so that someday I can make my life and the lives of those around me better than you ever could imagine. And my wife DID thank me for my hard work—many times. So take your faux indignation and shove it up your ass. I choose to make living amends. Put that in your bong and smoke it.*

My recovery voice, apparently, had woken up and joined me. *Hi! Welcome to the team.*

CHAPTER 5

FIVE MINUTES BEFORE
THE MIRACLE

"How'd you do it?" was the universally shouted question.

How was I to know when a miracle was happening? Was I supposed to be struck by some skull-rattling bolt of blue lightning? Was some tunnel of illumination going to appear before me, or maybe a Gandalf-like figure, staff in hand, flowing white hair undulating in the mist?

In the early 1980s, when I was thirteen, my stepdad and I had a conversation about sex. That afternoon, we were the only two home, sitting around the kitchen table. I was not particularly interested in chatting, since it was World Series time and my Yankees were once again in the playoffs, the perennial matchup against the Kansas City Royals set to begin.

I sat there respectfully, mainly just indulging him, paying barely enough attention to convince him of my interest. His descriptions of the act of intercourse seemed somewhat mechanical, as if he were reading out of some instruction manual for the design of a backyard swing set. He had moved through the steps where clothes come off and bolt P inserts into slot V. His long-winded narrative concluded with a description of the culmination of *the act.*

"You will both reach a point where you experience something called orgasm."

Sigh. "How long will *that* take?"

"You will want to try to make things go on as long as possible before that happens."

"Why?" *Will Guidry's power slider be able to silence George Brett's bat?*

"Because you want to make sure that your partner arrives before you do."

Crap. Seems like a lot of work. "How will I know when I am having one?"

His expression changed to one of amusement. "Oh . . . *you'll know."*

A somewhat crude analogy, but so it seemed to be the case with my miracle. At age fifty, I was once again a thirteen-year-old boy learning about some laborious process that was supposed to culminate in some grand payoff, some ground-shaking release. How would I know when the miracle happened? I posed the question to my sponsor.

"Oh . . . *you'll know."*

▲▲▲▲▲

My introduction to "the rooms," as those in the Fellowship call them, happened well before my bottom, the day I refer to as Implosion Day. About a year prior to my stint in rehab, when it became clear to me I was a serious alcoholic, I decided to quit drinking—again—and give Alcoholics Anonymous a try. On some level, I realized that stopping on my own was impossible, completely beyond my capacity. I attempted all the usual maneuvers—tapering my consumption, switching from vodka to wine, substituting Valium for vodka, and even going for longer and increasingly intense runs to achieve a more prolonged runner's high.

Inevitably—which usually meant by lunchtime—the palpitations, shakes, and racing thoughts intensified, eventually overwhelming my ability to resist. Driven by my alcoholic voice, I would sneak down to my hidden basement stash and take two gulps straight out of the bottle. *Where's the harm in feeling better?* It was a nasty, vile, bitter liquid that burned in my chest and made me shudder, but it did the job. Within minutes, I would feel like my left big toe had been unscrewed and all the molten lava of my boiling brain hormones had poured out into a fiery puddle on the floor; my body would instantly cool, my mind quieted. I felt "normal," back to my new set point, my new baseline. *You see? Was that such a big deal?*

The problem was, like a quintessential alcoholic, I needed to take things further, beyond the stabilizing buzz. Back upstairs, maybe five minutes later, the *voice* would call again, and I would make an about-face, rush back down the steps (looking around, of course, to see if anyone noticed my movements), and take four or five more swallows to help my brain get beyond feeling just OK to heavily buzzed. I was chasing the dragon, always aiming for that sweet spot on the euphoria spectrum nestled somewhere between boringly normal and staggeringly drunk. Mine was a moving, shrinking target, and becoming less and less sustainable as the years wore on.

Step One of Alcoholics Anonymous presented itself to me, and I may have recited it, but I half-assed the follow-through. On some level, I had admitted I was powerless over alcohol. But had my life become unmanageable? Not so much. I was still doing well with the people, places, and things in my life—I was working shifts, getting paid, serving in leadership roles, and being a dad. I felt like I could secretly manage my alcoholism and still control my personal and professional life: I just required the right formula of daily dodging, deception, and cover stories.

I had searched online and located an AA meeting in an outlying county—far enough away from my home turf so that I would not be recognized. For years I had hidden my drinking, and the moment had arrived to admit I was an alcoholic—anonymously—to a small gathering of other alcoholics whom I'd never met and who knew nothing about me. I would eventually learn, in treatment, that "we are only as sick as our secrets." My alcoholism was a mammoth secret whose big woolly body I hid, traveling thirty miles to the south to a room full of people who probably didn't give a shit.

I drove down on an off day at a time nobody needed me, when I had no major work or domestic obligations. The AA club was nestled along a row of storefronts on a nondescript street off the central district of the city, much like a main street barber shop or hardware store, with no more than a small sign with the trademark blue AA triangle marking its presence on an old screen door. I walked in fifteen minutes early. It was dark, and the wood-paneled room was quite large with a low ceiling. A long wooden table sat in the center with various mismatched chairs around it. Along the periphery of the room were equally mismatched sofas and worn, plush chairs one could have easily seen in a fraternity common room or secondhand store. In the corner was a counter with a coffee maker and a box of Krispy Kreme doughnuts. Hanging on the far wall was a large white poster listing the Twelve Steps of Alcoholics Anonymous.

As I skimmed over each step, the first word to impact me was "powerless." Over to one side, a handful of people were milling about, holding coffee cups and chatting. Others were filing in and taking their seats. I tried not to judge them offhand, but I couldn't help feeling I had landed on the Island of Misfit Toys.

I'm not sure I can do this. Yes, yes I can. I can talk to the room about my alcoholism, have my catharsis, and repeat this a couple of times a month and then go back home and manage my life. A half measure for sure, but it's at least a start. I'll ease into the program until I don't drink any more, then I'll shake their hands and say farewell. And if I ever get a craving to drink again, I'll come back for a meeting or two to touch up my willpower and strength.

Faces at the table, at the coffee machine, and on the sofas began to turn in my direction. *It must be because I'm a newcomer,* I surmised. *This gang is going to chew me up and spit me out. I'm going to admit in a room full of alcoholics that I'm an alcoholic and they're gonna say that I have no idea what I'm in for. I bet they're going to go through some sort of initiation with me, some sort of hazing process. Your Delta Tau Chi name is . . . Flounder.*

A pudgy middle-aged woman walked up to me and took my hand. "Welcome, friend."

"Uh, thanks."

She introduced herself to me as Sarah and asked who I was and where I was from. I told her, mentioning that it was my first AA meeting. The moment I said it her eyes lit up, as if I had infused her with a milligram of epinephrine. I said it loud enough so that multiple nearby faces also lit up like Christmas trees. I found myself suddenly surrounded by a crowd of alcoholics in recovery.

Zombie drunks, feeding off the fresh newcomer meat.

A guy named Trav offered me a cup of coffee. I was having my hand shaken and people were throwing names out at me, none of which registered. They asked me how long I'd been sober, and I responded by giving them an honest answer—just a few days. This seemed to energize them even more. Virtually every person who approached me touted double-digit years of sobriety and was not shy about letting me know it. I looked around with a moderate degree of disappointment. I must have been surrounded by a combined one hundred years of sobriety, and every one of them looked like complete shit. Ragged T-shirts, unkempt hair, flip-flops, halitosis . . . And they were the ones who were going to show me how to stay sober?

The man leading the meeting sat down at the far end of the table, we all found a seat, and he called the meeting to order in a way that, unknown to me then, I would eventually hear hundreds of times.

"Hello, my name is Bob, and I am an alcoholic."

I had plopped myself down on a peripheral sofa. Sarah sat next to me, thigh to thigh, trying to hold my hand, whispering advice in my ear close enough so I could feel her warm breath. With the number of other side conversations happening around me, it was clear that most of the people in the room knew each other very well.

A laminated page of AA dogma was passed around for people to take turns reading.

God help me if this is my fucking fate.

The preliminary readings were completed, and it was time for people to "share." It was an open discussion meeting, and the topic was chosen from the participants. The leader called out for discussion and an uncomfortable silence hung in the air. Finally, an ancient guy in the corner rocking chair began to speak, and the conversation began.

This is silly. I feel like an imposter, like I don't belong here. I'm not a week sober and these people are going on decades. What do I know? How can I possibly contribute, and to what end? This whole thing is useless crap. A bunch of drunks sitting in a room talking about how they were born a drunk and will die a drunk and hopefully with the help of other drunks won't do any drinking today so they can piece together a string of no-drink days in

their sorry pathetic lives, in their grimy, tattered T-shirts, with
their mottoes and platitudes and bad coffee.

The old man's share ended. More silence. Impulsively, I
opened my mouth.

"Hello, my name is Joe, and . . . *(pause)* and. . . I'm an
alcoholic."

"Hello Joe." All faces locked onto mine.

I hesitated. After initially drawing a long blank, my mouth
finally blurted out the only words I could think of.

"I woke up in a SoHo doorway, a policeman knew my
name."

Laughter all around. I loosened up, and continued.

Still, I felt like such a phony in a room full of puny and
irrelevant, yet sober, souls. Holden Caulfield from *The Catcher
in the Rye* came to mind. It wasn't just the opening statement
about being an alcoholic who wanted recovery that made
me feel phony, but every syllable I uttered over the next two
minutes. The room seemed to eat it up, all of it; maybe it was
just because they had a new guy. I supposed there were some
redeeming aspects of being present. I just had to try to believe
some of the philosophy, the core stuff, and maybe that would
be enough to get me to stop drinking. I could then retain my
job, keep my sanity and my present life. Then, after a year or
so of no drinking, or maybe six months, when my liver had
regenerated and my brain reset, I could go back to controlled
drinking—but only when out with friends. If I would just not
drink nine out of every ten days—that should be fine. Ninety
percent; that's an A minus and I'd be good with that. Low As
got me through high school. From time to time I could make
an appearance at a meeting, touching up my sobriety. Perhaps
two or three a month—that should hold the line.

An hour later, right after we circled up for the Lord's
Prayer, I departed the room with a giant list of men's telephone
numbers on a sheet of paper, relatively uninspired but happy

that I could check off the "went to a meeting" box. The phone list was ditched into the first trash bin I saw on my walk back to the car.

How'd that strategy work out for you in the end, Remy?

▲▲▲▲▲

My second AA meeting was one year later, less than a week after my hospitalization and subsequent transfer to the treatment center. I was voluntold to attend my next meeting. That first evening, I sat in that circle in the darkened lecture hall of the Big House with the other early detoxers, not permitted to leave the property for an established meeting in town. I was fresh out of psychiatric lockdown at Penuel, still trembling, tachycardic, and living in an emotional wasteland. We sat there, a dozen strangers, in our first days in recovery boot camp. Although I had read about it, I had no idea of the meaning of AA's first step. I was a finished man—beaten, absolutely clueless about what had happened over the previous week and terrified of the difficult days to come.

Fears are what dominated my shares in those early meetings. I spoke of the accomplished emergency physician who got caught in the vortex of alcohol and how life pressures built up until they exploded. I was desperate over what my future might hold. I was told by RoboKarl that evening that I need not look beyond the horizon of tonight's bedtime. That sounded like perfectly good advice to me, but easier to grasp conceptually than to put into practice. My dorm room, fifty steps away, contained all my immediate worldly possessions—a pair of sweatpants, underwear, hospital footies, a pair of socks, a toothbrush, and an orientation binder. That was it. Despite the group circles and the sharing of painful experiences on those first cold evenings, all I felt was lost and alone. I desperately tried to follow Karl's advice and not think beyond today. Had

I lingered in my imagined future, the weight of my situation would have surely collapsed on top of me and suffocated me to death. So there I sat, staring at the other faces nightly, trying not to contemplate too much.

It took me a few weeks to recognize the meetings where I felt most comfortable. My tremor had largely subsided, but my panic had not, and the nights were still largely sleepless. By early December I was thoroughly immersed in the residential recovery culture and had the daily routine down. I thought of the other program on campus and wondered how any recovering alcoholic could feel ready to be released into the world after only twenty-eight days. I felt like I was just getting started.

The Williamsburg meetings, I soon found, were warm and engaging, the townsfolk vibrant. I found myself almost looking forward to certain days of the week, particularly Friday evenings.

Williamsburg was a charming, historic Virginia city, but I wasn't exactly in a position to take full advantage of its tourist offerings. I had no car (or freedom to move even if I had one) and spent my days on campus and my nights being shuttled downtown into the basements of various churches. I was on a "recovery tour of Williamsburg." I would look out the window of the transport van at the festive trappings of the holiday season—handsome wreaths adorning the entrances of stately colonials and brick row houses; tiny white lights glistening on the trees lining the quaint main street; families bundled in the brisk weather, walking along the cobblestone sidewalks and window shopping; young children running to and fro. I felt like the Johnny Cash character in "Sunday Morning Coming Down."

The Friday night meeting at First Baptist was one of the more intimate gatherings. Unlike the Saturday night "zoo" (as my first sponsor coined it), held the following night in the same locale, the Friday meeting was usually no more than fifteen or twenty of us, with a nice mix of fresh-out-of-detox newcomers and veteran old-timers who were perfectly ready to retell stories of their younger drinking days and impart wisdom to the rest of us. This was exactly what I received, and that was perfectly acceptable to me. It was at that meeting where I met my first sponsor, Doug, toward the end of my first week of treatment, once I was off detox status. He took me by the hand, figuratively speaking, and guided me through those initial terrifying weeks of life in recovery. I would try to get a ride from a peer going to that same meeting (always a nice reprieve from the rehab *prison van*) so I could get there early to help Doug set up the chairs and make the coffee, and he in turn would teach me about the Steps. Early recovery focused on the first step. Good thing, because it was all I was capable of even attempting to comprehend. I was powerless over the drink and my life was unmanageable.

Like the game of chess, this would take a minute to learn but a lifetime to master. The crusty silverbacks seated in the circle around me understood it to their cores; they had mastered Step One and thus had earned their right to sit in those chairs. It is said in the program that the newcomer should take the cotton out of his ears and put it in his mouth; that is, listen to the wisdom coming from those "with a few twenty-four-hour periods of sobriety" behind them.

And so I did, or tried. Being quiet took practice for me, though. Sometimes I played the cool professional and used my shares to impart medical advice to my peers. I was quickly shot down after pissing off a few of the old-timers. Doug reminded me that my ego was creeping up on me, and that it had been my "best thinking" that had landed me exactly where I was. After a couple of verbal smackdowns, I learned to shut up and listen to those who had worked their program one day at a time for many, many years—more years than I imagined the alcoholic in me could possibly ever stay sober.

Once I was released from treatment and transferred to the Oxford House in Charlottesville, the habit of meeting attendance had stuck. During my "ninety in ninety," (number of AA meetings in as many days) I quickly learned, through word of mouth, my housemates, and the local recovery community, where the more engaging meetings were held. My friend Chris from back home had delivered my truck to me, giving me badly needed mobility. Since my car was the only vehicle at the halfway house that did not have its ignition connected to a court-ordered Breathalyzer machine, I quickly became the designated driver of our little crew of alkies for meetings—not because anyone was actively drinking, but simply out of convenience.

With Langston, I did experience such a device. To engage the car's engine, the driver would get behind the wheel and blow into the straw sticking out of the machine attached to the dashboard. A windshield-mounted camera recorded the action. If the reading was zero, the device would complete the ignition circuit and the engine would start. Then, at random five- to fifteen-minute intervals, a shrill alarm would sound, signaling the driver to pull over and blow into the straw within sixty seconds. If the driver failed to do so, or if the breath test was positive for alcohol, the engine would shut down, and the device would electronically notify the operator's supervising authority.

As in Williamsburg, my chosen Charlottesville AA meetings were active and energetic. Attendees cut across all educational and socioeconomic demographics. The crowd was a mix of laborers, professionals, old-timers, and a revolving door of youthful students. Coffee and snacks seemed a bit more luxurious (scones instead of doughnuts, Starbucks instead of Folgers), and there were more young lads around with man-buns. There was a particularly dynamic meeting of hipsters and artists that I enjoyed, just a few blocks from my job at the supermarket, and after clocking out for the day, I frequently made the short hike over.

On the difficult day I was served with divorce papers, I stumbled to an evening meeting on the edge of the University of Virginia campus. I was delirious with grief, in an emotional tailspin. Within minutes I had vomited the events of my day to the room in an incohesive share, not sure how long I rambled on, and with no recollection of exactly what I said or if I cried. What I did remember was a group of sympathetic men surrounding me after the meeting adjourned, hugging me, handing me their phone numbers, and escorting me back to my car. That night I called and spoke with several of them. This was the essence of the rooms and why they would become such a touchstone in my life. For the time being, at least, they were a great place to hide.

Murphy, my second sponsor, was a sixty-two-year-old therapist with three years of sobriety. He possessed a nice mix of experience and professionalism, and we got along well. He had survived one major relapse and made a point of regularly discussing it with me, which initially surprised me. *We are only as sick as our secrets.* By sharing his fall, he was providing me with his experience, strength, and hope. This was the great advantage of a good sponsor. That, and long sessions of kicking my ass working the steps in his office, while his yellow Labrador, Michael, snoozed next to me on the sofa.

It was Murphy who hammered into me the concept of "Let go, let God." My entire life, I'd been focused on setting up my own stage and running my own show. Yet here I was, living the final outcome of my forced strategies and grand plans. In the end, I was an alcoholic emergency physician living in a sober house, stocking shelves, and assisting UVA students in locating yogurt. (*Hi! I'm new to the team!*) Yes, my brilliant, egocentric, self-absorbed thinking had placed me *exactly* where I belonged.

It was just before I made the move out of the Oxford House that I discovered my hometown's local AA club. Finn, my long-time friend and children's pediatrician, had invited me to move in with him, and I began to spend overnights at his spacious townhouse as I made the slow transition back to my home area. Finding meetings in the age of the internet was easy, and I downloaded the Meeting Finder app, which used GPS technology to locate the place that would eventually become *recovery central* for me, the room where I would bury myself for the next year and where I would find my "home group."

The AA club was located along a little-traveled, somewhat industrial secondary road on the other side of town. Low and flat, resembling an oversized prefabricated shed, its interior walls were painted urine yellow, and the place reeked of stale cigarettes and Pine-Sol. It fronted close to the street, and in the rear, attendees could be found congregating at the picnic tables before or after meetings, chatting and smoking. It was a ragtag bunch, even for alcoholics in recovery, but just about the most gracious people one could ever hope to meet. Despite their unkempt exteriors, club members were, for the most part, hardworking and honest people who went out of their way to shake hands with a newcomer or console someone in crisis. Their makeup reflected the cultural cross-section of the area— farmers, contractors, painters, machinists. The noon meeting also had its complement of retirees, and the gatherings were peppered with members of the local university community. I felt comfortable there. "Early on, it is not a sin to hide in the rooms where it is safe," as Lara, my cousin (also in recovery), mentor, and pinch-hitter sponsor, stated.

And hide I did. Meetings were held at noon and seven o'clock in the evening, seven days a week. My budding career stocking shelves had ended and was now behind me. I had been offered a short gig by a local college to be a guest lecturer of emergency medicine, and soon I was engaged in writing lectures to present to physician assistant students. I was elated. The job's hours were very limited, allowing me ample time to build my program of recovery, which included showing up early before meetings, attending two each day, and lingering afterward among the crowd to further discuss that day's meeting topic or other matters pertaining to recovery (aka the meeting after the meeting). When I wasn't sleeping, eating, or preparing my PowerPoint slides, I could be found at the AA club, and that suited me just fine.

No school buses pass by the club, which is perfect with me. A good place to hide, indeed.

The club was full of special characters, as all recovery clubs seemed to be, but a few of the members in this one particularly stood out in my mind. Most men were named Bob (when they weren't named Bill). There were also plenty of generic (and geriatric) Johns, Jims, and Davids.

One of my favorites was a man they called Cowboy, his nickname the result of his extensive collection of western-style hats. A country boy in his sixties, he was a regular attendee, always sitting up front for meetings. He took me under his wing early, imparting to me snippets of *Big Book* wisdom on a regular basis. No matter what my immediate crisis was (and they were all too frequent), he had a *Big Book* quote handy to help me reflect and smooth over my emotional disarray.

There was Lauren, a somewhat flamboyant middle-aged woman with a warm heart, whose shares were always very eloquent and well presented. Although most in my evolving network were men (appropriately so), she became my female perspective.

Fat old Bill sat quietly in the corner with his forty years of sobriety and his ample snacks. Due to his near deafness, he had a severe speech impediment. Most of the time I couldn't understand a single word he was saying (except maybe when he read the AA preamble, which he did virtually every day).

Dennis sat against the far wall, aged and with a Parkinsonian tremor. He had a resonating voice and was so amazingly on the money with his shares that he could pack powerful meaning into a mere few sentences. He possessed a real knack for story-telling in a concise, impactful way. Frankly, some of his stories of mental illness and criminal activity simultaneously amused and intimidated me.

There was Bob, a limping, aged, crotchety man with a Yankee accent so thick that when he introduced himself as "Bob, I'm an alcoholic," it came out as "Bawbama-alcoholic." He was usually dressed in a ratty gray cutoff sweatshirt, cargo shorts, and unmatched white socks pulled up to his knees, and he seemed to have endless anecdotes about his now-remote drinking days from the sixties and seventies.

I enjoyed my meetings with all of them and others, and I found most sessions at least marginally beneficial. There always seemed to be at least one share that served as my take-home message for the day, some golden nugget that I could savor until the next meeting. I "joined" the club, and within a few months, found myself leading meetings.

It was my third recovery community in my third city, and I obtained my third sponsor. Bobby was a long-sober silverback with a heavy Shenandoah Valley accent and a no-nonsense attitude. He could usually be found sitting quietly along the back wall, not speaking unless called upon. I had been attend-ing club meetings for a couple of months, and during an open discussion meeting where the day's topic was self-pity (one of my personal specialties), he opened up, allowing his hard-nosed opinion to rip through the room, hammering home how life isn't all about our own personal self-absorbed needs and desires. In other words, "Suck it up, buttercup." His message, and the way he delivered it, resonated with me big time. It was as if I was on the floor in an emotional fetal position and he had strolled over, yanked me up by my collar, and shook me, waking me up out of my self-absorbed spell. I needed this guy as my new sponsor. Immediately after the meeting adjourned, I asked him.

Bobby was the strong, silent type, with a chronically pissed-off look on his face and an economy of words that he used wisely. Gruff and often short-tempered, he made it clear he was neither my friend nor my therapist; he had little interest in hearing how sad my pathetic little life was. The loss of my marriage, kids, and job concerned him only with respect to how my indulging in self-pity could lead to me picking up a drink. He was a guy with long-term sobriety who had worked the Steps and was going to help me learn how to keep myself sober by quieting my inner crybaby. He had no patience for so-called justified dismay or whining. "You made this bed, you gotta lie in it" was a common saying in his repertoire. He was exactly what I needed. Sponsor number one woke me up; sponsor number two brought me to the classroom; sponsor number three would be my sergeant in basic training.

There is no doubt Bobby's methodology (if you can call it that) enhanced my recovery; over the months with him, I continued to stay sober and worked diligently on ego reduction and self-pity control. We spoke on the phone regularly, and I found that whenever I devolved into despair over my life situation, I was immediately cut off and given a reprimand. Recovery was much bigger than my petty little sadness and self-centered fears; as my sponsor, he kept me cognizant of this and on track with the Steps, doing what it took to tear me down so I could build myself up.

▲▲▲▲▲

On the first Saturday of every month, it was a tradition at the club to celebrate anniversaries with a cake, decorated with the names of those celebrating a "sobriety birthday."

In November of 2017, my name was written in icing underneath Bobby's, as we happened to celebrate recovery anniversaries in the same month. For him it was his tenth year; for me, my first. The evening meeting was "open," meaning nonalcoholics could attend, and the room was filled with members and their families and partners. There was a speaker, and we all sat and listened as James, four years sober, told his story. I enjoyed the speaker meetings immensely, hearing how other people in recovery used to be, what happened, and how things played out for them afterward. Upon adjournment, the usual ritual of handing out chips to mark time in sobriety was performed, from white (new in the program), through a rainbow of colors, ending with bronze anniversary medallions. On that night, Bobby stood in the front of the room and presented two medallions—one for me and one for his other sponsee, who was marking three years. I relished my moment as he called me up, placed the heavy bronze coin in my hand, and gave me a firm handshake. The crowd shouted the standard question.

"How'd you do it?"

The answer was a canned response.

"One day at a time."

Bobby and I parted ways after about a year together; it wasn't that either of us "fired" the other, as sometimes happens; it was more of a slow drifting apart. As I changed and evolved in recovery, so did my areas of focus for continued growth.

So it happened that at a Sunday morning meeting of another AA group, which gathered across town from the club, I met Wally—a seventy-one-year-old native of Maine. His demeanor was quite different from Bobby's. He spoke softly, with a relaxed, cheery delivery. His shares in meetings seemed to strike a nice balance between program dogma, compassion, and gentleness. After listening to him a few times, I asked him to be my sponsor, and he accepted. Wally was short, round, and approachable, and he usually had a welcoming grin on his face. He loved working in his home garden and seemed to mysteriously pop in and out of meetings without being seen coming or going. My new sponsor was a garden gnome.

I had been through the Steps twice in my recovery, and Wally guided me, using his interpretation of the *Big Book*, the third time. In Alcoholics Anonymous, it is encouraged to continuously work through the Steps and upon completing Step Twelve, start over again at Step One. Many of the steps were passive and required thought, meditation, and mental processing: We admitted we were powerless . . . Made a decision . . . Were entirely ready . . . Other steps felt more like homework assignments that necessitated putting pen to paper, such as Step Four, writing out a searching and fearless moral inventory. I found these active steps much more arduous, both logistically and emotionally. The fourth step, for me, was the biggest challenge. Even Steps Eight and Nine, which are all about making amends to others, were not nearly as intimidating to me as the process of digging down inside myself to learn what made me tick, as the fourth step demands.

The fourth step is much like cleaning out a closet in an old, neglected house that has fallen into a state of disrepair and has accumulated decades of clutter. The first pass-through was like opening the door to air it out, looking around, and pulling out the larger items. The second time through felt more like shining a flashlight into its deep corners and high shelves to see what had been forgotten or left festering. Going through the third time was the *deep clean*.

Wally pulled into my driveway one bright Saturday morning. My notebook was open and ready, its pages filled with an inventory of fear, anger, and remorse over virtually every negative life situation I'd experienced, going back to childhood. Like a term paper assigned by the professor of my least favorite but mandatory class, I had continuously conjured excuses to avoid sitting down and writing it out. This was more than just procrastinating on a school assignment; it was avoiding having to mentally dig into memories I would have much rather kept buried forever, ones that were profoundly upsetting and agonizing to drag out of my vault. The exercise of shedding light on a long-buried sinful act, admitting to it, mentally processing it, and writing it down felt akin to a painful radiculopathy of the back. They say that the disease of addiction dies in the light, but exposing myself this way made me feel like a vampire outdoors at noontime in May.

Despite my love-hate relationship with the fourth step, I recognized the vital importance of this mental closet-cleaning. It felt horrible going through it, but when it was over I would—and did—feel lighter on my feet, emotionally liberated. I became mentally freed as I vomited out my sins, as opposed to how I used to puke out my stomach contents in my dark basement.

Wally lounged in the cushy chair in my living room and I sat on the sofa. Out of my notebook, I recited entry after entry of some ugly secret, some vile act, some thorn in my soul. Every disruptive interaction with another human being was pulled out and exposed to the light that day, kicking and screaming. Fifty years of stealing, lying, damaging, disrupting, and putting my own self-interest over others' were piled up in the room for Wally and me to discuss. My dark closet was scoured as I spoke of memories I had suppressed for decades. Step Four was the act of writing them down. Step Five was the act of confessing them. The purge required no less than six hours. I completely understood why it was tradition, after the fifth step, to physically burn one's fourth-step notebook like in some pagan ritual; it was symbolic of the destruction of the "old ways" of the alcoholic behavior as one evolved in the program.

The fourth and fifth steps would, so long as I was in long-term recovery, inevitably have to be performed again. Since I was a fallible human being, my closets would not likely remain clean and tidy forever. Unsavory acts would undoubtedly begin to once again accumulate, cluttering my dark shelves.

Beyond the fourth and fifth steps, I could maintain my supposedly healthier soul through the daily routine of continuing to take a personal inventory, as is required in Step Ten, and admitting faults, as they presented themselves, on a daily basis.

▲▲▲▲▲

It was another Saturday night speaker meeting at the club. It was November 2018, and I was on the cusp of receiving my second anniversary sobriety medallion. I had been sober exactly 730 days. (I had a cell phone app that reminded me.) I sat in my chair, quietly absorbing the spirit of the room as our speaker told her story. She was seventeen years sober, and I still couldn't help but feel a bit like an imposter.

Do I deserve this? Have I worked my program, practiced my steps diligently and comprehensively enough? When does my miracle happen? Why am I not feeling happy, joyous, and free, like I have heard about in so many shares over hundreds of meetings?

My miracle was not going to strike me in some flash revelation, some divine bolt of blue lightning from the sky causing me to leap out of my chair and scream "I'm saved!" evangelist-style. No, my miracle was going to be more of a slow, steady awakening. *They* say not to abandon the program five minutes before the miracle occurs. I came to the realization that my miracle *was* happening, but I couldn't see it because it was unfolding around me slowly, and I was in the middle of it. There was no flash-bang, only the continuous, almost imperceptibly slow illumination of my universe.

My miracle was one of relinquishing the bondage of self, letting go of operating out of absolute self-reliance. My entire life, I'd chosen to depend on myself, and only myself, to surmount life's ongoing daily challenges. By staying in the rooms and opening my mind to what others had to say, I was learning to permit the power of the program to work within me.

My sober network, my sponsors, and God could now assist me in life's decisions for this day because I was letting them in. I was no longer sacrificing my *here moments* to panicky, egoic future thinking, frantically chasing after decisions that did not yet need to be made because they were the product of some imagined future. I finally began to allow God and people to inspire me to calmly make only the decisions that needed my attention *in the moment*.

This was an epic shift in thinking for me. I was now strolling and breathing instead of sprinting and gasping through life.

It was an imperfect miracle, if such things exist. I had not yet completely rid myself of the self-pity or ego character defects. Hannah, Robert, and Toby's estrangement from me continued to weigh heavily, to pull me away from inner peace. Until I could completely "let go, let God" with them, I could never be *happy, joyous, and free*. Even so, I had made real inroads toward serenity, and I was able to count my blessings. At the two-year mark, sitting there in the club, I mentally conjured the all-important gratitude list as espoused by the treatment center's counselor Nathaniel.

I am alive.

I am physically healthy.

I am sober.

I am gainfully employed in a profession I love.

I have a nice house and a sweet dog.

I love people.

People love me.

My children are healthy and secure.

Perhaps most important that day, I was grateful for being able to pick up my two-year chip, not for self-promotion or narcissistic self-congratulation, but for using it to work the twelfth step: helping other newly sober alcoholics at the meeting remain so by sharing my experience, strength, and hope.

Somewhere in the crowded room that evening sat a terrified newcomer who, just maybe, would watch me receive my medallion and perhaps be inspired to keep away from alcohol another day, today.

After a kind introduction, Wally held up my medallion. I rose and walked slowly up to the podium to genuine goodwill applause. He placed the chip in my palm and hugged me. Wally's hugs were always warm, and I let his comforting arms envelop me for a moment. Feeling reaffirmed, I heard a single voice from the crowd.

"How'd you do it?"

I answered.

"I stopped relying on myself."

CHAPTER 6

SWIPING RIGHT

An entire generation had been born, raised, and entered adult-hood since I had last been a single man in the dating world. Over that time the universe of coupling up had not just changed—it had evolved, morphing into a process virtually unrecognizable to the midlife-crisis crowd. As teenagers and college students in the eighties, we met each other in high school parking lots and at church socials, the mall, or in fraternity barrooms. If an attractive someone caught our eye, we may have initially attempted to make the connection through intermediaries. If and when we finally summoned the courage to make our move, we simply smoothed down our mullets, adjusted our Members Only jackets, and approached our targets, communicating to them face to face.

In every American generation until now, boys were required to physically stand in front of their prospective mates and open their mouths to let out real words. We were either rejected or accepted, got a phone number or didn't. There was no text to hide behind, Facebook profile to stalk, or background to google. We were forced to be brave and risk a bruised ego or mild embarrassment for the chance of the big payoff of a new girlfriend, or at least a date.

Once an established pair, we would tie up our home phone lines for hours with mindless babble just to hear the voice of our new, exciting infatuation. This usually annoyed the hell out of our parents, siblings, or dorm mates. If no phone was available, we would make excuses to walk or drive by her house, to "be in the neighborhood" on our bikes or in our cars. We would go to the hangouts where we knew she would be with her friends. We would tan our gym muscles in the late spring warmth of the college quad in front of her sorority, vaguely knowing her class schedule. We would hit the good parties and take her to dance.

Dating without a protective technology shield required time, effort, and chutzpah. There was no online process or quick-clicking; it was a slow, methodical trial-and-error ritual that often led to eventual romance, whether for a night or a year. While on a date, at a dance, or in the back seat of our beat-up sedans, we were certainly not reporting the play-by-play in real time on social media for all the world to see. The connections were made with each other, privately, without the distraction of selfie uploads or Facebook likes.

I was out of the Charlottesville sober house and back in my home area living with Finn—recently divorced—along with his dog, Jake. I was not yet employed as a practicing physician but had acquired work teaching emergency medicine to physician assistant students at a local college. Several times a week I found myself in front of a classroom full of vibrant, young, attractive people. Although my conscience and professionalism kept my students off limits socially, so to speak, I felt like more than my academic enthusiasm was awakening.

In the evenings, Finn and I relaxed in his living room watching reruns of *Seinfeld* or *Dexter*. By this time, I was legally separated and in the full throes of divorce proceedings while still adjusting to my new life in early sobriety. I was relieved to be out of the Oxford House and back in my hometown. My social life to that point had consisted of dinners with my sponsor and any meetings or events involving the AA club. My animal spirit was, for the most part, still hibernating.

Finn and I had a mutual friend, Jerry, a local business owner and poker buddy who was obsessed with online dating, so much so that he virtually never stopped talking to us about it. Many evenings, when he was over at the house, we would sit around the living room, half paying attention to the TV, while he displayed to us pictures on his phone of amazingly attractive ladies of international flair advertising themselves for companionship and romance. Finn wanted no part of it; I found myself both amused and intrigued. Jerry's primary go-to site displayed a fine selection of Ukrainian women interested in marrying American men; their only apparent requirements were that the men had to be American and had to be men. These young ladies were gorgeous, if the photos were anything close to legitimate. Jerry assured me they were, as he had traveled overseas and met a few. He would scroll through his selections as I looked on, slowly waking up to the reality that the dating scene had been forever revolutionized. He persuaded me to start an account with one of the more reputable mainstream dating sites, and so I did.

Who in my generation had time to go out and meet people? At the moment, my loose schedule did allow for it, but so much surrounding the dating game involved alcohol, and I simply was not ready for that. Online dating certainly seemed to be the safer and more efficient way to go, and so I decided there was no harm in looking. There were the legal ramifications, but the separation was officially inked, and I was informed by my attorney, Mr. Hitschmeiser, that at this point dating would have no impact on my divorce proceedings. My multifaceted loneliness did not have to go on, even if filling the void with single-serving internet dates was a rather superficial remedy. Jerry was no George Clooney yet seemed to have some good success, so I figured that for me, it couldn't be too challenging. There were bound to be some nice women out there willing to date an underemployed alcoholic, right? I thought of a coffee shop scene from a *Seinfeld* episode in which George approaches a woman and says the opposite of what his instincts tell him.

"My name is George. I'm unemployed and live with my parents."

▲▲▲▲▲

The more I went online, created accounts on dating sites, and researched what was out there, the more I began to see the online dating process as an experience akin to the online shopping process. One set up an account, signed in, and created a personal profile; there were premium versions of the website where, for a nominal fee, one could be featured and displayed near the top of a search list, and could even access real-time chatting software. On the home page, one was presented with a spectrum of profiles, usually with the most popular candidates at the top, based on the software algorithm's analysis of search traffic. Often the "premier" people displayed would be in seasonal attire, such as a bathing suit in August or a festive dress around holiday time. With a few mouse clicks or on-screen taps, one could adjust the search parameters for demographics and specific qualities tailored to one's personal interests, such as "age thirty-six to fifty-five, athletic, college educated," within a seventy-five-mile radius (when one's GPS feature was enabled). Style, color, material. It had all the feel of shopping online for a bathrobe or kitchen appliance.

Click here for more options and brands!
People who liked Cynthia also liked Janice and Darlene.
Add to shopping cart?
Ready to check out?
It all seemed so . . . virtual. As photoshopped pictures of women looking their best flashed in front of me, my cynicism outpaced my libido. *And what's the deal with all these cartoon cat-ear and bunny-nose add-ons?* During one evening's search, out of absolute sheer exasperation, I went onto Amazon.com and searched for an Orgasmatron, but came up empty. *Damn.* *Is* it possible that these dating sites are excessively deceptive, even a complete scam? What do these women—especially the midlife-divorcée crowd—really look for? What do the young ones want? What are their intentions? What the hell am I getting myself into? Should I click on someone? *Oy.*
Click here to piss away money on one-off dates!
Click here for a cash-grabbing sugar baby!
Click here for a chlamydia queen!
Ultimately, I came to the conclusion I could sit there on Finn's sofa and allow my paranoid fantasies and unfounded fears to relegate me to a life of erotic websites, or I could take a chance with a real human. I decided I was not going to live as an autoerotic hermit while our horny friend was busy dating half of Ukraine. So I took the plunge, opting for a more American experience.

▲▲▲▲▲

My first dating experience was actually not from an online encounter; it was with a nurse I had known for some time. I had always admired Celine from afar. She was in her late twenties and very attractive, and she always kept a subdued demeanor at work. I had an inkling she had a wilder side, based on some of her Facebook posts. She had a fantastic body, athletic yet feminine, and was uninhibited about posting pictures high-lighting her toned physique in swimwear and sexy negligees. She was educated, clearly intelligent, and had a strong work ethic (something I found curiously appealing). A well-rounded woman with a built-in professional overlap with me seemed like a good opportunity to connect, relax, and have some fun. Since there was no ice to break, first contact was not going to be a cold call. I took a chance and texted her my interest in a get-together. To my relief, and mild surprise, she responded positively.

The fantasy of Celine excited me, and our date—my first one since 1992—could not have gone better. I felt no awkward-ness despite the fact that my life situation was an open secret back at the hospital. I didn't have to sheepishly explain why I was not drinking with dinner as we sat across the table from one another, engaging in lively conversation. Even better, while she sipped on her mojito, I felt no cravings (well, no cravings to *drink*). I was drawn in by her smile and general warmth. We laughed a lot, and after dinner, walked through downtown, stopped into a bar for a little bit of dancing, and capped off the evening with a warm, soft goodnight kiss in front of the apartment building where she was spending the night with a friend. As I walked back to my car afterward, I concluded that the post-divorce single life might not be so bad.

Celine and I quietly dated for about six weeks, and we seemed to genuinely enjoy each other's company. For me, it was a nice reintroduction to dating after a quarter century. I found myself far more comfortable than I thought I would be at this tender early stage of my reemergence. In the end, the realities of our different stations in life became apparent, and we discontinued our brief but pleasant run of get-togethers, parting on good terms. There were no regrets. The seal had been broken with someone familiar and gentle. For a damaged guy like me, it was an ideal start. I was able to practice living in the moment, and she was a great person to keep me there, however briefly.

▲▲▲▲▲

I was "back on the bike." It didn't take long before I was connecting online with some of my internet hits—like-minded women with whom I matched up well on paper. My main dating site seemed to screen well and permitted online chatting, and I was off to the races. I began to meet some of the women in real life, but as expected, many dates went nowhere. However, I learned something new from each one, and in time, some short and some not-so-short relationships ensued. Early on, my criteria were overly restrictive, but as I loosened up, I found myself immersed in a wide range of . . . experiences.

After Celine, my confidence began to percolate, and my pendulum swung in the other direction. Things got a bit crazy. The divorce proceedings were in fifth gear, with the lawyers on each side progressing through the discovery process; I was still not gainfully employed, and life was a cacophony of multiple moving pieces. I was utterly controlled in many other facets of my life, so when it came to dating, I eventually chose to throw a little caution to the wind. What did I have to lose?

A disease-free groin, you idiot.

▲▲▲▲▲

My first notable online match was with a respiratory therapist who lived an hour's drive away. Chandra was older than me, in her mid-fifties, and was crystal clear about her dating objectives from the get-go. It became apparent to me that some of the more . . . mature . . . women were attempting to make the best of what was left of their sexual physiology before their hormonal countdown timers sounded, stuffing in as many men as possible. Our first live telephone conversation devolved into highly charged sexual banter dripping with innuendo, and it was only forty-eight hours later that I found myself driving to her locality to see her for "dinner."

Danger, Will Robinson!

We did meet at a restaurant, and actually made it almost completely through our entrées. Apparently I passed some sort of qualifier screening, because within the hour we were back at her place under the pretense of viewing *Fifty Shades of Grey*. We barely made it through the first three shades.

Click here to enlarge!

It was a bit disconcerting to me that she was a mother to a thirty-two-year-old son and a twenty-nine-year-old daughter, who herself had two kids (and whose grade-school portraits were proudly displayed on the wall). I lay there on my back in her bed for the first time, next to the nightstand adorned with an antique candy dish and vase of dried flowers. My head was propped up against a needlepoint decorative pillow embroidered with the words "World's Greatest Grandma." I couldn't help but recall a scene from Steve Carell's movie *The 40-Year-Old Virgin*, in which Cal tells Andy to do it with his hot grandma girlfriend on her plastic-covered sofa while watching *Murder, She Wrote*.

Alas, Chandra soon became my go-to guilty pleasure. As dangerous as a trigger like sex could be for a recovering alcoholic, I found that I had no alcoholic cravings.

Over the next few weeks I acclimated to my newfound boy-toy role. There were some nights I'm not even sure she remembered that there was a living, breathing human being underneath her. Poor Emily was the recipient of my guilt-ridden texts sent from the interstate as I left AA meetings in Charlottesville and, instead of going home, diverted southwest for booty calls. I justified my actions by saying I was practicing acceptance and riding a wave (actually, it was riding me).

Eventually the wave's energy depleted, the momentum ended, and the relationship, if that's what it was, burned itself out. After our final, final parting (it took a few tries), I was back online, searching and probing.

▲▲▲▲▲

Lylah was from Charlottesville and worked in the local university's IT department, helping hospital personnel to acclimate to the new electronic health record software. Like Chandra, she was in her fifties, but that's where the similarities ended. She'd never married and had no children. Her online bio depicted a confident-appearing, pretty face, much younger looking than her stated age, and a photo displaying her thin, muscular build while sitting at the overhead-bar pulldown station in a health club. We seemed to match up well online, and within a day were off the computer and speaking on the phone—or rather, she was speaking at me, talking about her job, her house, what she ate for breakfast, her ukulele, and her previous summer's conference in Tulsa. With Lylah, I served primarily in the listening role, simply because she would never shut the fuck up. When we met on our first date, she carried the conversation, which was perfectly acceptable to me. She was petite, with a mousy voice that flowed like a creek after a thunderstorm. I ended up spending the night at her place after our third date.

Her home had the look and feel of an oversized dollhouse. It was immaculate, and she decorated in pastels, country-style, with a kitchen one might see a photo of in *Southern Living* magazine. Shiny copper pots hung in place above the food preparation island, white and sky-blue tiles were everywhere, and just the right number of knickknacks made the spaces feel homey without looking cluttered. Her shelves were meticulous and she had every conceivable variety of coffee and tea, neatly organized in matching decorative jars. We would come downstairs in the morning in her plush, oversized cotton robes, and she would prepare eggs Benedict, thick-cut French toast with apricot marmalade, or blueberry porridge; each meal came with an accompanying reference to a family recipe, cooking class, or discovery of some rare baking spice found in a farmers market while touring old Europe. She cleaned all the while she cooked and spoke. I'd never seen a home so spotless.

All of this, of course, came with a curveball. As if to contrast with her sophisticated demeanor and surroundings, she would sporadically and unexpectedly unleash a string of horrific profanities while speaking—often in midsentence, seemingly uncontrollably.

"This particular English jam was imported from South Wales, *motherfucker!*"

"The antique quilt, *you fucking jerk-off*, was inherited from my maternal grandmother."

"While on holiday in Monaco, I came across a nice set of European spa towels for the guest bathroom, *asswipe!*"

It didn't take long before I realized I was dating Martha Stewart with Tourette's.

For a full two months, I enjoyed top-notch accommodations while sampling homemade, world-class cuisine, served by a dainty aristocrat with a mouth as foul as a drunken sailor's. A few nights, just for fun, I tried to get her to talk dirty to me in bed; unfortunately, the curse feature could not be activated on demand. Plus, she was way too shy. As the weeks passed, our mutual interest waned, as did my amusement with her crude outbursts, particularly during theater performances and double dates. Our last night together preceded a very mature and unemotional breakup conversation. Lylah was an experience I will never forget. Ya can't make this stuff up, folks.

▲▲▲▲▲

Along came Inga, a German-born nurse practitioner who worked at the aforementioned university medical center. A lifelong U.S. resident, she was fluent in English but maintained a heavy Bavarian accent. She was tall and statuesque and had straight auburn hair well past her shoulders. She had Barbie-doll physical proportions; for fifty, her body was holding up quite well. She had caught my eye on the dating site fairly early in my searches, and I had messaged her, but weeks elapsed before I received any response; apparently, she had stepped away from dating for some time. She would later tell me mine was the first profile she'd found interesting upon returning. As per protocol, we connected initially by website messaging followed by texting, then we finally set up a live meeting. I scrolled through her photos with frat-boy, testosterone-dripping enthusiasm.

Click here for a stacked Fräulein!

With medical careers as common ground, Inga and I made a connection right away. Our first meeting took place in a coffee shop on the Charlottesville walking mall, and I felt chemistry that, admittedly, was skin deep. Our thirty-minute rendezvous led to a second date, a dinner engagement in Staunton. She quickly made me feel comfortable around her and took notice when I ordered a sparkling water with my entrée. It had been my practice to wait until a second encounter to bring up the subject of my recovery from alcoholism.

Revealing to a date that I am in long-term recovery took some practice. Much like with the job interview process, I developed a keen sense for when to broach the topic to the new woman seated across from me: too soon and I might frighten her off or weird her out, too late and I might come off as being deceitful. The second date, much like the second job interview, seemed to be the sweet spot for the revelation. We would be past the "screening interview," conversation would be more relaxed, and she would know just enough about me so that I was not a complete stranger. I never went into much detail, and certainly never made the evening a preaching session about long-term recovery or AA.

When the drink orders were taken, I simply let her inquire as to why I chose a non-alcoholic beverage. I would state very matter-of-factly that I was in long-term recovery and allow her to pursue the topic if she chose. Sometimes the subject would be immediately changed, but more often my date would ask a few follow-up questions, which I would answer honestly and generically, without gritty detail. If the relationship progressed to the next phase, more would be revealed during pillow talk.

Inga and I did have a brief conversation about it during that second date, and it seemed to fold seamlessly into the wider discussion about our respective life challenges. She was a divorced mother of two teenagers who split their days and weekends between both parents (like most normal divorced couples, where each parent actually supported the other for the good of the children). We covered significant ground over that dinner, and I was quickly smitten with her intellect, European flair, and fun-loving attitude. Dinner seemed to fly by, and afterward we took advantage of the warm spring evening to stroll the streets of downtown, talking and holding hands. We went into an ice cream shop, and our conversation deepened. We walked out with our vanilla cones, and the *kiss me* look came—the one every man in every stage of life should learn to recognize and respond to, as it is a window of opportunity that can close very fast. The smooch was warm, sweet, and delicious, and as the evening went on, it was followed up with many more. We walked arm in arm, eventually finding ourselves wandering through a church cemetery, intermittently viewing the graves and making out. The area was quiet, and events were progressing rapidly from warm to hot, but the mature man in me quashed the horny boy, and I walked her back to her car before we committed sacrilege over one of the sturdier headstones.

Inga and I became exclusive to each other late that spring and into summer. I spent my spare time with her at her house in Albemarle County, and she would occasionally spend nights with me at Finn's place. It was during this period that the monitoring program approved me for a position at an urgent care center, and I was moving through the laborious task of professional credentialing, a process that usually takes months before a work start date can be set. I lived with the relief and comfort of knowing I would be working in medicine again soon, yet I still had the flexibility to see Inga for lunch, after work, or any time we chose, and we made the best of it. We took full advantage of the Virginia Piedmont, going on trail hikes on warm afternoons, attending the local Shakespeare theater, and dining in Charlottesville. On weekends, we relaxed with some quiet time at her house. Inga became an embodiment of serenity and sanity in my otherwise fast-moving, turbulent world of recovery and change.

As much as I tried to keep my two worlds apart, they inevitably began to overlap one another. Several weeks into our relationship, I met her son, a quiet, well-mannered boy who played on his high school football team and enjoyed his video games, as boys his age did. Meeting a girlfriend's teenage child was a completely novel experience for me. It had been a quarter century since I had a "girlfriend," and as a younger man, parenthood had not factored into my dating matters; now it was the norm. The middle-aged dating man (or woman) had a unique challenge: whereas earlier in life, it had been to gain acceptance from the parents, now it was approval from the children.

I apparently passed the initial screening. Her son, while not thrilled with the idea that his mom was dating, nevertheless expressed tentative approval of me. Still, I felt awkward around him, much like a third wheel when he was in the house. Learning a bit about me, he excitedly asked me about my children, and despite the sting, I answered him honestly and with poise. I had no contact with them myself, so the chance of fulfilling his request to meet and hang out with them was slim. At one point I gave him a small gift—a quality multitool, which won me major points.

Inga seemed to initially handle my long-term recovery situation well, even coming with me to an occasional AA meeting. She kept the wine in her house hidden, and even removed from sight all the alcohol at Finn's place. There appeared to be genuine interest and compassion on her part, and she clearly demonstrated it in her actions. Over time, however, the issue of my children began to take its toll, weighing heavily on our relationship. My complete lack of contact with them angered and frustrated her; my emotional lows over the issue detracted from our time together with increasing frequency. Still, we managed to enjoy each other's company enough to offset my difficult moments of self-absorbed distress.

The relationship started to significantly erode when Inga became less my companion and more my self-ordained therapist. She started to advise me on the nature of therapy I should seek and what I should focus on. She had contacts in the local recovery community, and apparently had a good friend who had been sober for more than twenty years; her attempts to impose another's sobriety success formula on me led to friction. I began to openly rebel and then disengage.

"Joseph, your success in sobriety hinges on your success with the children. I see that. You need to go to therapy more, at least twice a week, and get your children into sessions with you."

Every girl that I go out with becomes my mother in the end.

She just didn't get it. My kids were nowhere close to wanting to be anywhere near me, let alone opening up in therapy sessions. That would require the preferred parent to subscribe to co-parenting; my ex was doing just the opposite, implementing a scorched-earth policy when it came to me. Our children had a full-blown case of parental alienation syndrome, and their mother considered alcoholism my personal moral failing as opposed to the family disease so well described in the therapy community.

Passive-aggressive interactions led to fights, which led to cooling-off periods and short stints of reconciliation, followed by more fights over unresolved conflict. I needed Inga to be my oasis of fun and relaxation, not my life problem solver. I recognized her approach, though—at times I would become so distraught over my children she would tap into her clinical side and offer assistance, which I rejected. It wasn't long before she began to discuss my character defects with me and judge me. I sensed the relationship death spiral. The end was near. After a great three months, our days together concluded with a single phone call. In the final tally, my emotional baggage was just too heavy a burden for her, her impositions too inappropriate for me. A few days later, while at work (I had begun my urgent care job), I received a text from her asking how I was "holding up," and I provided a cordial but curt response. That was the last time Inga and I ever communicated. It was great while it lasted, but it was clearly time to move on for both of us. Still, losing her presence hurt. She was the first woman I had a full-on relationship with whom I found both physically and intellectually exciting. I dreaded the lonesomeness of the days that followed.

▲▲▲▲▲

One evening a few weeks later, I was back with Finn and Jerry in our living room, feeling dark and lonely and staring at the TV as Jerry scrolled through pictures on his Ukrainian websites.

Still mourning the breakup with Inga, I was contemplating my next moves with regard to my dating life, including whether or not to take a break. My program promoted a one-day-at-a-time approach, to accept events as they unfolded and make choices as they appeared in the *now*.

Peeking over his shoulder at Jerry's cell phone, I saw the mindless appeal of bikini-clad Eastern European women. How hard would it be to carry on with a woman who was interested in nice dinners and travel, with whom I could keep a relationship casual and firewall off my emotions, uncaging them only where appropriate—with my therapists and in the rooms of AA? For me, this was difficult. Companionship for me meant sharing more than a fancy meal, a bed, and a few orgasms. It meant really sharing, allowing myself to be open and emotionally vulnerable with a partner who permitted the same. It meant keeping the relationship on an even keel, with neither partner vying for the power position, or conversely, allowing domination. I had yet to experience this balance in a relationship, ever. I had always been controlling or controlled and wondered if it was even possible to achieve a healthy, "horizontal" companionship, one that maintained a steady state of mutual respect, openness, and honesty, without the relationship slipping into a power struggle or unhealthy codependence.

Click here for a kind woman looking for a balanced relationship!

I got up from the sofa to go to bed. I said goodnight to Finn and Jerry and began to walk upstairs. I abruptly stopped and turned back around toward them.

"I need an intellectual equal with some hard-knock life experience. Perhaps a divorced university professor." Finn looked at me and nodded in approval.

"I agree; that would be good for you. Well, good night, old man."

Jerry never responded, his eyes remaining fixed on the phone screen in front of him. I climbed the stairs and went into my bedroom, slid under the covers, and opened the dating app, sitting there in the dark, mindlessly swiping right and left without any real enthusiasm.

Then her picture appeared.

She was sitting on outdoor steps in a summer dress, alone, looking down, her arms around her knees, a sweet, wistful look on her face.

CHAPTER 7

FIRST, KINDNESS

I stared at the screen. She was cute and had the look I had always been attracted to—thin, fair, Anglo-Saxon; however, it was that sweet, wistful downward glance that captivated me. I stared; there was much behind those eyes, behind that look. I scrolled to her bio. She was a university professor here in town. Her profile contained no red flags. She was over forty, posted no party pictures or cat pictures, and did not Photoshop in animated kitty ears or a tail. She was the only one in that single picture, sitting knock-kneed on those concrete steps, looking like . . . looking like she wanted *out* of something. Needed *out* of something.

I not only swiped right but used up my last "super like," a special version of approval that alerted the recipient of my existence without requiring her to also right-swipe me. It allowed me to let her know that I was out there and genuinely interested. Once I did it, her profile disappeared. Our match was then in the hands of fate and the software algorithms. I closed out of the app and slid under my comforter to get some sleep. It was late.

I had a couple of days off work. That next morning, I woke up early as usual, went for my morning run, and planned on a day of laundry, relaxing, and attending my regular noon meeting. By the time I returned from my standard loop, Finn was already out of the house and at the office seeing patients. I showered and continued my day-off routine. I appreciated my routines, as they made for nice, comfortable, structured days. My job at the local urgent care center was a twelve-hour shift, from eight in the morning to eight at night, four days a week. Patient issues were of a common low acuity—colds, the flu, bladder infections, ankle injuries, and other problems that never taxed me intellectually or stressed me out. On days off, I always hit my AA meetings, then ate lunch and had a nap. Evenings usually consisted of dinner with Finn, an episode of *Dexter*, and bed.

Having showered, dressed, and put the laundry in the dryer, I plopped down on the sofa next to Jake the Jack Russell and fired up my dating app. A notification was waiting. Wistful Girl had made contact, an introduction. Her message contained a few lines of information about herself. She was separated and a mother of two. She was a faculty member in the biology department and provided me a link to her university website profile. I clicked over and read extensively about who she was in her professional life. She asked me what a "super like" was. On paper, at least, things seemed like a good match. She opened the door to a response, and respond I did.

I immediately wrote back, letting her know a bit more about myself beyond my bio, providing her a link in kind to my old hospital's website profile and to my blog, which was a travelogue of my annual medical missions in Haiti. There, she would be able to view plenty of pictures and read descriptions and accounts of my overseas adventures. She could also see a couple of shots of my children. I normally would not have given an online match so much information, but my spider-sense told me this woman was honest, upfront, and wholly legitimate. Not only was she a PhD, but she was involved in STEM (science, technology, engineering, and math) outreach to underprivileged public school students. She seemed entirely authentic online, complete with official university shots of her assisting students at a microscope in a public school biology lab.

Again, there is something about her look. . . .

Our first meeting was at a popular coffee hangout on the edge of campus. Playing the game properly, I made sure to arrive first. Blind dates were now antiquated; with internet dating, everybody knows what everyone else looks like before they ever set foot in a room together. I went to the men's room for a quick check in the mirror to make sure I had no unsightly skin blemishes or food particles in my teeth. Just as I emerged, I saw her in the doorway, chatting with a student, one foot in the entrance.

She is more beautiful than her picture.

I stood there in front of the coffee counter for what seemed like several minutes as she finished up her conversation, and she eventually turned around and saw me. She introduced her-self as Cassie and we awkwardly shook hands, ordered a couple of coffees and sandwiches, and made our way to a corner table. Icebreaker conversation topics bubbled up easily with a large helping of intellectual overlap and caffeine.

In the blink of an eye, two and a half hours had passed, and the coffee and sandwiches were long finished. We wrapped up what had become a very pleasant afternoon of dialogue, and enthusiastically made plans for another date. We kept to the universally accepted dating protocol for a second meetup: a dinner date over the weekend. We said our goodbyes and parted ways in the late afternoon. I was excited.

Cassie and I didn't seem to follow protocol, though; the second time we saw one another was later that day, seemingly by random, fortuitous chance. She happened to be purchasing one of the newly constructed townhomes on the same block as Finn's, only a few doors down from him. Three hours after we had said our goodbyes at the coffee house, I received a text from her saying she was swinging by the neighborhood to check the status of the construction. I was home, so within the hour, I was meeting her out front. Finn was working late, and I invited her in; we sat on his back-porch steps, watching silly YouTube videos and laughing. She showed me the scene in *Big Bang Theory* in which Sheldon attempts to teach Penny physics; I responded with a video of a "professor's" explanation of women, using the "hot versus crazy" graph. We both had our inner nerds openly on display. (A week later I would describe Cassie to my sister over the phone as a cross between Sheldon and Penny.)

Afterward, I accompanied her down the lane to her nearly completed townhouse. We walked through the construction, inspecting the carpentry, drywall, and fixtures. I helped her look for any defects she could report to the builder. We stood facing each other in what was to become her kitchen, near the center island. We had been enjoying each other's company immensely, and there was that pregnant pause in our conversation. She gave me the *kiss me* look, and I moved in—even though this was not a formal date (playfully reflected back on by us as "date 1.5"). There was no passing up the moment. She responded to me, and our lips pressing together felt unforced and natural. Boom.

A few days later it was my turn for a new house inspection. Since I was gainfully employed at the Med-O-Matic, I put a contract on a modest ranch home in the county with four bedrooms—one for each of my children for when they . . . *come to visit.* The builder had agreed to let me move in a few weeks before the official closing date. Cassie and I sat on my front porch eating subs from Jimmy John's while movers unloaded a truckful of newly purchased furniture into my new place. We relaxed in the sunshine, sharing more of our backstories and basking in each other's company. We talked, ate, and kissed. I finished off half her sub (which would become a standard practice), and after the truck departed, we went inside, smooching and giggling like teenagers on my new sofa. We were living in the moment, so much so that when I was with her, past and future disappeared. I permitted myself to float off to a place of genuine excitement. Here I was in my new home, sharing playful intimacy with my new girlfriend. Darkness be damned—thoughts of drinks or divorces or children not only were absent but didn't even exist.

Our relationship instantaneously became exclusive (she and I swapped dating stories, and it sounded like her crazy dating life easily rivaled mine), and within weeks our evenings were filled with each other's company. She shared her children with her ex, having them two nights a week and every other weekend. On the other nights, we were together. We kept things simple on weekdays, binge-watching *Big Bang Theory* and *The Office* in each other's living rooms, eating pizza or ordering Chinese. She visited me at work, often swinging by the Med-O-Matic for a quick kiss and a lunch delivery; over a short time I met and got to know her daughters. We would text each other *Hello I'm thinking of you* with smiley or bashful emojis. Everything seemed so naturally comfortable for us. I basked in her warmth and kindness; I had a compassionate, loving person providing cool, pure water for my parched soul.

It wasn't long before we had leveled up in our commitment to be long-term partners. We got to know each other's friends, had clothes at one another's places, and escaped for romantic weekends. I learned about her career and she, mine. For the first time in many years I was feeling truly happy. One Sunday morning, lying together lazily in my bed, we declared our love for one another.

I was initially very tentative about exposing her to my troubles—my divorce and complete estrangement from my children in particular. She had a giant bag of crap to deal with as well, and at times when we were together, all our woes poured out of us and seemed to fill up the room. I couldn't help but feel that my issues stretched her thin, even overwhelmed her. I was an alcoholic in long-term recovery, separated and getting divorced (more like destroyed). For her part, she was also separated (although on much better terms with her ex), dealing with the prospect of an exciting but stressful job change at the university, and trying to guide her children through their conflicting emotions. She was moving out of her rental and into her new home, and I tried my best to stay out of my own head and support her. More times than not, it didn't work very well.

Probably the first true test of our relationship's strength was the weekend of my son Robert's bar mitzvah. Coming up on a year of sobriety, I was physically and mentally as healthy as I'd been in years. My doctor had taken me off all my meds, I was working a solid program, had the prospect of returning to emergency room work, and thanks to some financial help from my family and Finn, had scraped together enough money for the down payment on my beautiful new home.

On the other hand, I was an emotional disaster when it came to anything having to do with my children. It was this singular issue over which I had decompensated emotionally more often and with more intensity than everything else combined. I had been through unsuccessful family sessions with the kids in a family counselor's office (the only time I ever saw them) and was dealing with a court-appointed guardian ad litem who seemed to be completely ineffective at facilitating any co-parenting.

When it came to Hannah, Robert, and Toby, my heart remained perpetually on my tear-soaked sleeve. Bar mitzvah weekend fell on the eve of my one-year anniversary of sobriety, which seemed to magnify the severity of my distress. Cassie had to bear witness to this *and* meet my family for the first time—no easy feat. I saluted her for her efforts.

My son requested that I stay away from the bar mitzvah service. My family was coming into town and staying with me at my place, not only to attend but to participate in the ceremony. My oldest boy was performing a centuries-old coming-of-age ritual, the biggest moment of his young life, prepared for over years, without his father. The morning of the big event, I watched from my doorstep as my mother, sister, brother-in-law, and stepdad departed in their suits and dresses. The gravity and emotional severity of the situation were not lost on Cassie, who, with all of six weeks of experience with me and my situation, had been forced into the role of emotional caretaker. This sweet, delicate woman was, literally, placed on her new boyfriend's suicide watch.

▲▲▲▲▲

I was diagonal on my bed, facedown, unmovable. She was beside me, touching me, torso to torso, right arm around my waist, her face pressed against the side of my neck.

"I'm so sorry. I can't imagine what this feels like."

"Thank you. No, you can't," was all I could muster. She was doing all she was capable of. I so desperately wanted to go unconscious, or at least numb. But it was not a drink I was craving. Cassie's warm body against mine seemed to draw out some ache, and for that I was grateful. It was the fire in my chest that remained.

My thoughts took me to my bedroom closet, to the high shelf where I kept some of my medical supplies. There was a plastic bin with surgeon's scalpels. I thought of the icy bite of the blade as I used it to slice into my right shoulder only a few months prior. How wonderful it felt at the time; my brain's pain center had been distracted. It likely would have worked again, extinguishing the chest fire just a little bit. But as I played that scene through in my head, I envisioned Cassie making a 911 call. Then where would I be? In the ER, and then the psych ward. No, I've made it this far; I can live with the fire. Bloodletting was not a good idea. Rather, I focused on the warmth of Cassie's skin, her breath. . . .

▲▲▲▲▲

On that horrendous day, she was as sweet, warm, and comforting as any lifelong companion could have been. While the ceremony proceeded over at the temple, I remained in my bed, buried in my pillow and covers, blocking out the day. She did her best to comfort me, nuzzling up next to me, softly stroking my head and back, speaking softly to me. Her voice was delicate, and I recalled the words on a T-shirt I had seen her wearing just a few days before: *First, kindness.*

She handled me with poise and compassion well beyond anything I had ever experienced in my life. Indeed, it was that day I recognized her for the special human being she was, and still is.

▲▲▲▲▲

As the months passed, our relationship continued to mature. A few weeks after the bar mitzvah, we were in Williamsburg for my "triumphant" return to the treatment center, where I had been invited as an alumnus to speak to the current residents in recovery (I skipped the walk down memory lane in the psych ward). My guest appearance took place in the very lecture hall where just twelve months earlier I'd sat day in and day out like a frightened rabbit trying to make some sense of my upside-down world. Although very nervous, I was able to fill up the hour and get my story across, Cassie anchoring me with her encouraging presence.

Cassie was adept in her support role, and I tried to be the same for her. Above and beyond our deepening emotional intimacy, there was an outer layer of professional respect and support that I relished. When I sat in on one of her STEM Outreach program engagements, listening to her profess with passion to those in attendance, I felt myself brimming with pride and admiration. I loved being inside her sphere, whether she was in front of an audience or at a group dinner with faculty.

Our relationship energized me in all aspects of my life. Cassie and I rode each other's momentum and were firing on all cylinders—physically, socially, and professionally. The months passed and we both transitioned to better jobs, making the adaptations to our new realities fluid and seamless. She had gone from biology professor to the university's STEM Outreach director, and I moved from being a doc-in-the-box back to being an emergency physician. My new primary job (I also had a part-time gig) was one hundred miles out of town, and I was holed up in Airbnbs for multiday stretches. She would drive down to see me and spend the night, then drive back to make it on time to work in the morning. We found the time for each other, for evening activities, generally enjoying our moments together, be they intimate weekends at some country inn or simple drive-by kisses on a busy day.

▲▲▲▲▲

We were (ostensibly) driving to a restaurant for her birthday dinner as we pulled into my neighborhood. She thought this curious, since all the half-decent restaurants were in town, in the opposite direction. Granted, I had billed her birthday destination as a surprise as we approached my house. I sensed her confusion, yet she never openly questioned my moves. Her best friend and I had orchestrated the maneuver perfectly. Nearly two months prior, Denise and I schemed an elaborate surprise party, and this evening was to be the culmination of our efforts. The catered event was kept on the down-low, and thanks to the magic of social media, her circle of friends were kept informed. This was to be our first of Cassie's birthdays together, and I was determined to make it special.

We pulled into my driveway, and out of the corner of my eye, I could see the quizzical look on her face, lips pursed and pulled to the side. I said nothing and cut the engine, quietly relieved that the invitees were all alert enough to park their cars well down the block. Just as she opened the passenger side door, they came pouring out of my front door, cheering her, smiles on their faces. Finally, it hit her.

"What the fuck?!"

Before she made it out of her seat, Denise, Susan, Abbie, Kara, Steph, and the rest of her gang had fanned out on my front porch, shouting "Surprise!" in a delightfully unsynchronized manner. She turned to me, first shocked, then beaming. My chest warmed with satisfaction.

"Wha—when did you have time to do this?!" A question she would repeat many times throughout the evening.

She emerged from my truck to grand applause, and her friends enveloped her in one giant group hug. My eyes moved past the cluster of women to see Finn standing on my porch, a wide grin on his face. Just inside my house, the caterer's hot plates were steaming with birthday party entrées waiting to be enjoyed. I was feeling, at that moment, like quite the good boyfriend. That evening she would be the special birthday girl, the prom queen, celebrating with her friends, eating, drinking, and enjoying. I don't think this is exactly what my program meant when it professed service to others, and I did get a not-so-healthy ego boost, but what the hell, it was a happy victory in the moment, nevertheless. A good time was had by all, and the next morning Cassie and I departed from Dulles Airport for a glorious week in Paris—my birthday gift to her. For the first time in my recovery, I was feeling bliss—the bliss of giving, of loving, and of sharing a memorable moment with my partner. Gratitude, indeed.

CHAPTER 8

PASSIONS AND PROCESS ADDICTIONS

A skilled musician, I was not.

Throughout my childhood and adolescence, I avoided my guitar. It always seemed like such a chore to pick it up and practice. I just didn't have the tolerance to play scales and do finger exercises that bore no resemblance to an Eddie Van Halen or Alex Lifeson solo. There always seemed to be a good excuse to stay out of the basement where my instrument lived. Instead, I chose to run around in the streets of my New Jersey suburban community and play pick-up football by day, then after dark climb the water tower to drink beers with Marc and Scott.

Like many aspects of my existence, I tried to get by with doing the minimum. My passion for beginner learning was simply not there. Right before my guitar teacher showed up for my weekly lesson, I would stumble through the obligatory assignment from the week before, doing just enough not to catch any grief. The thirty-minute session would end, my guitar teacher would collect his ten bucks, and the music book would stay closed for one more week. I had other teenage priorities that took me elsewhere.

Thirty-five years later, right after I became a single, childless man, unemployed and homeless, filling the hours became a real effort. The highlights of my days were usually my noon and evening AA meetings. I ran daily but could only exercise so much. Finn's dog, Jake, was entertaining enough, but the townhouse quickly became my new low-security prison cell. I passed the time while the world was off at work and school trying to be productive, doing some home repairs, assembling some of my housemate's furniture, and cleaning (the least I could do; Finn wasn't charging me rent). Sitting idle felt neither comfortable nor healthy. I was still waiting for official clearance from the monitoring program to return to work in a medical setting, and my fledgling patience was stretching thin. Described so beautifully in *Oh, the Places You'll Go!*, I was in "The Waiting Place." And I despised it.

One afternoon, I sat with my back up against the wall in the corner by the table with the flashlights and a shriveling houseplant, staring at my old instrument. It seemed to follow me for years, decades even, this guitar. I remembered back to my early doctor days, before children, when my wife and I were exploring our interests, I dusted it off and found myself a local instructor who taught me a few of the latest popular songs. He let me try Stone Temple Pilots, U2, and Marcy Playground. I briefly became interested in practicing. I flailed, but I tried. Even when I became reasonably proficient, playing in front of anyone else was simply out of the question. I completely lacked confidence in my musical abilities.

Eventually, my short attention span caught up with me, and the next big thing on my agenda elbowed out my practice time. My enthusiasm fizzled, and the guitar was returned back to its dark case, where it stayed for another twenty years . . .

until the afternoon I sat bored and lonely, cross-legged on the floor of Finn's living room.

Open the case. Pick the damn thing up.

The urge to play it struck me. Suddenly I felt the need to strum. I had toyed with my musician brother-in-law's acoustic during a recent visit to Philadelphia and realized I had some music memory still waiting for the chance to come out and be nurtured, spiffed up. I reached for the case and unlatched it.

Just learn a few songs, maybe just one song.

I began to pick at the intro to Pink Floyd's "Wish You Were Here" and found myself surprisingly adept after such a long absence. I moved on to "Me and Julio Down by the Schoolyard" by Paul Simon, a song I was taught back in med school by my musically talented friend Joe, a popular guy who was an open mic regular at our favorite hangout in Northern Virginia, where he dazzled the crowd weekly with his guitar and voice.

I played for Jake, all curled up on the sofa. I wasn't horrible, all things considered. Here I was, by my lonesome, with my life upside down and everything that ever mattered to me gone, but I could remember how to bang out a couple of classic tunes. Over the next few weeks, the guitar became my new old friend.

I am gonna choose my favorites and brush up on them and be fantastic! I will dazzle everyone at some open mic somewhere just like Joe used to, and all the people who matter will come to their senses and take me back into their lives so I can once again be a husband, a physician, a father! All I have to do is play songs in front of them and the evil spells will be broken! I'll be popular and loved *and famous as famous can be, with the whole wide world watching me play on TV!*

Except when they don't. Because, likely, they won't.

Tap the brakes, dude. Get out of your delusional fantasy skull. How about, in this moment, in the here and now, just

strumming a few simple songs in front of Jake the dog? Start
with that.

▲▲▲▲▲

It was early spring, and I was about four months sober, and
I started spending quality time with my guitar. I began with
the stuff from my past: Pink Floyd, Tom Petty, and the Beatles.
I had been hitting my meetings like clockwork and incorpo-
rating some of my AA teachings into my practice sessions:
Accepting that I kind of suck. Accepting that I really only have
a handle on the open chords, and still struggle with bar chords.
Accepting that my fingers are painfully sore. Accepting that
the guitar that I own is badly warped and horribly out of tune
from years of sitting in a dark basement and humid garage.

Joe, try this on for size: Accept with gratitude that you are
alive, sober, and have the luxury to strum a guitar, because
you have a good friend who let you move in with him rent-free
while you try to piece your life back together. Accept that you
can learn song after song in his comfortable townhouse with
his fully stocked refrigerator. You can practice while keeping
yourself faced away from the front window, so when the yellow
school buses pass and stop to drop off children after school, you
don't have to look.

And play I did. I found myself picking up songs that I
listened to on my Pandora station on my way to work. I had
an affinity for nineties alternative music and quickly got the
basics down to Eve 6's "Inside Out," Green Day's "Welcome to
Paradise," and STP's "Plush." It didn't matter that I stumbled
and fumbled and missed strings, buzzed and rattled. I was
playing, and it felt nice. Not only was it a good distraction but
it gave me a sense of accomplishment and satisfaction. I was
thinking and doing *in the moment*, fingers and hands moving

in a pattern that vibrated taut strings across a wood neck that made a noise that crudely resembled music.

What really mattered was that when I played, I was not leaping into the *next* moment before my hands and head were ready. In addition, when I focused on keeping up with the chords and lyrics, my mind was unable to ruminate on the past. Staying inside a song prevented me from both mentally torturing myself with memories and conjuring fear for the future.

As I progressed, I moved on to Red Hot Chili Peppers, Bush, and Third Eye Blind. Their melodies seemed slightly more complex, forcing me to stay on task even more, out of my head and away from unnecessary anger, self-pity, and fear.

I found I needed a confidence booster, something to keep me motivated to continue practicing and cultivating my new-found interest. I had a mortal fear of audiences, but at the same time, yearned for applause after I played. Like with all fears, my monkey brain had a terrible case of the what-ifs. What if I froze up? What if I just kept making mistakes, and people laughed and pointed, or shouted insults? What if they all got up, en masse, and left mid-performance? Such was the nature of my flawed thinking patterns, and not just with playing guitar.

It didn't take long searching to find an open mic night online—a small venue downstairs from a popular downtown restaurant. They advertised for amateur musicians, poets, hip-hop artists, and comedians to perform fifteen-minute sets every Wednesday night. *Amateurs. We all have to be in the same boat, right? I mean, if everyone else sucks as bad as I do, and we are all each other's audience, won't that mean lots of support and love? (Just like an AA meeting where we all suck at life, so nobody ridicules and everyone supports.)* Mentally committed, I made sure I had four songs I could finish without falling on my face, and then planned to show up. Then I practiced some more.

▲▲▲▲▲

It was a brick-and-concrete, windowless cellar that had the nostalgic look of a fraternity barroom. The layout was rectangular, much longer than it was wide, with a bar counter off to one side and cushy, low-lying sofa chairs and high tables with stools lining the room. At the opposite end of the stairs leading up to the main restaurant was the "stage," really nothing more than a little alcove, on the same level as the audience, with a couple of mic stands and a speaker system. It looked small, even when empty.

I walked in awkwardly with my guitar case and was immediately approached by the only other person in the room besides the bartender—a tall, skinny guy with a man-bun, wearing leather bracelets, tapered, ripped jeans, and a university T-shirt, who just seconds before was toying with an amplifier.

I'm here, the main act, proclaimed my ego.

He introduced himself as Chris, the MC for open mic, and directed me to the clipboard sitting on the bar. I tentatively approached the counter and viewed the sign-up sheet. It was blank except for one entry: *Tom, poetry.* I wrote my name down in the number-two slot: *Joe, guitar.*

I ordered a club soda with lime and found a seat away from the bar. It was quiet. The TV mounted in the upper corner was playing a *Men in Black* movie, closed captioned, and I stared. Sign-ups opened at eight o'clock, with the first act at nine. It was 8:04. It was me and Chris Man-Bun and the bartender. I supposed somewhere, Tom the Poet was lurking.

Over the next hour, people filtered in and the clipboard filled. There were acoustic guitarists, poets, a rapper, and a couple of comedians. I engaged in nervous conversation with whoever was around me. Everyone seemed so young and hip; I felt out of place. I let a heavily pierced young lady know it was my first time performing and received a "right on."

Chris opened the evening with an original acoustic song to warm up the crowd, all twelve of us, and then promptly called Tom the Poet, a skeletal old man who was easily pushing seventy-five. He was obviously an open mic regular, because everyone seemed to know him. He read his three well-crafted but rather depressing poems out of a dirty, tattered spiral notebook and after finishing each, received scattered applause. He looked perfectly content and at ease. *Good for him, but if he can do this, so can I.*

"Next up, Joe, who will play us some nineties tunes." I was trembling badly as I walked to the front. I put the shoulder strap around me and plugged in. I could feel my legs shaking. I said a croaky hello and without pause began to play. Green Day's "Welcome to Paradise" followed by Eve 6's "Inside Out." I finished with "Closing Time" by the one-hit wonder Semisonic. With each line played, I gained a bit more confidence. I had practiced my three songs about a hundred times in front of Jake, the last ten or so, flawlessly. That night I made some mistakes, singing a few lyrics wrong and occasionally botching a chord. Nobody seemed to take notice. When I finished, I received a moderate round of applause. I was neither laughed at nor the recipient of a standing ovation. People pretty much acted as people act—receptive but talking among themselves and doing their thing. Newsflash—I was not the center of their universe.

I thanked the room for listening, unplugged, and departed the stage with the same number of limbs I had arrived with. The two extreme possible outcomes I had built up in my head never materialized. I quietly declared victory and sat in the audience to listen to the other acts, another unfounded fear dispensed with.

Open mic night became a great regular distraction for me, and I made new friends, including Corie, a young woman with a cheery disposition who recited poetry and who provided me with incredible support and encouragement. Granted, I was under no pretense that I was particularly talented, but for me, playing was more about finding the courage to perform in a public venue. It was a fear I was able to slowly chip away at over a period of months as I stood up on that makeshift stage week after week and stumbled my way through some popular cover tunes. It was never about the applause (although it did feel good at times to get some positive reinforcement); it wasn't even about being particularly proficient. No, it was something deeper. It was about that need to face the fear, plain and simple. Like jumping out of an airplane or stepping back into an emergency department, I recognized that my fears were what limited me and retarded my advancement in every facet of my existence.

▲▲▲▲▲

In reality, my new hobby replaced an older one that had taken root and dominated me before I got sober.

My enthusiasm for firearms started very slowly but grew steadily.

I was raised in the Northeast region of the country in a liberally minded household where guns in the home were not in the equation. As a kid, I always felt a small pang of jealousy whenever I read a passage in a book about a Southern dad handing his rifle down to his son in keeping with a family tradition. It seemed to have a certain charm and manliness to it. Being a relatively wimpy kid who was afraid of his own shadow, I was painfully self-conscious of my inability to defend myself. After years of schoolyard bullying, a couple of school cafeteria fights, and ongoing intimidation by bigger, stronger boys, I decided I had had enough, that it was time to confront the wimp factor that seemed to define every academically minded Jewish boy in the New York area. I wanted to be different, to be tough and stand up for myself. I wanted to be less like an American Jew and more like an Israeli Jew—like the courageous Sabras who wielded automatic rifles and defended Israel. It wasn't until much later in life, however, that I would actually hold a gun in my hand.

My first firearm was purchased from Najif, a good friend and medical colleague in the emergency department: a high-quality Onyx over-under shotgun. My wife grudgingly allowed me to have it so long as I stored it out of the house, at Najif's place. I tried to learn how to shoot skeet but frankly did not have the coordination. I seemed to do pretty well as long as the targets were stationary, but I missed every time they whizzed through the air. *OK, intruder, just stay very still for a few seconds so I can properly place this double-aught buckshot into your torso.* Ultimately, that first purchase disappeared along with Najif's house, which one night burned to the ground.

My next acquisition was a beautiful 1911 Kimber Raptor II pistol, also purchased from Najif. I stored it at home in a safe, hidden and locked away. It was a superb quality firearm, well built and far more accurate than I was. I used it during my Virginia concealed-carry course, passing the proficiency component of the exam easily. I tricked it out with a laser and glowing night sights. I felt strong and somehow complete, like I had achieved some goal in life that my studies could never provide. Not only could I have a badass forty-five, but I was able to legally conceal it. In my mind, my wife and I would now be safe. I was confident that in the event I had to defend us against the bad guys, I could pull that trigger without hesitation.

Unsurprisingly, threats to my life occurred with alarming frequency in the emergency department, usually by unstable, mentally ill, or sociopathic patients. There was one particular instance when I had to commit an overtly homicidal patient—a clear danger to others—to a state psychiatric facility. Some weeks later, I was informed by the authorities that the patient had been scribbling my name in crayon on the walls of his hospital room and expressing to the staff psychiatrist that when he was released, he was coming to kill me and my family. Local police and hospital security were notified, and I was called into the nurse manager's office, where the hospital's chief of security informed me of the threat against our lives. The patient remained on official watch for a period of time (how he was released from the institution remains a mystery to me to this day). Any lingering doubt regarding firearms ownership was, with that one circumstance, completely eliminated in my mind. I felt vindicated and kept my gun close. Close and concealed.

Try it, fucker. Just try to come for me and my family. I will show you who's boss. No more wimpy school kid here. This Jewboy will rip some holes in you without a second thought.

From that day, my interest in firearms grew into a full-fledged hobby, turning into a passion and then ultimately an obsession. Unbeknownst to my antigun wife, my pistol collection grew, and I soon added rifles. I became proficient with each type, going out to remote areas of the county to target shoot. I accumulated a wide variety of hardware: guns that would do different things under different circumstances—the right tool for the job. Each acquisition created a hunger for the next. I would justify each purchase under the pretext that I was "rounding out my collection." Revolvers, pistol-caliber carbines, tactical shotguns, Old West lever-actions, AR-10s, bullpups. I even found myself a gold-plated Desert Eagle .50 caliber, buying it for no other reason than it was made by *badass Hebrews.*

With all the gun purchases came ammo, loads of ammo. I had joined an online survivalist forum and learned that one should begin with one thousand rounds of every kind of caliber one needs (although some posters indicated three thousand to five thousand was a good base). When the pillaging hordes or Chinese army arrived after the inevitable collapse of the U.S. government, it was gonna take that much ammunition to defend family, friends, and other innocents within my protective compound. I stored everything in safes, five-gallon buckets, the ceiling, filing cabinets, hidden storage spaces, and underground in the backyard.

When I surrounded myself, physically and online, with other firearm "enthusiasts," it was easy to justify every purchase. We validated each other's obsessions, rationalizing away our extreme behavior. I viewed every mass shooting incident covered in the media as an excuse to stockpile even more, because in my mind each tragedy was the result of people being prevented from defending themselves. I committed never to allow such a tragedy to happen to my family, friends, or neighborhood. I was determined never to end up a statistic, so I had to be prepared. Plus, guns were cool and shiny.

My hobby became an obsession, and then an addiction. I had gone over the top, to the extreme, driven by paranoia and unfounded fear. I was cherry-picking my facts to conform to my mind's narrative, rather than self-reflecting on what I was becoming.

Little did I realize that what would destroy me in the end could never be defended against with a gun, because the enemy attacked from within. No, ultimately the safety and welfare of my family could be secured only through trust in God and having the spiritual well-being to make the right decisions as a sober man.

▲▲▲▲▲

How does one wake up in the morning devoid of what matters most? How does one lift one's head from one's pillow and set one's feet on the floor without a left ventricle, that critical chamber of the heart tasked with pumping blood every second, one hundred thousand times per day, three billion times in an average lifetime? How does one drive to a job, play a guitar, do laundry? How can I even open my eyes or author a page with an incomplete heart?

I know my left ventricle is there. I've placed the ultrasound transducer on my own chest just to the left of my sternum and directly viewed it: mitral valve on one end letting in newly oxygenated blood from the lungs, aortic valve flying open as blood is piped down the aorta to the rest of the body. It is definitely there; it's just that it occasionally goes on strike, proclaiming a self-declared Union of Cardiac Chamber Workers break from its other responsibility as keeper of the love emotion, outsourcing that task to its weaker, right-sided colleague.

There are mammals on this planet with three-chambered hearts that seem to get along just fine, but I am not one of them. I require every last muscle cell in my four-part pump to perfuse me through my day. The majority of the time, I depend on that left ventricle to be on its A game; whether damaged by heartache or not, it needs to be present and accounted for. It must live up to its contract, so every morning I can rise from my bed in my new home. My feet can hit the floor and I can shuffle into the kitchen, where my reliable Mr. Coffee machine stands at the ready atop the counter.

It's predawn, black outside, as I dump the damp, gravelly remnants of the previous day's filter into the trash, place a new one in the coffee pot, and scoop in fresh grounds (no K-Cups here). It is the start of my morning ritual—brewing the caffeine, my last remaining chemical vice. The goal is to get the coffee going quickly, pour a few ounces into my oversized Yankees mug with the broken handle, and gulp some down before the *dark thinking* begins.

Before you think of them, of another day in an endless ocean of days without them. Before that bottomless grief consumes you and sets the tone. Before you question why you even bother with a routine, or bother with anything for that matter.

I put the ice cube in the empty mug so I can pour the steaming liquid over it and hear the satisfying *crack* of frozen water expanding way too rapidly to stay whole. It takes seconds to melt; I watch with satisfaction. Half a cup of pure ebony, bitter goodness flows down my gullet. Ninety seconds later, the first stirrings of that comforting, familiar waking up of senses, along with an immediate elevation of mood takes hold, quashing any grim emotions in their embryonic stage, just like a good drug is supposed to. It's officially on—the daily morning battle for possession of my head.

I retreat back to the bedroom, lose the boxers and cotton T-shirt, and put on my running clothes. Skipper sees me and gets excited, his insightful doggie brain telling him we will be on a run soon enough. I sit and lace my shoes as he twirls by the door and whines. The caffeine has permeated my brain's limbic system, awakening my excitatory neurotransmitters and artificial enthusiasm for whatever comes next. Through the front-door window, I see the glowing red taillights of a neighbor's car in the driveway. Maybe they think I'm crazy for heading out this early. Maybe not, probably not. Is my ego still so dominant that it really believes neighbors are thinking of me at five in the morning as they drive off to work? I'm not sure I give a shit; I know *they* don't.

I clip the orange Day-Glo leash onto Skipper's harness. The happy pup's excitement is now at a crescendo; he knows he will go miles with me over dark roads in the calm, sweet quiet. We exit the front door and descend the porch steps. Down the dark street and through the sleeping neighborhood we shuffle. I can tell Skipper feels satisfied, and he settles into his trot. I feel the relief that I once again made it out of my house . . .

. . . and once again away from the scalpel.

We move at a comfortably slow pace that first mile. The cozy blanket of night that swaddles me feels nice. I feel safe, comfy. Wrapped in the darkness that recedes well before sunrise, my soul increasingly awakens with each passing mile. It needs this gradual acclimation, this fragile baby soul of mine, and so I nurture it with steady, consistent movement and fresh air. The only sounds are of feet on pavement, the wind rustling leaves, and distant cars driving off to their morning destinations. Sometimes a train whistles in the distance. Those are nice; Baby Soul likes those. I trudge along my serene road of happy destiny.

But I am not alone, not quite. I try to think as little as possible. I remember once from a share in a meeting that we hear God's messages to us most clearly in the quiet between our own noisy thoughts. This comforts me; I want to hear what God has to say, so I try to clear my head. I get an idea about something—maybe work, maybe the house, or a new song to play on my guitar. I allow it to present itself, then pass.

An hour goes by, sometimes more, sometimes less. I always try to finish the run with a sprint up the steep hill leading to my house. It's a routine I have repeated many, many times. Getting that heart rate up, pushing that trusty ventricle to pump out blood to oxygen-starved muscles 170 times per minute is my end goal. I purge the body and mind of their extraneous energy early in the day, so that a relaxed, calm feeling can remain for hours afterward. Getting Baby Soul's wiggles out at play time prevents temper tantrums later, a spiritual daycare routine, if you will. For my toddler soul, this seems effective.

If I'm not going to work right away, I get my household chores done: the routine of laundry, bills, dishwasher, and cleaning up the accumulated household piles. The dog and fish get fed. Distractions mainly come in the form of my guitar and texts.

I also enjoy truly mindless activities; *Bubble Shooter* is an example. This silly little cell phone game, downloaded for free, I find surprisingly addictive. Shooting little colored balloons at other little colored balloons seems to fill a hole. I pull it out when between larger tasks, and it works for me. Fun, free, and distracting. And, unlike skeet, I almost never miss.

Any favorite activity has the potential to transition from habit to addiction if it takes control of my head and detracts from the rest of my day, but it seems that I have found some balance in my post-recovery living. Balance—that is something alcoholics and addicts lack in their behaviors. One can enjoy running, or playing guitar, or target shooting without any single one of them devolving into another destructive addiction; unlike chemicals or alcohol, it just takes balance. All my activities that could once have been labeled process addictions, in the end, with a little spiritual reprogramming, have the potential to even out.

How do I wake up in the morning without what matters most? By rephrasing the question: What matters most to me in *this moment*? And the answer I find is, unsurprisingly, what is right in front of me.

CHAPTER 9

PHYSICIAN, HEAL THYSELF

I stood awkwardly in front of her, feeling like a spaceman walk-on in some second-rate 1950s science fiction movie. The nurse sprayed a noxious vapor in a small opening in the hood, and I was asked to "just breathe normally" and inform her if the protective mask she was fitting me with was keeping out the odor. If it fit properly, I would smell nothing, confirming that the respirator was effective. I would then apparently be equally protected from both coronavirus *and* bad farts.

My hometown hospital had mandated these N95 face-mask fitting sessions for all its employees on the very same day the first case of COVID-19 was declared in Virginia. I laughed to myself at the irony of the situation. I had been out of emergency medicine for eighteen months, fought all the way back, jumping through endless bureaucratic hoops along the way, was hit with a divorce, and worked a rigorous program to stay sober. As if that were not enough, suddenly, and without any warning, I found myself on the front lines fighting the biggest global pandemic the world had seen in one hundred years. *I used to be disgusted, now I try to be amused.*

▲▲▲▲▲

"The first job back will feel incredible." Such were the words of wisdom from Carter, a resident in recovery whom I met briefly near the end of my stay at the treatment center. A neurologist hooked on fentanyl and alcohol, he was a habitual relapser. After rehab he'd be standing trial for grand larceny and assault with a deadly weapon (quite literally, he shot a man while robbing his castle). For some strange reason, I found him mesmerizing, routinely listening intently to what he had to say. So when he suggested that my first job out of treatment practicing medicine would feel glorious, I put stock in it.

Naturally, I would be thrilled to go back to medicine. It was just four weeks earlier, in my first few days of recovery, that I had convinced myself that my doctoring days were over, that there was no going back. I recalled sitting in the community room of Penuel, scribbling calculations of my net worth on a napkin to determine how long I could stretch our family savings. I envisioned a nonmedical job—hopefully. My wife, who had long ago chosen to be a stay-at-home mom, would find some work, and we would be OK. A silver lining of my alcohol-induced apocalyptic paranoia was an ongoing compulsion to sock away as much money as possible and retire all debt. In my crazy worry over impending world economic collapse, I had paid off our mortgage two months prior. We wouldn't be wealthy, but we could stay in our home and send our kids to college. As far as my professional life, I was convinced I was all washed up.

As the weeks passed and I increasingly mixed with the other residents, I discovered that my alcoholism did not have to spell the end of the line for my career, not even close. I spent free time speaking in depth with my fellow recovering physicians, particularly the relapsers, learning about how various state monitoring programs had been created to rehabilitate doctors, nurses, pharmacists, and therapists back into their careers. My alcoholic brain, still quite volatile and panicky, had already written my career obituary. Slowly, I learned that with patience, and by putting my recovery first, things could slowly fall back in line.

The practice of learning patience was excruciating. Just working my program daily and staying sober—that was within my new capabilities. Waiting for institutions and prospective employers to judge me worthy of returning to medicine was *completely* beyond my control. But I had hit bottom, or so I thought. Learning and understanding the tools in recovery would, I hoped, teach me how to have the patience to pace myself, so that in time, I could once again be a clinical physician.

The Virginia Health Practitioners' Monitoring Program (HPMP), in existence for decades, was the means to provide the structure and oversight for impaired providers. The program was created and run under the Virginia Department of Health Professions, and they were in the business of guiding an impaired provider with a license in the healing arts back to work. Through a program of continuous accountability— monthly addiction-counselor reports, employer reports, meeting-attendance reports, random drug and alcohol screenings, and regular case-manager call-ins—the HPMP kept their professionals on short leashes while we practiced under a microscope. I enrolled in it while in rehab, and from that day on and for the next five years, they would own my professional ass.

After an extensive initial phone interview with an intake caseworker, all my medical records, rehab facility records, letters from counselors and psychiatrists, and other pertinent information were transferred into their files. I signed a seven-page contract outlining in detail their requirements and which violations would get me expelled from the program, and my medical license suspended or revoked. Working any job without express written approval, failing or not reporting for a drug screen, neglecting to file a monthly report, not checking in online every day, and incomplete AA meeting attendance were all grounds for dismissal. It was rigorous, requiring daily vigilance; it had to be. We professionals in recovery needed it. In this sense it paralleled a successful personal program of recovery, and it worked—nine out of ten enrollees, research showed, completed the program successfully. The rebellious part of me wanted to reject giving up all the control, but the recovering side of me knew it was exactly what I needed if I ever wanted to return to and remain in the medical profession.

I wasn't out of rehab twenty-four hours before I was sitting in HPMP headquarters in Richmond with my newly assigned case manager. Anne, a petite woman in her midthirties who looked ten years younger, sat at her desk across from me in her cozy office while orienting me on policy and procedure. Fail a drug screen and I'm out; work a single day in medicine without approval, I'm toast. No traveling out of Virginia without prior notification; no traveling out of the country in the first year; attend and log the required number of AA meetings every month; meet with an individual counselor; meet in professionals' group therapy; keep work hours under the cap; accept decisions of the HPMP without challenge. . . . I sat and absorbed all her information, not as Dr. Remy, but as newly minted Client #5301.

Seemed fair.

▲▲▲▲▲

It was a full three months before I received the back-to-medicine call from Anne.

I had finished my stint as supermarket stock boy (*Hi! I'm new to the team!*) and had been teaching a course in emergency medicine to physician assistant students. It had originally been offered to Tom, but he'd declined, instead referring me to the course director. It was a temporary gig, but one I enjoyed immensely. I prepared the syllabus weeks in advance, creating basic lectures on topics in my specialty. It was an exercise that got me opening my old textbooks and reacquainting myself with the science behind the profession that seemed hardwired into me. In addition, I was able to concentrate on a task that required my complete attention, focusing my stabilizing mind. I had the opportunity to stand in front of a room full of enthused, attentive medical students, ready and willing to scarf down everything displayed in my PowerPoint slides.

Nostalgia for my medical school days wafted over me as I discussed arrhythmias, basics of airway management, trauma, and principles of shock to the class. The substance of my talks was taken from the textbook of my own medical training twenty-three years earlier: *Tintinalli's Emergency Medicine*. Pulling it out of a storage bin in my damp basement room at the Oxford House, I recalled cracking it for the very first time between operating room cases on my anesthesia rotation in the early days of my internship back in Baltimore. . . .

▲▲▲▲▲

It was the summer of 1992 and I was assigned to a young anesthesiologist who taught me the finer techniques of endotracheal intubation—the act of placing a secure breathing tube down a patient's windpipe to secure and protect the airway. For ER docs, it was a vital skill, and was the first letter in the emergency physician's alphabet: *A* is for airway.

Three years later, in my final days as chief resident, just before I departed for my new job in Virginia, I intubated that very same anesthesiologist in the same Baltimore hospital. It was before his doctors realized his cancer had metastasized, before he'd designated "do not resuscitate" status for himself. As he'd instructed me years before, I placed his ET tube with ease and without complication. Days later, I was told, he was made DNR, and succumbed to his illness.

▲▲▲▲▲

While teaching, I was able to step outside myself and watch a group of fifty younger versions of me eat up information and ask for more. I found it exhilarating and a nice respite from my life outside the classroom. My zeal for teaching may have gotten the better of me to some extent, though, as half the students failed my final exam. The course director restored the kids to sanity by scoring it on a bell curve.

▲▲▲▲▲

I was in the Pantops area of Charlottesville, heading to a meeting with my sponsor, when her call came in. Anne had "staffed" my return-to-work submission in committee, and they'd granted me permission to seek employment in a clinical setting. Four hours later, I was mailing out my curriculum vitae to prospective employers. I signed up for a physician job-search site and made a few phone calls. I knew on many levels I was not ready to go back to work in the high-stress, fast-paced world of emergency departments, and instead focused my efforts on securing a position in a more basic, low-key urgent care center.

Even as damaged goods, I was able to land a few offers relatively quickly. The delay in my getting back to work would not be a lack of job offers; opportunities would flow in. It was the credentialing that always took time, often months. Background checks, professional history reviews, procedure log audits, license evaluations, and professional reference checking had to be performed. Medical credentialing committees had to meet and make decisions. Making matters more complex for me was the fact that all my personal professional files were *back home*, where I was denied access. But I persevered and managed to get what was required through saved emails, my old hospital, and friends who were permitted into my old house.

I ultimately accepted a job with an urgent care company with sites throughout Virginia. These were basic walk-in clinics where a patient could stop by and be checked for the flu, have an ankle looked at, or get an antibiotic for a bladder infection. A full-service Med-O-Matic, if you will.

I was grateful for the opportunity, regardless of its simplicity; finally seeing patients again after nine months was a dream come true. From the first day I was there, I found the nature and pace of the work comfortable. I relished the time with the earache babies, hand lacerations, knee sprains, and sore throats, twelve hours at a time.

My ego would have previously scoffed at such work, considering it the lowest rung in the ladder of professional medicine. But that ego had been mitigated, at least partially. Still, I thought of other physicians in the world surgically removing brain tumors and discovering cures for cancer while I processed a waiting room full of common colds, back pains, and school sports physicals. Putting matters in perspective helped. Given that only months earlier I was locked up in a mental health unit, I embraced my new environment with a dose of genuine appreciation. Gratitude taught me I should appreciate having a license and working as a doctor and doing so just a few miles from home. I was making a small difference in patients' lives—maybe not curing their cancer but helping them feel relief from their nuisance ailments on a day-to-day basis, and that felt good.

It was very foreign to me, ending clinic and turning out the lights at eight o'clock every evening. The entirety of my career had been spent in a 24-7 emergency department, so closing an office was quite novel. We worked very hard during those twelve hours—a physician assistant, nurse, X-ray tech, clerk, and me making our way through a steady stream of patients. Also strange to me were job tasks I had never experienced—employment drug screens, school physicals, and medical certifications for truckers. I particularly liked examining the truck drivers. They had many cool stories of the road to tell, and I found my time with them pleasant and enlightening. One older driver had trouble passing his hearing test but was relieved when I pulled an earplug out of his ear canal, which he had forgotten was there after a hunting trip eight years earlier.

I worked about fifteen twelve-hour shifts per month at the Med-O-Matic, and unlike emergency room work, I had every evening free for a social life. Inga and I were in the twilight of our relationship when I began work; Cassie arrived in my life soon thereafter. She and I would text each other during the day (with *nice* emojis) and she would leave campus on her lunch break to see me. I would meet her in the employee parking lot out back for a hello and quick kiss. On my off days, since the hours were regular, I had the energy to spend more time with her, play guitar, make my meetings, or get together with friends. Divorce and kid issues aside, between work, Cassie, and friends, for the first time in many months, or even years, I felt like I was living some semblance of a normal human life. The work environment was comfortable, and I made friends with the youthful, warm, and receptive staff.

▲▲▲▲▲

The Med-O-Matic was convenient, easy work, but in my mind's recesses I could hear my inner ER doc beckoning, though I wasn't quite ready. As my professional confidence grew, I recognized the importance of remaining connected to my hometown hospital, the "Rock." I had been on staff there for twenty-two years, and it would have been imprudent to relinquish my privileges. After reporting me to the state medical board, the administration had granted me medical leave, a temporary designation. I had to retain my status as a member of the staff while accepting the idea that returning to the emergency department, with all its associated challenges to my fragile recovery, was not yet a good move. I didn't know if *they* even wanted *me*. Part of me wanted to think they didn't. Deeper down, I knew there was more to it—my old job still intimidated me, for many reasons.

Because of room twelve.

Because of Maggie and the Kidney Stone Lady.

▲▲▲▲▲

Long before Implosion Day struck, as shifts in the ED increasingly became a mental struggle for me, I'd been considering transitioning to the hospital's wound care center. The clinic had been aggressively recruiting, and I thought it might be a comfortable pathway out of emergency medicine as my professional death spiral accelerated. Feeling my expiration date rapidly approaching, my wife and I had been discussing "wind-down" career options for months. After my abrupt departure from work life, while I was still in rehab, she mentioned (in one of her rare phone calls) how one of my colleagues had suggested that a position in the wound management clinic might be a good option for me. I was working full-time in urgent care, but I also deeply desired getting back under the roof of the hospital, even as a part-time wound clinic doctor.

Formidable professional challenges lay ahead of me. My flameout and hospitalization was an open secret among the medical staff. There would be panels to sit before, committees to appeal to, and a mountain of administrative red tape. Any approvals were predicated on the assumption that the HPMP would even approve me. On the bright side, my recovery was proceeding solidly, and I was feeling strong enough to carry two jobs. I wanted active staff status, and with a divorce in front of me, I needed the extra income for legal bills. There was also the opportunity to mix with old colleagues, some of whom were not privy to the gossip and probably wondered where I had disappeared to.

I wanted to prove myself worthy to them, and to myself.

▲▲▲▲▲

The Rock's wellness panel, consisting entirely of my physician peers, had convened to hear my case. Opposite me, sitting at the boardroom's long mahogany table, were doctors I had known for years; a few had served with me when I was president of the medical staff. In my mind, my self-destruction had been epic, happening right before their eyes. I sat there feeling a combination of fear, guilt, and hope. The current president of the medical staff was present, as were two other physicians I had once socialized with; I knew others through professional collaborations. Several, including a staff psychiatrist, were new to me. Jamie, chief administrator of staff services, a woman I had known for decades, sat at one end with her laptop and notepad.

For the next two hours I was questioned in a cordial but interrogative way about my activities the prior twelve months. By this point I was accustomed to telling my story to groups, having done it many times, but it had always been in front of empathetic AA members in meetings. This time it seemed different because it *was* different. These physicians—some sympathetic, some not—listened with a discerning ear, and appropriately so. While they wanted a willing and competent doctor back in their midst, their ultimate objective was to ensure patient safety, protection of the medical staff, and the hospital's reputation.

Was I going to relapse while on duty? I could sense the groupthink weighing the risks and benefits of a Dr. Remy back on staff. While I believe they cared about me as a physician, they had the wellness of an entire medical center and community to consider. I answered their questions carefully and truthfully, permitting myself just enough emotion and vulnerability to demonstrate my authenticity. Finally the interview portion of the session ended, and I was dismissed for them to deliberate behind closed doors. I departed the room with a feeling of cautious optimism.

▲▲▲▲▲

One week later, I received a letter recommending my reinstatement. The decision of the physician wellness panel was reviewed by the credentialing and executive committees, and I was formally returned to active medical staff status. A sense of satisfaction came over me, as I had been granted permission to practice back under the very roof where, a blink of an eye before, I lay in a hospital bed with shattered hopes of ever working in medicine again. Some weeks passed, and after additional training and approval from the monitoring program, I was a full-fledged part-time woundologist.

I found the wound care clinic quite foreign at first. It was, clinically speaking, the complete opposite of what I had practiced my entire career. As a part-timer, Friday was my clinic day and I would see the same fifteen to twenty patients weekly, attending to their diabetic foot wounds, pressure ulcers (bedsores), and postoperative incision infections. The patients were chronically ill with numerous comorbidities; almost all had diabetes, and many were debilitated residents of nursing facilities. Their wounds were large and multilayered and would not heal naturally due to chronic tissue damage, poor circulation, or a general state of immobility. After an initial first visit assessment, we would implement a long-term strategy for healing, pulling in a combination of state-of-the-art topical dressing materials, hyperbaric oxygen therapy, and supplemental medications. We sometimes performed simple skin grafts.

I developed a pleasant, ongoing dialogue with my patients, learning their underlying medical and social conditions, engaging them in a way I never could in a fast-paced emergency department setting. This type of healing was measured in weeks and months—and sometimes years—with progress recorded in millimeters. Early on, care usually involved weekly sharp debridement—literally, the scraping and clearing away of devitalized (necrotic) tissue with a scalpel to expose and free up healthy underlying tissue, over which we would then apply our fancy medicinal dressings. Patients returned on a weekly basis to see us. They were given explicit home care instructions for continued progress. It was only when the wound was completely healed—covered over with a full layer of healthy skin— that we discharged them from our care. For many patients, these moments were a long time coming, and momentous enough that when they left us after their final visit, they would ring a special symbolic healing bell in the clinic's hallway to mark the happy occasion.

I drew parallels with the healing process required in my personal relationships. In my sickness, I had developed broad, deep wounds in my relations with virtually everyone around me. I could only treat them patiently and methodically, merely assisting in a natural process of healing and wound closure. The shallower lesions closed up more quickly; others were deep and infected, and would take years of ongoing attention to heal. Sharp, painful debridement was required to remove necrotic emotional tissue. When the underlying viable wound bed began to "granulate in," I knew we were on the right track. Some wounds, I had to accept, would never heal. Others, even if they did, would leave ugly, disfiguring scars that would forever remain present.

My children's wounds—how broad and deep are they? I can't even get them into a therapy clinic so they can be assessed and worked on. Their lesions are painful and festering under a thick, foul-smelling layer of decaying tissue that badly needs removal; the healthy wound bed of our recovery is suffocating and in desperate need of sharp debridement. There are medicated dressings just waiting to be applied; healing could progress if the smothered cells were uncovered, allowed to see the light of day. The virulent bacteria that kill the nascent growth of reconciliation hate the light because they die away in it.

▲▲▲▲▲

The Med-O-Matic had temporarily assigned me to their facility in Winchester. One of the physicians had abruptly departed, and the site was severely shorthanded. I didn't really mind the hour-long drive; it afforded me the chance to quietly do my morning devotions while driving and listen to my nineties alternative music on Pandora. The clinic was not nearly as hectic as my home site, giving me a chance to make phone calls, answer emails, read the *Big Book*, or socialize with the very personable clinic staff. The shifts were also a refreshing reprieve from the endless flow of local college kids—and their mothers—demanding antibiotics for chest colds and making medical suggestions based on Google searches. The citizens of Winchester were hardworking, salt-of-the-earth people who seemed to genuinely appreciate the care we provided, and I found my time there fulfilling.

Everything happens for a reason, I had begun to accept that. My program taught me that nothing happens in God's world by mistake. I was still in the infancy of what I hoped would be a lifelong process. I was blessed with a new home and a promising relationship; on the flip side, my children were still not speaking to me and my divorce was turning downright nasty. I found the experience of the seventy-mile drive to Winchester, the twelve-hour shift, and the journey home a nice way to fill the days.

It was right around Thanksgiving that I worked a couple of days alongside a nurse who hailed from Southwest Virginia. As is the case when working closely for a shift, we became chatty and learned each other's backgrounds. When she discovered I was a trained emergency physician in the Shenandoah Valley, she informed me of a freestanding ER—a full-service emergency department unattached to a hospital—about to open its doors in her hometown of Roanoke. My interest was piqued. Its director, Dr. Pasthegas, happened to be a previous colleague of one of my old ER partners back home. The one degree of separation in the emergency medicine world never failed to impress me. I was more than interested, and I felt the invisible hand guiding me.

So maybe going from shelf stocker to classroom teacher to urgent care doc is my Higher Power's way of moving me forward, gently immersing me back in my longtime specialty?

On my next day off, I made telephone contact with Dr. Pasthegas, and we arranged for an interview meeting. The facility was brand new and he needed board-certified emergency physicians to staff it. I don't even remember deliberating about it in my head; the decision-making just seemed to flow. After the holiday season I found myself sitting across the booth from him in a coffee shop, discussing the details of the job. Just like dating, this was our second contact, and it was time for my *revelation*. During the Q&A, I broached the subject of my battle with alcoholism, the monitoring program, and my long-term recovery. My future boss never flinched as he absorbed my story; that familiar, warm sense of gratitude filled me. He offered me the job on the spot, and I accepted.

After five hundred days away, I would be returning to the world of emergency medicine.

Once again, there would be some minor hurdles to clear, but we managed them smoothly. I was given the go-ahead by the monitoring program and submitted my ninety-day notice to the Med-O-Matic. Things were happening, changing again, and it didn't even feel like I was trying. Effort, yes; trying, no.

This is because you got out of the way and let God handle it; she operates on her time, not yours, and she indicated it was time to move forward.

Three months later I found myself working a shift in an emergency department in Roanoke, Virginia. I did not arrive my first day and set the place ablaze with the power of my presence, nor did I suddenly forget all the knowledge and skills I'd accumulated over my lifetime. I simply walked in, said hello to the staff, signed in to my workstation, and walked into a room where the first patient was waiting, as I had done one hundred thousand times before in my career. It was nothing more, nothing less.

▲▲▲▲▲

Life became much busier with my new job at "the Cave." I was waking up in the predawn darkness (a habit I was accustomed to), driving two hours, working my twelve-hour shift, and crashing in an Airbnb before returning to report to duty the next day. I often worked in blocks of three or four shifts, lodging locally to minimize the long commutes from home. I bunked in a host of private guest rooms, basement apartments, and suites. I made a concerted effort to sample different neighborhoods and speak with my hosts about life in Roanoke. Half the days of the month I was living there, and half the days I was back home. Fridays were still reserved for the wound care clinic.

Emergency work had always been an exercise in chaos management, and my Roanoke job proved to be no different, albeit a bit more subdued. Since it was a new facility, it had not yet been widely discovered by the city's population. It was very well laid out and optimized for efficiency, particularly when compared to the "main" emergency departments of my past. It housed eight treatment rooms, including a large trauma and critical care bay, a dedicated lab with a tech, and its own CT scanner and ultrasound machine. Like all ERs, we saw and treated our complement of "clinic" patients (sore throats, coughs, ankle injuries), but chest pain and trauma cases punctuated our day. We were a full-functioning emergency department equipped to handle all comers, but in reality we received ambulances with two basic patient types—Grandma fell and Grandma vomited (sometimes Grandpa too). It may have been emergency medicine *lite*, but it was emergency medicine, nonetheless. Every shift, I was able to put aside my "clinic doc" mindset in favor of the "ER doc" one. I saw the usual array of emergencies—appendicitis, arrhythmias, geriatric falls, respiratory distress, shoulder dislocations. A few of my colleagues had intubated there, a baby was delivered, and one doctor even did an emergent cricothyroidotomy (cut a hole in a patient's neck to emergently access an otherwise blocked airway). My long-slumbering inner adrenaline junkie began to awaken.

The nursing staff at the Cave was top-notch. Because many of the nurses were longtime veterans of busy main departments and trauma centers looking to throttle back in intensity, the vast majority of our patient care interactions went smoothly, and I felt a growing confidence that we were fully equipped for anything that showed up at our doors. My skill set may have been on the back burner for almost two years, but it sprang to life quickly; my emergency medicine mojo was fired up.

▲▲▲▲▲

One particular evening, a few months into the job, I had finished up an unremarkable shift at the Cave and had signed out to the oncoming night guy at eight o'clock on the dot. Having just completed a string of three straight shifts, I was ready for getaway night. I would be traveling back home, looking forward to crawling into my own bed with an awaiting Cassie. It was a clear, warm night, and within a few minutes I was cruising on the I-581 beltway, passing the brightly lit Mill Mountain Star and heading toward I-81. Traffic was scant . . . until it wasn't. Just up ahead, perhaps a quarter mile, a trail of bright red brake lights suddenly appeared like a Christmas tree lighting ceremony. It was a few seconds before I realized the cars hadn't just slowed, they had stopped completely.

Crap. Must've been an accident.

Upon closer inspection, peering through the last of the September dusk, I saw open car doors and people on the road, running around on the highway asphalt, arms flailing.

This was not good. In the same way an off-duty cop is never completely off duty, neither is an emergency worker. I slowed and veered my truck onto the left shoulder, came to a stop, cut the engine, and jumped out, hastily making my way to the commotion only yards ahead. Moving closer, I saw that I had not been mistaken; before me lay a horrific scene.

Just a few yards up the road, in front of the first line of cars, scattered debris littered the road. High-pitched shrieking noises filled the air. The headlights of the lead cars illuminated the remnants of a motorcycle—badly twisted and surrounded by shards of its own metal and plastic. The noxious smell of spilled gasoline assaulted my nasal passages. Ten yards beyond that, two helmeted bodies lay motionless in shadow, sprawled across the asphalt, lifeless.

I looked around and saw no flashing lights of any color, anywhere. I heard no sirens. The scene could not have been more than a minute or two old. I sprinted up to figure number one. Based on size and shape, he looked to be male, wearing full riding leathers. His body was badly contorted, left arm impossibly twisted behind his neck, deformed and disfigured. I moved closer and kneeled before him. His face shield was smashed, blood trickled from both nostrils, his eyes were open, his face lifeless. His other arm was against his side in full extension, rhythmically jerking, wrist in flexion. He was decerebrating—a neurologic response that occurs when the brain is badly damaged or deprived of oxygen and the brainstem is in its final bursts of electrical activity, shutting down. I recognized him as a Priority 4: dead or near death with zero likelihood of survival. I reached under his helmet and felt a weak carotid pulse. A half circle of bystanders stood behind me, cell phones out recording and snapping photos. I shooed them away.

Another few yards or so beyond victim number one was a woman, I guessed, based on the sound of the shrieking. She was obviously alive, sprawled on her back. Also in full motorcycling attire, she was in more of an anatomically appropriate position, with the exception of her left femur, which was painfully angulated at a forty-five-degree angle. At her head, kneeling, was a middle-aged woman in hospital scrubs, holding victim number two's neck steady. Sirens in the distance became increasingly audible. The victim was crying, shrieking, trying to form words. *Airway, check.* Her chest wall was rising and falling in rhythmic fashion. *Breathing, check.* I felt her carotid. It was strong. *Circulation, check.* The woman in scrubs and I spoke without introductions or pleasantries.

"Keep holding c-spine while I reduce her femur."

Our eyes met and she gave a nod of understanding. In my peripheral vision I saw blue flashing lights. The cell phone crowd had backed off. I moved to the patient's badly deformed lower extremity, crouched, grabbed her booted ankle, and leaned my weight backward, swinging slowly to my left. She screamed. I aligned her left foot with her right, revealing the massive swelling of her thigh. A shard of shattered bone had likely perforated the femoral artery, and she was bleeding heavily into that leg.

We talked to the patient to calm her; she was in a state of oblivious shock and crazed confusion. The first responders arrived and poured out of the fire trucks, closely followed by the ambulance units and teams of paramedics. Police were suddenly everywhere. I identified myself and gave a quick report to the first medics on scene as we "packaged" the female victim for transport on a backboard. A hard cervical collar, spider containment straps, and leg traction device were implemented; she was quickly hoisted and loaded into the back of the ALS unit, which sped off to the local trauma center. Woman in Scrubs (whose name I never got) and I gave as much information to the police as we could. All the while, the apparent driver of the motorcycle lay dead in the road, now covered by an EMS blanket. We had come upon the trauma scene and done what little we could, Good Samaritan–style. My role in the scene complete, I got back into my car and resumed my trek home. Although I was having strong emotions over what had just transpired, I felt surprisingly unfazed by the entire event. Only thirty minutes earlier, while I was signing out of work, a couple was out on a motorcycle ride; in the blink of an eye, he was dead, and she was in a trauma bay about to be operated on, likely looking at months of excruciating rehab and physical therapy, and a lifetime of coping with emotional pain. That's how fast life can change, or end.

Later, as I drove north and the mile markers passed, I reflected on the event, and prayed for the victims and those close to them who would be forever affected. I also recognized in myself, based on my responses and my ability to switch into provider mode, that I was back professionally, and perhaps even more emotionally prepared to return to emergency medicine than ever before. I also said a quiet prayer of thanks for my children, who were likely at home in bed, with Mom downstairs, safe. I arrived home, shed my clothes, and slipped under the sheets next to Cassie, who was on her side, asleep. I wriggled beside her; her body was warm.

▲▲▲▲▲

Over the next year I worked over a dozen twelve-hour shifts per month, traveling to Roanoke, learning the people and places, running on the riverside greenway, and enjoying some of the local restaurants. I signed up for area road races and ran up to the Mill Mountain Star many mornings in the wee hours. Cassie would often visit me and spend the night with me at the Airbnb. She drove four hours round trip, despite work in the morning, to spend maybe half an hour of awake time with me. I learned the neighborhoods of Old Southwest, Grandin, Salem, Cave Spring. If I did a string of nights, I would attend the afternoon AA meetings. Roanoke had become my second city, my new Charlottesville.

As it turned out, old Charlottesville would also become my new Charlottesville. Six months into my tenure at the Cave, I caught wind of an opening for an emergency physician at another freestanding ED north of the city, by the airport, thirty-six miles from my house. My professional confidence continued to gain momentum, and I had been thinking of leaving wound care for a part-time job with another hospital system. It didn't pay as well as Roanoke, but certainly more than wound care, and I had developed an intense appetite for as many ER hours as possible; I had fallen back in love with my old profession.

There were several advantages to picking up work in Charlottesville. Not only was this position commutable from home, but I knew and liked the city. It was where I participated in Kenneth Dovel's bimonthly professionals-in-recovery group, and I was already familiar with the AA community from my Oxford House days. The work environment was similar to the Cave and, of course, I loved the patients. Over a three-month time span, I applied, went through the customary vetting process, and was accepted as a member of the medical staff. What enhanced matters for me—from a confidence standpoint—was that the ED director, Dr. Romano, knew my background before I ever set foot in his office for the interview, and he hired me anyway. With a fond adieu, I bid farewell to wound care.

For the first time in my career, I was a member of three separate hospital systems.

Be careful, Dr. Remy . . . all work and no play makes Joe a du—

▲▲▲▲▲

Like Roanoke, my days in Charlottesville's freestanding ER were comfortable, the environment customary and familiar. As in Roanoke, I worked alongside a highly skilled, competent, and welcoming team of nurses and techs in a well-functioning, efficient department. The acuity was generally low, although I had the opportunity to routinely employ advanced procedural skills to resuscitate and stabilize patients. Given the shorter eight-hour shift, if working during the day, I finished up with plenty of time to see Cassie and take her out to dinner at our favorite restaurant.

The weeks passed and I found myself content; I had two great ER jobs, a loving girlfriend, and a great dog. The anguish of missing my children occasionally even receded into the background. Life was pretty good. Yet it was only a couple of months before I found my restless thoughts drifting back over to "my side" of the Blue Ridge. I began thinking more about my old job at the Rock.

Not in my wildest dreams did I ever think that I could go back to my old emergency department, the place where I grew up, professionally speaking. A lifetime earlier I had completed medical residency at the tender green age of twenty-eight, having gone straight through my schooling since kindergarten without coming up for air. The Rock had been my first and only doctor job, and I'd remained there full time for twenty-two years before Implosion Day. While at the recovery center, once I realized that all was not lost, I spent time reflecting on new career paths—wound care, primary care, urgent care. As far as I was concerned, it was a miracle I was holding a license to practice medicine at all, let alone working in my specialty. The idea of being permitted back to the scene of the crime—well, it didn't even register as a blip in my most extreme fantasies.

I was just off the treadmill at a Planet Fitness when the phone call came from Dr. Ryan Steinberg, the ED director there and my old partner. He informed me I had been a topic of discussion at a recent group meeting and without a pause he asked me if I'd like my old job back.

▲▲▲▲▲

Dr. Steinberg had a firsthand account of my flameout. Months before my hospitalization, I had been flailing badly in the department—short tempered with nursing staff, hostile with patients, constantly sleepy and nauseated, with shakes so bad by shift's end I couldn't get out the door quickly enough. This behavior did not go unnoticed by my peers; although my secret was still hidden, the partners approached me and requested that I take a few weeks off, rest, and be seen by my doctor before returning to work. I did exactly as I was instructed, deceiving everybody—my family doctor, my neurologist, my colleagues . . . and myself. Before long I was back at it, mildly improved, working and hiding my drinking. Three weeks for a closet drunk to get his act together was a joke, but what did they know? In the end, it required over two years of a rigorous recovery program and healing for me to even set foot in the old department. When I was on the other end of the hospital in the wound care clinic, I avoided the ER.

After two and a half years of twelve-step recovery, extensive therapy, soul-searching, and discussion, I made the decision to make Roanoke a part-time gig and return to emergency medicine at the Rock. By then I had a one-year track record of solid post-recovery ER work, two years practicing medicine, and ten thousand patient interactions successfully completed over that period without any adverse outcomes. Management wanted me back, and I felt equipped—emotionally, intellectually, and socially. The gratification of having come full circle was overwhelming. Still, I had my fear-based self-doubts.

What will my kids think? Will they care?

Will I do a good job? Am I really the ER doc I once was? Have I been truly tested?

What will the staff who knew me . . . before . . . think? How will they relate to me?

What about room twelve? What about Maggie and the Kidney Stone Lady?

▲▲▲▲▲

The department buzzed with activity as Ryan gave me my tour. How strange it was, being guided through the hallways, nurses' stations, and patient rooms where I had spent seven years (the hospital had changed locations from downtown, where I had worked for fifteen years before that). The afternoon felt surreal. There I was, in my button-down shirt and khakis, walking with Ryan; my return was now common knowledge among the staff, and I was highly vigilant to any judgmental looks I would receive.

People at the Rock who knew me *from before* generally reacted to my return in one of three distinct ways. In the first, someone would recognize me, stop whatever it was she was doing, move toward me with arms extended, embrace me tightly, and give me an emphatic "Welcome back!" I enjoyed this approach for obvious reasons; it was an immediate positive reconnection. Samuel, the pharmacist stationed in the department who worked alongside us docs daily, was a perfect example of this. He gave me a prince's greeting, quietly told me how impressed he was and that he was proud of me. I accepted his openness and warmth unconditionally. I knew it was people like him who were not only good for me, but great for the functioning of the ER. Aside from his exceptional clinical competence in advising us on medications ordered in the department, he always emanated a caring vibe to all around, and for that the department loved him.

The second response type was the "double take," where after initial eye contact, there was a flash of surprised recognition, followed by a reflexive, robotic "Hi, how are you?" This would last a few seconds, after which the individual would return to his previous activity. This was the neutral response.

The third type of reaction disturbed me, and thus required the most self-reflection, the most reliance on my program. This was eye-contact avoidance. Although it was employed by a distinct minority of people, my spider-sense was particularly keen to it. They would spot me, and there would be that flash of sudden shock followed by the rapid look away, usually down at their feet. A mumbled greeting might follow, and a hurried shuffle past, providing me the wide berth every crazy alcoholic needs so as not to infect the innocent. It happened with a handful of nurses, doctors, and patient techs. It stung, but the pain was transient, and I recognized it as ego based. Not everybody had to like me or be happy I was back.

What other people think of me is none of my business. Besides, what a great opportunity to continue to practice my living amends, one day at a time!

▲▲▲▲▲

My first shifts back at the Rock were in the lower acuity areas, allowing me to acclimate to the environment. I treated abdominal pain, migraine headaches, coughs, and colds. I did not complain; I was flying high, emotionally speaking. I was back in my hometown emergency department, working with the old team, taking care of patients in my own county, many who remembered me from prior years. A few even shared fond memories of me during previous patient interactions.

After a month I had graduated to the acute-care side, neck deep in much of the critical pathology that defines emergency medicine—acute respiratory failure, head trauma, heart attacks, and diabetic emergencies. The city and county squad crews would be lined up out the door with patients, waiting for room assignments from the charge nurse. In the rooms, acute care teams would operate fluidly during an expedited check-in, each member knowing his or her role. My teambuilding skills in recovery translated well as I joined in.

As a physician in long-term recovery, there was a discernable difference in my approach to the patients. It was subtle at first but became increasingly palpable. After my primary evaluation and examination of a patient, I permitted myself just a little extra time at the bedside to make a human connection—that less tangible component of the needs of the person on the stretcher or backboard. Whether they looked frightened, dismayed, complacent, or oblivious to their surroundings, I took the time to do an emotional assessment. Was the patient alone in the world, crying over her demise? Did she have anyone to reach out to? Was family on the way? Did they care, or was this visit to the hospital an excuse to fast-track Grandma to the nursing home? I found myself, on a daily basis, looking to stabilize more than just anatomy and physiology.

I was particularly keen to the plight of the intoxicated. Whether it was a college student passed out on a hallway stretcher in her vomit-stained party dress, clutching her cell phone, or the old, crusty regular from downtown, I found that my approach contained a level of concern previously nonexistent. Granted, I'd always felt *some* degree of buried compassion for these patients, but now there was a new facet to my understanding of their situation—empathy. I had lived with these patients, had been in their shoes; I remembered . . .

. . . *room twelve.* Looking pathetic, screaming, with vomit-stained clothes, as the staff looked down on me in pity.

I attended rehab with these patients, lived with them, worked with them, went to meetings with them . . . they were my *comrades in alcoholism* now, and I quietly thanked God each time I took care of one, for the blessing bestowed upon me of newfound empathy. I was no longer the arrogant, authoritative physician who glared disdainfully down my nose at them as they writhed in their own secretions and moaned; I no longer cracked jokes about them to my colleagues with a misplaced sense of superiority. Not anymore. I was definitely one of them, always had been, only now I knew it. I was just as diseased and full of shit as them, and my chronic incurable illness was still there, only in remission but for the grace of God. Wearing scrubs and a white coat didn't make me anything special, nor waive my responsibility of compassion. My uniform was merely a role-playing costume, that's all. I may have been showered and alcohol-free, but there was no denying in my mind that I was them, and they were me, and we were imperfect.

▲▲▲▲▲

As if I needed more reminders of my imperfections, I had Maggie and the Kidney Stone Lady, forever. Little Maggie, the cute five-year-old from early in my career who came in with her croupy cough and low-grade fever, and whose chest X-ray was normal. She responded so well to racemic epinephrine, Tylenol, and humidified oxygen. The little dark-haired girl with the big eyes whom we all watched gleefully sashay out of the emergency department so many years ago, smiling and happy, waving goodbye to me and the rest of the nursing staff . . . and who, just twenty-four hours later, died of overwhelming sepsis. How I sobbed for nights in my bed, racking my brain as to what else I could have done, what subtlety in her presentation I could have picked up on, and wondering if I had discharged her too quickly instead of keeping her around for observation. It was back in the old hospital; I was maybe thirty-two at the time. Years later I was still trying to drown the vision of her ghost in cheap vodka.

But Maggie kept appearing, following me—sometimes alone, sometimes alongside the woman with the kidney stone.

The stone had shown up on the CT scan. She was a diabetic woman with flank pain whom I had seen a few years back. She had a normal urinalysis and bloodwork, but her urine culture grew out *E. coli*. The result was reported to me by the microbiology lab the day after she, too, died a septic death. That tiny pebble, stuck in her ureter tube, blocked the flow of urine in its normal journey from kidney to bladder. This caused the retained fluid, teeming with bacteria, to sit and fester, permitting germs to feast on stagnant glucose and proteins. The bacteria multiplied exponentially, and the resulting soup of piss and pus backtracked up to the kidney, creating a bloated, infected organ, which in turn invaded her bloodstream, overwhelmed her defenses, and led to cardiovascular collapse and death.

I spoke with her husband after the funeral. She had done everything we told her to do, and the day she died he had been trying to cool her off all day at home in the bathtub.

Now, in her afterlife, she occasionally accompanied Maggie on excursions into my head, usually at night. Make that a double vodka.

I thought I had finally learned in sobriety how to put them in the past, encased in a box, and keep them there. Still, sometimes they found a way out to visit me. The program taught me how to at least limit their appearances.

▲▲▲▲▲

I worked hard over the months, showing up for shifts with an energy I had not seen in myself for decades, a newfound enthusiasm I had not felt since my residency days back in Baltimore.

"Put your recovery first, and everything will fall back into line," was the advice I heard over and over, and it was coming true—at least in my working life. "God's time, not my time," was an additional caveat, one that took me longer to absorb. Every now and then, I opened the story box voluntarily to visit Maggie and the Kidney Stone Lady, mainly to say hello and pay respects, and to remind myself that everything happens according to a plan well beyond my comprehension. I possessed other story boxes in my mind too, happy ones—like the utility worker who fell from the telephone pole and fractured his spleen, arriving in traumatic shock, whom we stabilized for emergency surgery and who survived; like the baby that

Jessica from the satellite lab and I delivered together in room three; the blood pressure medicine overdose case who rolled in unresponsive and made it out of the hospital alive; the walk-in anaphylactic shock patient I resuscitated with help from an incredible nursing team, with extra kudos to our Johnny-on-the-spot pharmacist, Samuel.

The good with the bad, it was a lifetime of spicy brain stew spent in this godforsaken, amazing specialty, and I was ready for more. And more I was about to get, or more accurately, be clobbered with.

▲▲▲▲▲

Eight months to the day after my return to the Rock, I pulled into the hospital's Lot C just as the first light of dawn, pink and orange, appeared over the Blue Ridge. Two freshly assembled white biohazard tents, each the size of a tour bus and erected in the adjacent parking lot to screen the less severe cases, obscured my regular view of the ER's rescue squad entrance. I sat in the driver's seat for an extra minute, listening to the finale of the Foo Fighters' "Hey, Johnny Park!" and reflecting on how rapidly the change had happened. Fortunately, we all saw it coming.

Only two weeks earlier, my shifts were business as usual: fresh coffee in hand, I would put on my white coat and stethoscope, take sign-out from the night shift doc, and begin what I had done four thousand previous times in my life—see and treat a full shift's worth of acutely ill patients until my relief arrived in turn.

Today was day one of the "new way." COVID-19 was everywhere now, especially in the news and on social media, and our local community was in lockdown. The new hospital infection control measures were all in place. At no time in my career had I seen such extreme precautions—avian flu, SARS, flesh-eating bacteria, H1N1—none of those came close. This novel virus, creating an outbreak of panic and hysteria the modern world had never seen, had spread to every corner of the planet, and the health care community was desperately trying to contain it. We all knew it could not be stopped, only slowed.

Our objectives as nurses, doctors, administrators, and community leaders were far more modest—to control the virus's spread and limit the loss of life without exhausting all medical resources, all the while maintaining some semblance of a functional health system for everyone. I had no idea if we could accomplish our goals and maintain our own health in the process. As I peered into the distance, I had only a vague notion of what awaited me that morning once I walked into the department. It didn't matter; I was heading in. I had been given a blessed second chance in my specialty; fear be damned.

What I knew for sure, and with absolute clarity, was that never before in my adult life was I as mentally, physically, and spiritually prepared to play my small part in this global fight as I was that day. Ready for battle, I donned my respirator mask, grabbed my work bag, and got out of my car.

I walked across the parking lot and through the emergency room squad doors. No, I was never more ready.

CHAPTER 10

RESENTMENT, FEAR, AND PAIN

Titi me maryaj, maryaj la mizerab
Manmanm mouri maladi, papam mouri maladi
Mayiango eya, mayiango fe woch mache.
Ooo ooo mayiango fe woch mache

(This is the wedding, the wedding is miserable.
My mother dies from the sickness,
my dad dies from the sickness.
Mayiango makes the rock move.)
—Haitian children's folk song

They writhed and shook on the floor as they wailed, eyes squeezed shut, shirts and dresses drenched in perspiration. Their noises would cycle in pitch, from low, guttural belly grunts to ear-piercing shrieks. Some were entwined together in the middle aisle; others remained in their chairs, babbling their unearthly language, arms akimbo. It was as if the entire room was embroiled in one collective grand mal seizure. Had I been performing a neurologic assessment on any single one of them, the NIH Stroke Scores would have ranged anywhere from five to fourteen—enough for the clot-busting medications or interventional radiology suite.

From his pulpit, Pastor Geordany fueled their intensity, his robust sermon expertly timing a crescendo as only an experienced preacher of his caliber could muster. His flock was in spiritual ecstasy, the room heaving and spinning. My ears were buzzing. As his deep, impassioned voice approached a climax, I expected a rapture moment. The Creole words firing from his mouth were rhythmic and unbroken; as he spoke, Renel translated for us Americans. Converted into English, the content of his sermon was awe-inspiring, particularly for this suburban Jew. His passion stemmed from his unwavering belief in his God. His personal immersion in his faith that Sunday, and every Sunday, is what I believe connected him so strongly to his followers.

I remained quietly seated up on the front stage alongside my co-missionaries on what was just one of many sweltering mornings in central Haiti. The cinderblock church, with its roof of rusty corrugated tin, sat within a treeless orphanage compound, the rising sun converting it into a giant oven. There was not a single dry spot on my shirt in the one-hundred-plus-degree heat. None of us had showered in days, nor did we care; feeling the power of what was unfolding around us was far more intense than the Haitian weather. We sat there, witness to the packed house's simultaneous release of a week's worth of pent-up emotional and physical pain, from a people who lived a quiet life of hunger, sickness, and poverty. From Monday through Saturday they stoically held it all inside. But on that Sunday, like every Sunday, it was purged from their collective hearts with the help of their seventy-year-old spiritual leader.

In that moment, I was convinced that no people on the planet could process pain as successfully as the Haitians.

▲▲▲▲▲

It is written in the *Big Book of Alcoholics Anonymous* that for the alcoholic, resentment is the number-one offender. It took me some time and a degree of sober maturity to scratch the surface of that concept. If I am wronged, get angry, and hold a grudge against the offending person, group, or institution, am I justified in my feelings? If I get screwed over by my boss, get set up for humiliation by a coworker, or have my good idea stolen, don't I have the right to get fired up? Am I not then morally justified in running around to friends and confidants, vigorously making my argument from a morally superior vantage point to cement validation for my feelings of righteous indignation?

If I cherry-pick those around me who I know will support my anger, then I can feel vindicated. Being fully backed by those to whom I present my case and winning them over allows me the cover I need to simmer in my own self-justified rage and infuses me with a steady feeling of bitter conceit and superiority. *Now, doesn't that feel better?*

No. In the end, the satisfaction is fleeting at best. As it is oft repeated in the rooms of AA: *I'd rather be happy than right.*

The problem with holding a resentment, and its forced conversion to righteous indignation, is that it reinforces a thinly veiled sense of ego-driven personal entitlement. If I resent another for a perceived wrongdoing, it underscores an expectation of how I "deserve" to be treated, that I am automatically due a certain amount of respect or honor. This occurs all around us. It can be as basic as a parent's expectations of a grown child or a corporate CEO's expectations in a boardroom. Pilots, project managers, physicians, anyone in a power position—we often put too much stock in our titles and not enough in the responsibilities of those titles, demanding to be constantly paid homage for our authority instead of finding gratitude for having achieved the capacity to *serve* the goals our positions require.

Our self-perceived rules of engagement, based on our station in life and influenced by our professors, bosses, and institutions, subconsciously dictate how we treat the world and how the world "should" treat us. This is ego run amok. When the world fails to live up to our romanticized expectations of respect or meet our personal emotional demands, we get indignant, angry, or passive-aggressive, or we simply withdraw. Each one of these responses underscores a certain sense of trumped-up self-worth, attributable to an overinflated ego, and is just plain selfish.

This bloated sense of entitlement keeps us addicts intoxicated with our own egos and triggers emotional relapses, clearing the path for chemical relapses. We "deserve" the drug or drink, because, you see, the world is too stupid to understand us and how important we are. We get a case of the "fuck its." *The world can do without my great contributions for a night while I get sloshed. By golly, I'll show them.*

For alcoholics, addicts, and other members of the human race, holding resentments is the fail-safe way to block internal serenity. In the program, we often describe the concept of resentment as "drinking poison and hoping the other person will die." Another metaphor is "permitting the offender a rent-free room in your head." Allowing these so-called personal violations to bounce around the inside of one's skull at the expense of productive thought is off-putting at least, self-destructive at worst.

Deconstructing resentments is an exercise that requires practice and continuous vigilance, until it becomes a new pattern of thinking by force of habit. For me, I utilized the *Big*

Book to write out comprehensive fourth and tenth steps, which involve personal moral inventories and self-analysis. But one does not need to be immersed in AA doctrine to confront resentment issues. Learning how to incorporate gratitude, humility, and acceptance in any form works.

▲▲▲▲▲

My ex-wife's attorney, I was told, was one of the best in the county. During my divorce deposition, I sat directly across the conference room table from him. His legal team and my ex were present, frantically scribbling notes to pass to him any time I opened my mouth to respond to a question. (For the record, I chose not to attend my ex's deposition, not feeling emotionally equipped to watch my attorney question her. I preferred to keep the years of happy memories of marriage as pristine as possible inside my head.) Divorce attorneys are quite possibly the quintessential targets for resentment, and to me, hers was no different. The entire narrative he spun was that of the "husband as an abuser and evil family destroyer," intentionally exaggerating and mutilating the facts surrounding our twenty-three-year marriage.

He grilled me with his questions for hours, painting me as a monster of a human being while the stenographer obediently typed along. After the ordeal, forming a huge resentment would have been easy, and so I did. Channeling all my rage and frustrations of life into a single villain was simple and convenient, and for a while, my righteous indignation felt satisfying. However, as I processed my feelings mentally and spiritually, with the aid of my sponsor (and a thorough fourth step), I was able to reach a vital emotional settlement. First, the man was just a professional, performing the job he was paid to do to maximize benefit for his client. He was hired and compensated handsomely for the sole purpose of being an overdramatic

douchebag, and he did a first-rate job. Also, as my own attorney reminded me, absolutely nobody—including his own legal
team, my ex, the judge, or anyone else who read the deposition
transcript—would ever believe the extreme descriptions of me
as a malicious and disturbed husband, father, physician, and
member of the human race, who masterminded the decline of
Western civilization. Where there were kernels of truth (and of
course there were), wasn't it my responsibility to admit them
to myself, quietly, with my sponsor? My program required me
to own up to the facts: I was a closet alcoholic. I hid it from my
family. I cultivated my own paranoia. I stashed guns, Valium,
and vodka. At times, I lied and deceived to achieve less than
honorable goals.

In the end, I admitted to God and another person the exact
nature of my wrongs. I took the fifth step.

A powerful weapon against resentment is gratitude, and
Wally helped me employ it effectively. My family was safe and well
protected, physically and financially. Whatever the end result
would be for me, the four of them were taken care of. I was
grateful that I would retain shared legal custody of the children, that I had no DUIs, no criminal record. The police
were never called to our home, and we never needed Child
Protective Services.

I allowed myself to be humbled by the larger, mainly benign
powers at play and the intended fairness of the American legal
system permitting equitable divorces. However the division
of assets and child support formulas played out, in the end,
it would always be about taking proper care of the children.
After a quarter century of laboring as an emergency physician,
I employed gratitude to recognize that God endowed me with
the capacity to pay off a massive school debt and home mortgage while building up three college nest eggs. I was secondary; it was all there for them. That, in and of itself, gave me the

warm sensation that carries through to this day. But I have to give credit where credit is due.

If gratitude served in the superhero role against resentment, acceptance was its sidekick. Accepting that I was in a situation where my soon-to-be ex-wife felt she needed high-caliber legal counsel to protect her and the children against me took herculean effort, but this was her stance, and who was I to challenge her beliefs? Working on my own character defects was challenging enough. She had a damn good lawyer and a good situation: three healthy children on her side who could face the challenges of adolescence without ever having money woes. She could focus her attention on her own situation without ever having to fret over paying the bills. I may have been seen by them as nothing more than the goose laying the golden eggs, and I had to swallow that. As Alanis Morissette said, "What a jagged little pill." But it was acceptance or relapse, and relapse for me was death.

Nobody ever said practicing gratitude and acceptance was going to be easy; it was going to take lots of practice. "Spiritual progress over spiritual perfection," the saying goes. Resentments lingered. Such was the case with our so-called co-parenting counselor. We had been assigned this asshat by the guardian ad litem during the divorce proceedings. His sole purpose was to help us parents develop strategies to effectively raise our children during and after divorce, for the ultimate well-being of the kids.

The process was an abysmal failure. We spent two years in regular sessions with this pathetic excuse for a professional. The objective was to acclimate the children to an environment of being raised by a loving mother and father whose lives were separate, and over two years we made absolutely zero progress. It was very clear that this bumbling clown was as clueless about co-parenting as he was incompetent as a clinician. We were supposed to be laying the groundwork for civility in divorce, establishing a dialogue for the long term, and eventually introducing the children into the sessions so they could observe their divorced parents getting along.

He never even came close. Session after session we would sit on opposite sides of his office while he permitted the "Tribunal of the Sins of Joseph" to proceed. With his framed diplomas on the wall behind him, he would shift in his seat uncomfortably, saying little and enabling her to hurl accusation after accusation, rehashing over and over how I screwed up as a husband and father, reinforcing her claims with grotesquely muddied anecdotes.

Some of her stories were accurate, others embellished exaggeration, still others complete constructs of a struggling mind. Ultimately, it was not my ex-wife I formed a resentment against, it was that buffoon who slouched between us, with his ample gut hanging over his belt while he scratched his bald head and stared at the carpet. He provided no constructive alternatives to the kangaroo courtroom environment he himself created (and that I was paying for). Eventually, it dawned on me how intimidated he was by her. My resentment toward him thrived, and although fading, still exists.

However, even in resentment, I learned to take some responsibility myself for what transpired in the co-parenting sessions. My guilt over my actions in active alcoholism restrained me from responding to the attacks. I inaccurately blamed myself for everything, sitting passively while the shitstorm rained down on my head. At the time, I interpreted the happenings in that room as a badly needed catharsis for the woman I was married to for all those years. I was the only one receiving regular therapy, and she clearly needed help badly. My hope was that we would get everything out in the open, I would make heartfelt verbal amends, and then we could get down to the work we were there for in the first place— parenting children.

The counselor was clearly out of his depth in this situation. He was worse than useless, actually setting back a process that had gained some traction with the previous counselor the court had initially assigned and which had included meeting with the children. Supervised visits had been arranged, and the kids and I had spent time together in a neutral location. We talked and played games. I made a video tour of my new home on my phone for them to see; my ten-year-old excitedly watched with anticipation. On two different occasions, Toby announced his interest in coming to visit me at my house and seeing his room. One time, I brought my guitar and played; another time my dog accompanied me. I even threw a joint birthday party for all of us, complete with cake and presents. Dr. Buffoon's takeover of the process, admittedly permitted by me in a vain attempt to curry favor with opposing counsel, sank what had been an advancing process. My own character defect of people-pleasing was partially to blame. I took ownership of my role in handing a vital process to a complete moron.

The result was a catastrophe for our entire broken family. I held out, keeping the sessions going out of a false hope that things would turn around, that the blame game would end, and praying for a breakthrough. What a fool I was! I lamented having stuck things out so long, and in the final tally, felt the hollowness of loss—for myself, my ex, and the children.

For me, the loss of the three most important beings in my life, my raison d'être, was the mother of all resentment. I even went around to my therapists, consensus-building against this bastard, as if that would fix anything. It was an exercise in futility indulging my ego. After the sessions ended once and for all, I produced an angry, turbocharged resentment letter to Dr. Buffoon:

> *These so-called co-parenting sessions, supposedly engaged in for the benefit of the children,*

were permitted to devolve into a repeating nev-
er-ending looped track of the sins of the father,
taking some perceived infraction on my part
and using it as a pretense for making additional
excuses as to why the children have made zero
progress in developing even the most remote
improvement in attitudes toward me. In your
room, over and over again, as you mindlessly
nodded along, a case was built on how "well"
the kids were doing without me. Then we tran-
sitioned into my ongoing tribunal, recounting
years-old negative memories which have long
since been discussed, processed, and apolo-
gized for . . . at the expense of the real work that
should have been done these last two years. All
progress, and purpose, was stifled.

Please excuse me if the comments about
the children acting and thinking on their own
about me, without outside influence, with my
ex remaining a neutral party, ring hollow.
There are many very smart people out there
with decades of co-parenting experience and
basic common sense who have advised me oth-
erwise. Disingenuous is the word that comes to
mind.

One of the primary reasons my individual
therapist, group therapist, sponsor, and numer-
ous others are expressing their dismay at the
spectacular failure of your "co-parenting" ses-
sions is that there's never really been any true
co-parenting going on. My having the audacity
to actually be present in my children's lives has
been called out as a "violation of a boundary,"
a concept which has been bastardized in your

room and used as a pretense to prevent any progress from being made. While we should have been setting up a framework for more involved legitimate co-parenting, involving the children so that they don't get increasingly bound to a destructive narrative and cementing in their anger-fear cycle, we should have been working against the permanence of their condition known as parental alienation syndrome (look it up). This should have been the real work; work that was never done. Sandbagging and foot-dragging ruled the day. Maybe true progress was never the intention; perhaps acclimating the children to a life without a father was the actual objective. We heard her exclaim at least once that she wished to never see me again; how can this be good for a co-parenting process? She and I are forever tied together with the children and I for one will never give up on them.

If we are going to be honest, then we need to admit that these sessions have not only been a complete failure, but they have actually cemented the damage. A year and a half ago Toby and I were seeing each other, playing games together, and he more than once told me how he would like to come visit me at my house. Hannah and he were emailing me positive things. But instead of building on this we decided to use the sessions as nothing more than an excuse as to why they should be kept away. Where has their therapy been? What efforts have been made inside or outside your room to show them that they have a father who is getting healthy, improving his life, and cares? Why does our situation fall into the 4% of divorce cases in which one parent has zero contact with the children? Why are there others out there, many whom I know personally, who are divorced, having committed egregious crimes and sins too unspeakable to mention, some who have served prison sentences, who have some relationship with their children? We can sit here and say that . . . "oh every situation is different" . . . but I once again ask you, why is ours such an extreme case? I suspect your first thought will be to point at me accusingly and who I am and what I've done, but I encourage you to challenge that pattern of thinking. Everybody has a role in this disaster. The difference is that I take ownership of mine.

I have been told repeatedly by others that these sessions have been a farce, a sham, a pretense to set up a framework and a narrative to justify keeping the father away from the children. In the end, we should be able to have the vision to see this may cause far more damage than I ever could. I challenge you to show me a single study in which a child growing up with one parent in the end does better than a child growing up with two loving parents. Even the court-appointed guardian ad litem, who in the end I dismissed at my ex's request, repeatedly expressed that I needed to be in the children's lives.

I fully recognize that I am partially to blame here, don't get me wrong. I have prostrated myself, enabled these discussions in hopes to appease and satisfy, gaining me no points in Heaven but only serving to embolden this destructive pathway.

I want to assure you that there are other paths. Paths I will engage in to reinvigorate a long moribund process, a process you have long surrendered and turned tail on. Your backpedaling the last few months was embarrassingly apparent. I have freely admitted many times that I have been at fault here in many, many ways. Over these last years, as I have clawed my way back from the brink of oblivion to turn my life around, rebuilt a successful professional career and active social life, and with the help of many, many people, I have learned how to forgive myself. . . . And once I was able to do that, I began to learn how to forgive others. Forgiveness is the true salvation, true path to God's serenity, and I wonder if the children have been offered an opportunity for this vital lesson. I'm not saying that I am absolved, but are any of us?

I will continue to improve myself and hope God smiles upon all of us. I depart your sessions with my head held high in the recognition of what my Higher Power has allowed me the strength to accomplish these last three years. I pray for you to develop some real therapeutic clarity as time goes on. Doc, perhaps the mistakes made in this room will serve as a springboard for your professional development, and perhaps another family may be helped as a result of this two-year disaster.

Joe

My resentment was ablaze, my character defects out in full force, parading around in the letter like a crazed, trigger-happy soldier and full of rage, ego, intellectualizing, superiority . . . and fear. Getting over this resentment would take time. A very, very long time.

Thinking back, perhaps my letter was a tad harsh.

Resentment lives in the past, playing back for us the scenes of difficult situations we once found ourselves in, whether an hour prior or in early childhood. Emotionally speaking, resentment takes us back to the scene of the crime. The *now* ceases to exist while our heads are hijacked by the past. These flashbacks of anger are memory-based, but as time passes and we continue to relive them over and over, we rewrite the script to our liking, crystallizing our confirmation bias. In the scene's "retake," our emotions take complete charge to edit the memory. We reshape it so that the final product bears little resemblance to the original truth. Confirmation bias—the tendency to recall information selectively to validate our deeply entrenched preconceptions and prejudices—takes over. This gives birth to stronger resentment, resulting in even more potentially destructive thinking and behavior. The emotional mind overwhelms the logical mind, a Pyrrhic victory.

Your memories called. You need to be even more righteously pissed off than you are.

While resentment is busy eroding our serenity by rewriting the past, fear hides in the shadows of the imagined future, waiting to pounce.

▲▲▲▲▲

I was suited up with my helmet and goggles in place as I sat motionless on the jumper bench. Out the window to my right, the aircraft passed a wisp of a cloud. I stayed comfortably inside my head, meditating and praying. It was an idea I had

back-pocketed for years: if I was ever in a deep rut, with my
life stagnating and in need of shock therapy, I would engage in
this completely and absolutely terrifying act—stepping out of a
plane's open door and into the atmosphere fourteen thousand
feet above planet Earth. Strapped to my ass was an old dude
with a parachute.

A few months after Implosion Day, my motivation shifted
into action. It became less about breaking free of stagnation and
more about simply facing my fear of falling. My logical mind
knew that there was an overwhelming chance I would reach
the ground safe and intact, and that the most dangerous parts
of the day, statistically speaking, would be the drives there and
home; my emotional mind didn't care about statistics.

Fear in life is all about the what-ifs: *What if I get a poor
job evaluation? What if this rash is not just poison ivy? What
if my kid flunks the SATs? What if I bomb on open mic night?
What if coronavirus gets me? What if our parachute doesn't
deploy?* All possible permutations of all the answers to every
what-if question have one central truth in common—they all
exist in some imaginary future deep within our emotional
selves. Every last conceivable outcome of what-if is a construct
of our runaway emotions—every last one. Granted, when the
logical mind has a chance to get a word in edgewise, one real-
izes there are higher probabilities for certain outcomes than
others. According to the United States Parachute Association,
in 2018, there was a total of thirteen fatalities from skydiving. About three million jumps that year were recorded. That
would mean, for the rational mind, there is a 0.00043 percent
chance of a skydiver dying from any single jump.

The emotional mind called; it doesn't give a shit.

All the emotional mind knows is that descending thousands of feet in freefall is inherently unnatural, and some people have in fact died doing it, just like *"someone* has to win the
lottery." While many are up front about their fears ("I'm just

too damn scared"), others' emotional brains create elaborate rationalizations for not engaging in a given feared act. "I have a chronic sinus condition and cannot handle altitude changes," "I need to get a better guitar before playing in front of others," "I am having chest pain but won't go to the ER because of COVID-19."

I see fear all around me daily in the emergency department. While that would appear to make sense—it is, after all, an inherently scary place for the average person—it is not the patients with the obvious emergencies who seem most gripped by fear. It is those with the more routine walk-in complaints. The worry of a new mother with a feverish baby, a teenager's hand laceration, or a man's tick bite—all of these real-life scenarios generate fear, based on some negative imagined future outcome. This is a fabricated construct of an emotional brain. We feel a symptom and get online to google worst-case scenarios, talk to EMT friends, or call in to the doctor's office and are told to "go to the emergency room." *If this is a medical emergency, please hang up, and dial 911.* Playing the game in our minds, we manufacture emotion-driven possible outcomes at the extreme end of the possibility spectrum. Every cough is pneumonia, every headache is a brain tumor, every rash is Lyme disease, and no degree of professional assurance can convince us otherwise. Fear rules our thinking, controlling our thoughts and actions.

Just like we don't look up fatality statistics before deciding on skydiving, we don't speed off to the hospital in the middle of the night armed with stats about what ails us. We certainly don't consider the fact that in the vast majority of emergency department visits, patients leave the ER with nothing more than a prescription or two and some basic aftercare instructions. All we know is that we see a problem unfold and then our minds play out the extreme Hollywood-style fabricated scene continuously, until something changes. Fear, without a doubt in my mind, is the number-one reason people seek out emergency care (I would argue that impatience is a close second). It is only since the coronavirus pandemic that fear has, ironically, become a big reason *not* to go for emergency treatment.

Fear is self-centered; it is the relinquishment of logic, and it cannot be negotiated with. When I replace my fears with understanding, perspective, faith, and ego deflation, they seem to dissolve. Having experienced personal emotional hell with the estrangement of my family and the loss of my job—and having survived a near-death experience from the poison of chemical dependency—I had no choice but to confront my fears or succumb to them. I was months into my recovery, making healthy strides, when I committed to a skydiving experience. On the fateful day at the designated time and altitude, I simply stepped out of the airplane and let the constant of gravity (and the instructor I was attached to) do the work. Eight minutes later my feet were on terra firma, a parachute on the grass behind me, the instructor unhinged from my ass, all my appendages and cranium intact, and I was feeling exhilarated.

▲▲▲▲▲

When yesterday's resentments provide kindling and tomorrow's fears provide oxygen, the conditions in the present become ideal for a bonfire of pain.

Pain is a natural defense mechanism of all species, having evolved as a basic daily survival mechanism since the dawn of life. The claws of tigers and rocks at the bottoms of cliffs hurt, so we learned early on to avoid them, thereby avoiding the end of our existence by being eaten or having our bodies smashed. Fire scorched our skin, so we kept our distance from forest fires. The pain of intestinal cramps from eating the berries from a certain bush kept us from eating more and getting sick and dehydrated. The memory of pain was an integral

advanced-warning alarm of our seek-and-avoid early existence, and we combined it with our survival instinct through
basic mental processing to live another day.

Fast-forward millions of years to the present day, and our
modern conveniences and technologies have conditioned us to
believe that pain is dispensable, that it can be eliminated from
life altogether, made obsolete, processed out of existence by
technological innovations that cater to our creature comforts.
Running shoes have solved the problem of skin infections from
running barefoot through the forest, medical anesthetics have
made repairing wounds nearly painless, and advancements in
pharmaceuticals have "blessed" us with an extensive menu of
prescription pills to reduce every conceivable type of physical
and emotional discomfort.

We are afforded modern lifestyle enhancements and conveniences in which pain can be avoided altogether—sitting at
a computer workstation has replaced hunting and gathering
for sustenance; traveling anywhere beyond five hundred feet
requires us to simply sit behind a wheel, turn a key, and operate
foot pedals. We exist in an advanced society where pain need
not be a built-in reminder that our bodies and minds are fragile and require permanent, ongoing maintenance and upkeep.

Perhaps our advanced society has forgotten that pain has
not gone anywhere; our nervous systems are always attuned
to it, just as they were back in the days of tigers and dangerous
cliffs. It is merely our relationship with pain that has changed.
Whereby early in human existence, pain was a healthy message to avoid dangerous situations to help our personal brand
of DNA survive, nowadays it can be shut out by modern inno-
vation completely . . . until it can't. When pain finally and
inevitably bursts through our prescriptions, inventions, and
conveniences, ripping open our cocoons of comfort, we find
that, by and large, we have lost the ability to cope with it.
Whether we are hit physically, emotionally, or both, many of us

end up completely decompensating, balled up in a proverbial fetal position and helpless, simply because we never learned to confront, absorb, and process pain.

Of course, this is a generalization. When some of us do choose to bypass the environmental numbing agents and walk fully lucid through our own personal briars of discomfort, we find that great things are often waiting on the other end. Weeding a garden despite an aching back on a hot summer day, maxing out a heart rate during exercise, or submitting to the needle prick of a tetanus shot—all of these are basic examples of how transient pain leads to beneficial results.

Positive consequences can be even more significant when handling emotional pain properly. Whether we lose a job, fail an exam, or grieve a death, the anguish begins as a searing sharpness in our chest, head, or gut, eventually mellowing to a dull ache, which, over time and depending on our experience, transitions from continuous to intermittent. Healthy coping mechanisms include reaching out to those closest to us for emotional support, seeking peace through meditation and exercise, and seeking the aid of therapy through counselors or support groups. Eventually the painful event weaves itself into the fabric of our life story, becoming an essential component of our individual makeup. It provides us an opportunity to review the hurt and learn from it, grow spiritually so that we can bring the experience and wisdom to the next hurt—which *will* happen—so that when it does, we can utilize *that* experience to cope even more effectively with the next one.

We can choose to comfort ourselves with alcohol and prescription drugs—commercials, popular music, and our circles of enablers tell us so. We are led to believe a pain-free life is not only possible but the standard, full of comfort food, Xanax, marijuana, and wine. We never need to face the so-called misery that previous generations had to bear on a daily basis. We are brainwashed into believing we can achieve important life results without pain. We use digital watches to count the daily steps we were going to take anyway, eat candy disguised as protein bars, and head out to happy hours with our coworkers after a stressful day of sitting at workstations and "dealing" with bosses and uncomfortable meetings. We head home, watch Netflix, take a melatonin to sleep, and subvert the "stress" of repeating the process the next day. We fantasize about dealing with annoying family or boring social engagements on weekends by getting piss drunk.

At some point, we are blindsided by an unavoidable painful experience, and all the usual go-to anesthetics and analgesics fail to work. Lacking the most basic skills of healthy pain processing, many of us completely lose our shit. Not accustomed to the raw severity of daily necessary pain, we become dysfunctional and dramatic, or withdraw completely; we call in sick to work and reach for even more pills and alcohol. We cut out the very things most helpful to our recovery— exercise, healthy eating, human communication, mindfulness. We indulge in self-pity, victimization, and entitlement; our egos once again run amok. Yes, egos—we are so self-important, we are entitled to indulge ourselves in more drugs, booze, or pity from those around us. They make us feel better, temporarily, until the high wears off and the pain returns, still not dealt with.

As a result of our collective inexperience with handling pain, emergency departments are jam-packed, campus crisis centers overwhelmed, therapists' offices full. We, as cultured Westerners, having grown so accustomed to a minimized-pain existence, have completely lost the skills required to accept and experience pain as a necessary component of our human experience, learn from it, use it to grow spiritually, and move on. We have added an unneeded layer of anxiety and extreme emotional distress in our pain response. In other words, we have converted the pain into *suffering*, creating a "second arrow":

> *When touched with a feeling of pain,*
> *the uninstructed run-of-the-mill person*
> *sorrows, grieves,*
> *and laments, beats his breast,*
> *becomes distraught.*
> *So he feels two pains,*
> *physical and mental.*
> *Just as if they were to shoot a man with an*
> *arrow and,*
> *right afterward,*
> *were to shoot him with another one,*
> *so that he would feel*
> *the pains of two arrows.*
>
> —Sallatha Sutta

If the achievement of lifelong serenity can be boiled down to completing one task (and I'm not sure it can), it is our ability to form a healthy relationship with pain. It ain't going nowhere; it has always been here and is here to stay. In the end, we can't hide from it, outrun it, ignore it, or permanently lock it out. We can only *outgrow* it. But to do this, we must take the first step to *accept* it; but to even *accept* it, we must first *feel* it.

It is said that one of the most difficult pains to overcome is the loss of one's children; this is an anguish that I must actively process on a continuous basis. It is my own personal behemoth, still presenting a daily existential challenge for me. Only through my growth in the program of AA, support from loved ones, and intensive therapy have I been able to survive it. I am learning to outgrow it, and if I am successful in this pursuit, then all other forms of pain in my life will be, well, child's play.

▲▲▲▲▲

Night had fallen and the compound was quiet. The church was locked up, clinic finished for the day, and I was relaxing in the clear Haitian night air with the orphans. We were all together, in the dirt under the illuminated heavens, singing the grim children's folk song. The game we played while singing it involved squatting in a circle and passing small stones in cadence with the song's rhythm, left to right. The objective was to avoid losing control of the circling rocks as they moved ever more quickly while the song's tempo increased. One by one, players would mess up and get knocked out. The winner of the game was the last one able to maintain control of the final stone. The prize for that night's winner was my last Clif Bar, which would, for a brief moment, ease one child's hunger pain.

▲▲▲▲▲

The trips I have made over the years to Haiti for medical missions have served as a reminder to me of the reality of pain: *what pain is, can be, and should be.* Living alongside and helping care for Haitian villagers and orphans who live simply, whose daily doses of pain are handled without the aid of drugs or therapists, has taught me that pain is *not* my enemy. Rather, pain is my high school cross-country coach, my drill instructor, my seventh-grade algebra teacher, my college organic chemistry professor, my sweetheart. At specific moments in my life, each hurt me, and at the time, I despised them for it. Whenever I feel stronger and more skilled, life serves up the next round of pain, pushing my envelope. In time, a healthy relationship forms; my hatred dissipates and is replaced with a civil, respectful coexistence. I will not go so far, as some suggest, to make "friends" with pain, but rather I will walk with it at arm's length and in full view, grateful that as a result of its presence, I am evolving into a better, stronger human being.

CHAPTER 11

LAVENDER ROSE

The skies were quite atypical for a Shenandoah Valley July that day. The characteristic humid atmosphere normally obscuring the Blue Ridge range had given way to more of an autumn-like clarity, allowing me to discriminate the subtle reflections in the distant mountain hollows, a sight usually reserved for October. I viewed them with comfort, permitting myself this small passing gift from God as I sat on the steps of the elementary school. So fortunate, the children who went here, to see these views throughout the school year as they burst out of the building when the dismissal bell rang, full of laughter, moms and dads awaiting them.

I vividly remembered being a parent here. But did I ever truly appreciate it, inhale it and savor the moment, or did it get lost in the tumble of the daily routine? On a day as clear as this, we took Hannah to school on her first day of kindergarten in Ms. Ester's class. I was thinking the very same thing—*My baby girl gets a shiny new school nestled in a picturesque landscape, a shiny moment nestled in a picturesque homelife.* There was zero hesitation in her eyes as we followed her up these very steps ten years earlier; like with so many other first-time experiences, she proceeded with excitement and zeal. Courage never factored in to her first day because, I sensed, she never felt there was anything to be afraid of. Such an adventurous, fearless little girl she was at six years old. Now, I imagined, on the cusp of her sixteenth birthday, she would regard this day—the day she got behind the wheel of her first car—with that same enthusiastic sparkle.

I sat in the driver's seat, inspecting again every square inch of the interior. Was it perfect for my girl? I had placed the envelope containing the card on the console and hung the butterfly necklace from the rearview mirror. In the hatchback, after removing my bicycle, I had placed a complete roadside assistance kit, with a flashlight, glow sticks, tire pressure gauge, and work gloves. In the dashboard compartment I put the vehicle registration, insurance documents, emergency roadside contact information, and a tin of Altoids. I tried to envision how, months from this moment, the car might be decorated— colorful fabrics on the seats, maybe some charms dangling, a brightly colored steering wheel cover, a high school bumper sticker? It was her car and she could do with it whatever she wanted. I may have made the purchase, and the car may have been in my name, but it was *hers to do with as she chose.* My chest was bursting. My daughter was taking the next step on her path to adulthood—the freedom of mobility the first set of wheels affords.

She would be ready, I sensed it. Even though we had barely been in each other's presence in close to two years, I bore witness firsthand to her responsible nature and sense of awareness. I looked out the side window at my bicycle leaning up against the car's electric-blue exterior. She will more than succeed; she will thrive. *The way she did years before at this very school in whose parking lot I now sit.*

It was back then I had heard about the little boy in her class. We found it odd, given her hearty appetite, that Hannah had been coming home with a barely eaten lunch in her lunch-box. We knew it wasn't because she didn't like the food her mom packed. She always loved it. She was clearly very hungry after school and would wolf down her snack in record time. We were told by the kindergarten teachers that she just never had *the time* to eat her lunch. Ms. Ester told us there was a hidden, selfless reason. Hannah had been sitting next to a scrawny little boy from her class who was often in the same clothes several days in a row. They had become friends, and he had confided in her that he would be beaten by his father if he did not finish his lunch. He was told throwing it away was a sin and he would be caught. So Hannah sat with him and pushed him to eat his food, literally feeding him, so he would finish in the allotted twenty-two-minute lunch period. This, of course, left Hannah no time for her own food, but as I imagined she figured in her precocious little mind, Mom and Dad would not hurt *her* if she didn't eat.

So was the nature of my daughter. Proud, self-aware, confident, she was always ready to help the world at a young age. Navigating the roads in a 2017 Toyota RAV4 would, over time, literally be child's play for her. She danced like nobody was watching on auditorium stages in recitals as young as age four as I sat in the audience (sobbing); she played piano in front of her school at assemblies; and, when older, she performed at her bat mitzvah to perfection in front of a packed house. As early as age seven she proudly took on the role of mama's little helper with her brothers, especially little Toby. As far as I was concerned, there was nothing my self-confident, almond-eyed, empathic daughter couldn't accomplish in life.

She was a precocious child with a natural instinct to protect. As young as age three she would gather her dolls and stuffed animals and assemble them on the little beanbag chair in her room. I would go up to visit her and she would be sitting on top of them. "I am in my nest keeping my babies warm," she would exclaim. Included were her duck, her soft elephant, and a small plastic horse. She never called it a horse; it was always the "brown zebra."

I frequently lounged on the back deck while she sat on the jungle gym platform with paper and crayons drawing pictures (often of Chef Boyardee, oddly enough) or ran around in the backyard playing make-believe. She would speak in her dolls' made-up voices about taking turns riding the rocking zebra. "My turn to get on the rocking zebra." "Don't hurt the rocking zebra." You see, a plain horse was not good enough to Hannah; she wanted something more creative, more elaborate, and in her mind, zebras were more ornate than horses. She was my unique, precious girl.

She was our Hannah: Supergirl. As far as I was concerned, there was nothing she couldn't do. She was a straight-A student, always there for her friends, always there for her brothers. Throughout early childhood she was fun to be around—perhaps because she found no problem in dancing spontaneously. As a toddler she loved to twirl. She twirled to her favorite shows, twirled up in her room before bedtime, and after a few years, twirled with her dad to a dance trophy at the annual father-daughter Girl Scout dance. When she was four years old, she and I went on a trip to New York City. While I was at the check-in counter in the lobby of our upscale Manhattan hotel, she took it upon herself to dance and twirl for the guests. She did her thing, dancing and spinning her way across the floor, eventually colliding into the prominent belly of the Reverend Jesse Jackson. She looked up at him, all two-and-a-half feet of her, and giggled; I quickly went over to apologize to him, but he simply smiled, shook his head, and walked off.

Such was Hannah's happy way. She always found joy in the moment because she always found the party within herself. I would take her to the university's women's basketball games before her brothers were old enough to come along, and she would prance and twirl in the stands to the beat of the pep band, jumping around and mimicking whatever the dance team was doing during game breaks.

▲▲▲▲▲

It's OK to get a little bit angry, Joe. Anger is not always a character defect. It is just another permutation of internal pain, pain that you have learned to manage, to walk alongside in an uneasy truce.

In the months before Implosion Day, we had the texting trash talk going full force; I'd be at work, she'd be getting out of school. I'd tease her by sending her a photo of an open bag of potato chips next to my computer, she'd text me back a skull emoji and tell me I was an evil man. Mom wasn't big on unhealthy snacks. Sometimes I'd send her a short clip of me eating a handful of Fritos, and she'd respond with more angry emojis, probably finding her father quite silly.

Several years during Halloween time, we braved the local haunted forest attraction; she was a courageous preteen, and the live actors dressed up as ghouls and zombies never fazed her as we made our way through the dark woods. One year she even permitted some terrified high school girls behind us in line to join us. They were frightened out of their minds, and I could clearly see she was amused. I caught on and played along—every time we approached another "scare zone," I'd push ahead, exclaiming, "I'm just an old dude, but here comes a bunch of freaked-out high school girls." Hannah delighted in the knowledge that I was baiting the actors in the dark corners to time their jump-out-and-scream moments for maximum impact on the girls.

Those kids from the line called me Daddy. *I am not your daddy. I am only Hannah's daddy. The daddy that lets her be brave when there is nothing to fear, but who protects her with his own life against any of the world's true dangers. Because we almost lost her before we even met her, and* that *was true terror. You girls can be silly and pretend I am your daddy, but I am NOT your daddy.*

I am Hannah's daddy.

▲▲▲▲▲

Twelve years before the Halloween visits to haunted forests, before any children, I was online researching adoption agencies, putting together a couple's profile for prospective adoptive parents, submitting for background checks, and receiving social workers in our home. Seven years into our marriage, we remained childless inside a big house on a large tract of beautiful country land. Even though we had only been "trying" for about two years, my inner father was screaming to be a daddy. My wife, who was lukewarm about children early in our marriage, had come around to the idea of motherhood. After no initial biological success, despite fertility testing and maximizing our chances using every possible method, we were resigned to the idea that we might never produce a baby the old-fashioned way.

Adoption had always been a very real option. We had discussed having multiple adopted children with or without a pregnancy. I led the way and did the research, finding an adoption facilitator who seemed to be reputable, with a solid track record of placing children. I threw myself into the process; it became my other full-time job. Over months I wrote and revised our bio, gathered together the best pictures of us, our families, and our home, and constructed for submission a thorough professional profile of who we were for the agency. Once submitted and approved, our file became available for pregnant mothers to view. At that point, we had to sit on our hands and wait. We had been years without children; what was a few more months? I started a one-year countdown timer in my head, and promised myself to be patient, and to wait until eleven months to get truly antsy. This was in the winter of 2002.

Throughout my career, fate always chose for me to receive life-changing news while on duty in the emergency room. It was during a work shift I was given notice that the bid we made on our dream home was accepted. I was also informed, while working, of the deaths of two grandparents, and eventually, my father. It only followed the pattern when, one day in the spring of 2002, my wife excitedly called me while I was on duty.

"Are you sitting down?" I sat down. It was neither the first nor the last time in my life I would be asked this during a telephone call in the ER. As I listened to her, I processed the news; fortunately, I was assigned the minor care area that afternoon.

We had been chosen by a pregnant woman from Florida.

We were going to be parents in October. Nurse Scoobie, a longtime veteran of the ER, happened to be standing within earshot and was the first recipient of the news as I hung up the phone. I don't recall emotionally decompensating that day. Rather, I felt driven by a rapture that launched me through the rest of the shift and into outer space, landing back home a few hours later to my beautiful wife and the future mother of all my future children. There was never a hesitation in my mind; I was ready beyond words. My life was given new purpose.

Over the ensuing months, we learned the details of the biological mother and her family's background, health history, and the social circumstances leading to her decision to give her baby up for adoption. We provided all the prenatal care and made sure, to the best of our ability, that the mother was well taken care of. Days at home were electric. It was very hard to keep my mind on work, or anything else; patience was something I was always lacking but was forced to practice.

I had scheduled two weeks off work around the baby's expected due date for us to travel and get set up in a local hotel by the hospital; we converted the guest room into a baby girl's nursery, complete with a beautiful crib given to us by my very generous in-laws. Communication with the adoption facilitator assigned to our case increased from monthly to weekly and then daily. By early October we made sure the minivan was geared up for travel; we had also subscribed to a milk bank so the new baby could be fed donated mothers' milk. We couldn't have been more ready.

Two days before the due date, an excited, expecting couple got in their car and drove nine hundred miles south. We stopped overnight in Savannah, enjoying one final evening as adults without any real responsibility. The next morning, we finished the drive, checked in to our hotel suite, and immediately set up the temporary kitchen and put the bassinet in the bedroom. Within twenty-four hours the facilitator contacted us by email; the mother was in labor. In our makeshift temporary home, we did our best to relax, tried to eat, tried to sleep. I was up and out of bed through the night far more than I was asleep while we waited and waited for the next phone call, the only phone call in the world that mattered. Light came through the bedroom window; the sun had somehow risen without my noticing.

Early in the day, perhaps during the hour the rest of America had breakfast and drove to work, my cell phone rang; it was the facilitator. She said something, a few things. She wasn't making any sense. I listened again to make sure I heard right, then asked a question; she answered back. *This isn't happening.* I remember raising my voice in panic and screaming into the phone, then dropping it on the floor. I burst into tears. I looked at my wife and she saw my face and cried too. The world faded to gray, then everything went black.

▲▲▲▲▲

Six hours later, somewhere in the flatlands of inland Florida, I was leaning against the side of the minivan, gassing up for our journey home. A cooler full of breast milk sat in the back, next to an empty car seat. The bassinet was in the trunk. I was beyond numb; we both were. I forced my mind to remain quietly in denial, as if the past four months had never happened.

She had decided to keep her baby. We were sent packing.

A minute later we were home, breaking down the nursery and converting it as fast as possible back into a guest room. I moved the rocker and baby furniture into the attic while we had a conversation about booking a cruise. I was out of vacation days, so it would have to be sometime in the future.

Fate, God, or whatever, denied us Hannah, denied us parenthood.

Another minute later I was back at work, busily attending to patients, trying to forget everything. I was in the physicians' workroom dictating a chart when my cell phone rang. It was the adoption facilitator. The mother had changed her mind again; she wanted us back, wanted us to have her baby. I steadied myself with a hand on the counter to keep from passing out.

Another minute later I was at work again. My wife and her mother traveled to Florida to receive our child while I worked my required shifts. People around me were supportive and consoling; I mentioned nothing of the latest news to anybody. It was November 12, 2002.

Another minute later it was November 14, 2002. I was at home alone, lying in bed; the house was immaculate. I considered converting the guest room back into a nursery, but knew better. Another fake-out was coming, another disappointment. I waited for the phone call that would be coming from the adoption attorney's office where Hannah would be handed off to my wife.

The phone rang and I answered immediately. My wife said she had our baby, they were all there in the attorney's office with the birth family, signing papers and having a dialogue— my wife, my mother-in-law, and the baby's birth family. I simultaneously felt no emotion and all emotion.

The next day I called Tom, who had been on sabbatical from work for the month, and let him in on the news. I made a plea for him to cover my shifts for a few days so I could fly down to Florida and meet Hannah Anne, my new daughter. He agreed without a pause. Within the hour, I had my travel arrangements.

Another minute later I was in the back seat of a taxi as we pulled up to the hotel. I told the driver the entire story—I was an adoptive dad seconds away from meeting my daughter for the first time; my wife and mother-in-law were inside, waiting for me. I have absolutely no recollection of how the driver responded and have no memory of getting out, or walking to the door of the suite.

▲▲▲▲▲

I was standing in the suite's sitting area. My wife was opposite me, a few feet away, holding baby Hannah in her arms. Her eyes were giant and brown, so aware. She was wearing a frilly lavender dress. Even at three weeks old she had fullness in her cheeks and arms. Her eyes remained wide open, and she was looking right at me. My smiling mother-in-law receded into her bedroom. I moved forward and was handed our child to hold for the first time. She was warm and soft and smelled sweet. From that moment on she was our *Sweet Pea*. Mama held up a toy—a stuffed clown-like doll, blue with pink stars, pushing its fuzzy belly into Hannah's little starfish hand. It played a happy, beeping baby melody, a short song I had never heard before but that will echo in my head for the rest of my days. As I held my daughter for the first time, the universe fell away; the three of us were all that existed.

▲▲▲▲▲

After three blissful days and nights of bonding, I flew home, alone, to resume my shifts in the emergency department, telling not a soul of the events that had transpired. Everyone in my family and workplace was well aware of our having lost Hannah on the day she was born, and I was terrified. While my heart was bursting, my fear of losing her again to the system—the birth mom's legal rights remained intact until the judge gave Hannah the right to leave the state—was a strong emotional incentive to remain silent. I worked my shifts while an air of pity surrounded me. I focused on my job, my patients, the immediate tasks at hand. When I got home I called my wife and we discussed the events of the day, mainly what Hannah was doing—opening and closing her little starfish hands, making baby noises, taking a bottle, pooping. The day the judge would release Hannah to leave the state was open ended.

After an excruciating five days more, we were notified by the attorney's office that the judge had issued a ruling to permit Hannah to leave Florida. It was five o'clock at night. It then became a frenetic rush to secure a flight out of Dodge. Within hours the flight was booked. Ten hours later, I was at Dulles Airport with mama and child. My father-in-law, proud as a first-time grandparent could be, shook my hand and embraced me in the parking area. I loaded my little family into the minivan and we drove home. We walked through the door of our house with Hannah at around four in the morning. Mama passed out from exhaustion, and I played with my baby until it was time to report for my seven o'clock shift. I placed the sleeping baby in the bassinet next to her sleeping mama and headed to the hospital. It was time to trumpet our daughter's arrival to the world, to scream about it at the top of my lungs.

▲▲▲▲▲

As the years passed, Hannah learned to trumpet herself. I knew she was fabulous, but I did not need to remind her. Her maturing confidence took on a life of its own as she grew; it translated into helping other children and fearlessly performing onstage and in the swimming pool (she was a strong team swimmer by age six). She retained her silly side, striking poses in Times Square with *Sesame Street*'s Elmo or beside the characters from the Broadway production of *Wicked*. My daughter was very much her own person and would undoubtedly become her own strong, independent woman. This was, in my mind, beyond question.

▲▲▲▲▲

I stood in the elementary school parking lot, which was just around the corner from where she lived with her brothers and mom, and permitted the memories of Hannah and my previous life with her to wash over me like a tropical waterfall. Her new car, freshly waxed, glittered its gorgeous electric blue under the atypically blue summer sky. I knew that before the sun went down on this perfect day, she would be proudly and confidently behind its wheel.

I put the car keys in my pocket, strapped on my helmet, and mounted my trusty road bike. It was a quick thirty-second bike ride to the house. As I coasted up to their mailbox, opened it, and placed the car keys inside, I raised my eyes to the home in which she lived—the home where I had lived for all those years—quietly sitting one hundred yards up the driveway. Not a soul stirred; they would likely wait to come out and retrieve the vehicle until after I had pedaled off. The act of placing the keys in the mailbox was anticlimactic. I rode away in the direction of my home, breeze in my face, saying a quiet prayer that she use her car safely and happily. I imagined her getting into the driver's seat for the very first time:

Time to ride the rocking zebra!
She will twirl with joy before her first drive.
She will text pictures of the car to her friends.
She will drive it to high school.
She will drop her brothers off in the mornings.
She will decorate it with style and flair.
She will blast music during Saturday joyrides with friends.
She will litter it with books, papers, and swim gear.
She will pump gas for the first time.
She will kiss a boy in it.
She will go on a road trip.
She will drive off to her freshman year of college in it.
And maybe . . .

. . . maybe someday she will drive over and visit her old dad.

CHAPTER 12

GOLDEN BOY

I sat in the waiting room of the Toyota service center on that late September day in 2019 while my truck had its oil changed and tires rotated. It was an otherwise ordinary day, with its checklist of standard morning tasks to be followed by work that afternoon. I was biding my time, quietly pleased at the milestone my Tacoma and I had reached together—the one-hundred-thousand-mile mark. Toyotaphiles considered this just the break-in period, and I knew my trusty vehicle would last for another couple hundred thousand miles if I simply maintained it regularly. We were on the road quite a bit these days, continuously shuttling between the emergency departments in Charlottesville, Roanoke, and my hometown, so having a reliable means of transportation was a priority.

Between my Haiti adventures and watching the news coverage of various Middle East wars, I concluded that the Tacoma was the preferred truck of the undeveloped world. Its ability to carry a dozen men plus a gun turret over washed-out jungle roads or sand dunes was top-notch. Surely, mine could handle the smooth asphalt of Interstates 81 and 64.

I settled into one of the vinyl block seats in the waiting area, extended my legs, and pulled out my phone. I had recently blown past level two thousand on *Bubble Shooter* and thought I would knock out a few more to pass the time. It was seven thirty in the morning, the mechanics had just arrived for work, and I figured I could be in and out within an hour. My Gmail app indicated a few emails in my inbox, so I tapped it. In between the spam my eyes saw it, but my brain could not register:

hi dad

It was an email from Robert. Without even pausing to think, I opened it.

I think I'm ready to slowly work on a relationship with you. it's Rosh Hashanah and it's about atonement and forgiveness, and I feel like you've served enough punishment. I don't want to do this too quickly, but maybe we could get lunch or go to services together sometime soon, and there's a thing happening soon that mom can't help me with, but you might be able to.

I stopped breathing.

There is a rare neurologic disorder known as locked-in syndrome, in which a person's entire body becomes instantly paralyzed, completely unable to move or communicate, with the exception of vertical eye movements and blinking. For thirty seconds, I was there.

Celine, during our brief time together, had reminded me to *just breathe.* That I could try. My eyes closed, then opened again. Slowly, my fingers began to wake up. I closed the app and reopened it. Robert's email was still there. I did this several more times—opening and closing my email app. I powered down my phone and rebooted. The email was still there. Before my now-watering eyes appeared a note from my son, right there in my inbox. My paralysis morphed into a mild tremor.

I am in a reverse nightmare, I thought. *Perhaps I am misreading it, or maybe it's an online scam conceived by Russian hackers.*

After almost three years of complete absence punctuated only by occasional hostility, I had a letter from my son. He was interested in getting together with me. I felt emotion scratching at the door of my consciousness. My tremor began to intensify, becoming a noticeable shake. I had to get up. Others in the room were beginning to take notice. I didn't want someone calling 911 for "fifty-two-year-old man, conscious and breathing, with convulsive activity at the Toyota dealership." I regained some composure, rose, stumbled in the direction of the men's room and through its door, where it was (thank God) empty. I steadied myself against the sink counter and looked again at the phone's screen. The email was still there; it really existed.

Just a few weeks before, he had written to command me to stay away from all his athletic events. Now, out of the blue, just like that, he was offering to meet with me. My shaking may have steadied, but hyperventilation began; my emotional floodgates opened, and I completely let loose. I coughed up tears and saliva into the sink. Then I thanked God, the program, and everyone I ever knew who had advised me not to force things, to just let it all play out.

▲▲▲▲▲

He descended the stairs wearing a navy-blue hoodie and baggy athletic shorts; his teenage form was in its lanky, awkward stage. He walked down slowly, and we never broke eye contact. I stood below on the landing, looking up, feeling nervous. In the corner of my eye I could see a four-year-old Hannah sitting on the fireplace hearth, holding a sleeping baby Toby. Robert reached the next-to-bottom step and paused. His face, maturing now and dotted with mild acne, was my face. He was thin and tall, taller than me by at least two inches, and had that mop of a hairstyle all the cool high school boys had. His eyes glimmered like those of a truly brilliant, deep thinker. The expression on his face was serious, with a subtle hint of satisfaction. He was gratified that I was present, now just below him, less than three feet away. Without warning he leaped forward, his sinewy body adjusting to clutch me in a tight embrace of joy and love. I felt his arms grip my shoulders and neck; his skin was warm. His legs wrapped themselves around my waist, and I found holding his teen weight a challenge but manageable. My head turned. Baby Toby was awake now, and he and Hannah were looking at us; their stares were quiet and still. Robert's chin rested on my left shoulder and I felt his soft breath. He spoke.

"I love you, Daddy . . . youuu da best daddy ever. Youuu da best daddy in histowy." The burden of his weight began to ease; 130 pounds shrank to 40. I pulled my head back to look him in the face. He was three years old with his chubby cheeks and straight, blonde little-boy hair. "Youuu da best, youuu da best ever!" His face was inches from mine. My tears of joy and love began to flow. We were both smiling. His warm child's body began pulling away, and suddenly he was sliding down, and I tried to hold on but could not, and he slipped from me, receding into darkness. I could no longer make out his form and began to flail for him, but my fingers only managed a graze of his hoodie, which was not a hoodie at all but my pillowcase, the one that encased my pillow, in my bed, in my house.

I was drawn back into consciousness and found myself alone in my dark bedroom. The clock on the nightstand read 4:17. That familiar lonely aching rushed out of my gut and overcame me, as it had on countless previous mornings. *Please God, just take me now and be done with it.*

▲▲▲▲▲

"Reverse nightmares" was my term for them.

In a truly horrific nightmare, one freezes and shivers and screams inside one's head as terrifying scenes play themselves out—dark, horrible situations in alternate realities where there is no conceivable way out. There is seemingly no hope, but near the end, as the last awful sequence plays out, the escape hatch of wakefulness opens. Slowly the trickle of reality flows in and the nightmare state recedes. The moment of recognition that it was all a bad dream has to be one of the most underrated feelings of relief we humans routinely feel. For some time after, we lie in our beds, heart rate slowing, sweat drying, allowing the warm realization that we and our loved ones are safe to linger in the air above us.

For me, reverse nightmares are just as they sound; the emotional transition from dream to awake state is the exact opposite. The joyful, blissful movie fades, and the cold harshness of real life rushes back in with all the subtlety of an obnoxious drunken roommate storming in and puking up memories of his midnight romp. Muscular relaxation is reversed, replaced by an awake state of tension, palpitations, and cold sweats. Moving from the dream to the awake state feels like immersion into a cargo container of ice water, as if to say, *Welcome back to your* real *world, loser. Hope your dream joyride was nice while it lasted.*

▲▲▲▲▲

Finally, she was asleep. Her labor had begun twenty-four hours earlier, and as she worked through contraction after contraction, I assisted as much as a husband was capable. The epidural, administered late in the game, had provided her with waist-down anesthesia and a desperately needed reprieve. A strong and determined woman she was, my wife. From the moment she showed me the positive test stick nine months earlier to the moment we arrived at the hospital, she was determined to control the events of her pregnancy and labor. She read books and did online research. She kept the proper diet and selected the midwife and doula. We took birthing classes together. Her plan was for a home birth.

However, her uterus, combined with our son's cranium, laid her best plans to waste. After several hours of the birthing process at home, she threw in the towel and asked to be taken to the hospital. We were set up in a suite on the labor and delivery unit. The tortured look on her face as a contraction hit while I helped balance her on the birthing ball was almost too much for me.

"Please, help me out of this misery," she uttered.

This woman, who successfully competed in triathlons and maintained a strict dietary lifestyle, had been ready to take on the birthing process the way she prepared for a race. Fate had other plans. In her agony and exhaustion she finally acquiesced to the epidural, and she was able to take a break and fall asleep, and all was quiet . . . and I was very relieved. I sat motionless in the dark on the reclining chair across the room from her, staring at the oscillations of the tocodynamometer. Red LED lines rhythmically illuminated and receded as her uterus contracted and relaxed; I watched the baby's heart rate maintain its healthy cadence throughout. From my limited knowledge of obstetrics, things looked good, but it wasn't baby time just yet.

In the same week the Red Sox came back from three games down to the Yankees in the American League Championship to go on to win their miracle World Series, Robert arrived. He came that morning by C-section, well after the sun had risen. While I sat near my wife's head, Dr. A pulled him out. The blue surgical-paper drape that separated her body at the waist kept us from viewing the activity happening on the other side. I have no recollection of who handed him over to us. Baby's head touched Mama's cheek and she turned and kissed him on his scalp. She said a simple "Hi, Robert" as she lay on her back, the obstetrician already busy closing her abdomen. Then he was placed in my arms, and I carried him a few steps over to the newborn nursery, absolutely floating. Dr. Slosher, a long-time colleague, was there, but it barely registered. I was beyond emotion.

An hour later I was outside the room, letting Mama be alone with her new baby. I stood in the hallway, phone up to my ear, exhausted and elated; back home, my mother-in-law put two-year-old Hannah on the phone so I could tell her the news.

"Hi, Sweet Pea."

On the other end I heard her innocent, tiny voice. "Hi, Daddy." Tears flooded my face. Fade to black.

▲▲▲▲▲

He was my Golden Boy. My Mini-Me.

Even as a baby, he was something special. All loving parents feel like their kid is exceptional, but Robert *really was*. At eight days of age, he induced my father, his grandpa Neil, to do something I had never seen him do before—cry. It happened in my home at his bris (ritual circumcision) performed by Finn, with the rabbi, family, and friends looking on.

Robert emanated love and provided everyone around him copious amounts of hugs before he knew what they were. His capacity to snuggle up to his mother and me on a sofa, or between us in bed, was testament to his natural sensitivity.

He would stroke his big sister's hair or cheek from his bouncy chair at six months of age. As generous with affection as he was with the three of us, he could take or leave the outside world. My wife walked around with him nestled inside a Mayan wrap, and he seemed far more content with his entire body cocooned up against Mama's warm torso.

His intelligence also showed very early on. At eighteen months he would wriggle around on the floor, fake crying and "pretending to be a baby." He was a whiz with Legos by age two, building pyramids and cubes and intricate shapes, keeping to specific repeating color patterns. It took him mere days to potty train before his second birthday, and reading came to him as if he were born doing it. By the time he completed second grade, he had read the entire Harry Potter series. In third grade he composed his first piece of music for piano, "The Halloween Song."

▲▲▲▲▲

One night as I returned from a late shift, I heard Robert, then just a toddler, shrieking from his bedroom upstairs. I knew Mama must be exhausted with baby Toby, and before my backpack hit the floor, I was sprinting up the steps. Within a split second of opening his door, the problem hit me smack in the nose. The smell of vomit and stool was overpowering. Little Robert was standing up in the corner of his crib, holding the rail, looking at me with a distressed face, tears streaming down his cheeks. A big, bloated, brown diaper was sagging off his bottom. Pools of vomit covered his mattress and more was splattered below on the carpet. My heart sank; simultaneously, my self-centered drinking plans vanished and were replaced by an intense need to step up as a father. I felt that selfishness immediately evaporate. It was only at times like this, instances where I needed to be *present* and give of myself—as a father or husband—that my cravings for alcohol completely disappeared. As in, nonexistent.

I picked him up out of his crib, and he gripped me with his arms and legs as only a toddler can. A mix of puke, diarrhea, and saliva covered him, and then me. For a minute we just held each other, swaying back and forth, his face buried in my shoulder muffling his sobs. *My son, I am here, I am here.*

I carried him into the bathroom and drew a bubble bath, stripped him down, and placed him in. He vomited in the bathwater, so I just added more baby shampoo to the tub. He seemed to settle.

Throughout the rest of the night, he and I remained atop layers of old blankets and towels in the family room with him curled up at my side, intermittently waking to vomit. I simply stripped away a layer of cover with each episode. For a few hours, we managed some continuous sleep until morning. Together . . . my little boy and I.

▲▲▲▲▲

Robert's combination of intelligence and emotional warmth strongly displayed itself in preschool. He quickly endeared himself to his teacher, Ms. Sharon Elsbeth. He had completed an interactive counting game using beads called the "thousand chain," performing the task younger than any child ever before at the school. Sharon encouraged the children to think about large numbers, and, smitten with her, he took his assignment seriously. The next day, during snack time, he wandered over to her and asked how big infinity was.

"I believe it is the highest number in the universe" was her reported reply.

"Then what is infinity *squared*?"

"It's so high that if you think too much about it, time goes in reverse and we start to move backward."

"That's OK, Miss Sharon, because I love you infinity *squared*."

This exchange made a profound impression on Ms. Elsbeth. A bond between the two of them formed, beyond that of teacher and preschooler. They became true friends for life. Sadly, hers was cut short.

Later in the school year, as I was picking Robert up at dismissal, Sharon, then age thirty-two, confided to me, eyes full of tears, that she had been diagnosed with ocular melanoma, a rare type of aggressive cancer for which there was no known cure. Her oncologists gave her less than two years to live. With the aid of her doctors, ample friends in the Staunton artist community, my wife's "anticancer" soup, a fantastic attitude, and a zest for life, she managed to survive another six quality years. During this period, we saw her frequently, having her over to our home and visiting hers. The local community rallied around her cause; a play was written about her, with her as the main character. Its theme was her relationship and rapprochement with death, embodied in the form of a dinosaur. As a medical fundraiser, a jeweler friend created a pendant in her honor that was sold online and locally—a small silver rectangle containing an engraved heart and sideways eight inside brackets, with the number two in the far upper-right corner: *Love × Infinity Squared.*

Ms. Sharon Elsbeth passed away shortly after I was released from rehab. Godspeed, Sharon, we love you.

▲▲▲▲▲

Like his big sister, Robert joined the swim team. And like his father at the same age, he was physically smaller than many of his peers. In his seven-year-old wisdom, he made the decision to focus on and develop competence in the breast stroke, seeing that this particular stroke was technically challenging for undisciplined, flail-happy boys. He figured out quickly that this was not a stroke that required size and strength so much as finesse, and many of his competitors were routinely disqualified during the races because of technical violations. So he simply learned to do it properly, make it across the pool in reasonable time, let his competitors get disqualified, and land himself a high placing. For Robert, it was mind over brute physicality.

Robert excelled in his schoolwork and relished competition, but his sensitive nature was ever present, lurking just under his stoic exterior. At karate class one day, just minutes before testing for a promotion, he realized his belt was missing. Fully understanding the repercussions of not having it (no testing allowed), he stood frightened and upset, looking at me. The two of us jumped in the car and I raced home, running into the house and ransacking his room, searching. His tears turned into audible sobs. He had been solid in karate and had worked so hard to test. Just when we thought he would miss out, a text came through from Mom that she had found his belt in a practice room at the dojo. We jumped back in the car, and I returned him just in time for him to tie on his belt and test. He passed without a hitch. His beaming face afterward made me proud of him, and grateful to be his father.

In fifth grade he won his school's spelling bee and moved on to the regional finals. We all sat excitedly in the auditorium of a local high school as proud members of Team Robert. As the competition progressed, he was given a word that was not on his study list. It was a long, multisyllabic word, and he erred on a single vowel. Just like that, he was eliminated. He kept a brave face onstage, but later, as we left the school building, he let his emotions out. But he was as resilient as he was sensitive. The next morning he was himself again, ready to move on to the next challenge.

I pushed him academically, creating homemade quizzes for him. I used silver coins to reward high scores, and he managed to accumulate a nice stack over the years. With a small safe full of coins, he learned to go online to look up the value of silver and calculate his net worth, excited or annoyed depending on the rise and fall of the price of the precious metal.

Periodically I assigned him books to read. In fourth grade we studied Orson Scott Card's *Ender's Game*. He consumed the book with ease, passing my quiz, and asked for more. *The Lord of the Rings*, *The Chronicles of Narnia*, the Percy Jackson series—he buried himself in them all. Quiet Robert, sitting in his bed or on the sofa, nose in a book. He was our bright, content, sensitive, well-rounded, loving son. He was the Golden Boy.

▲▲▲▲▲

I was beyond emotionally exhausted. My two years of efforts of weekly writing to him seemed futile. Impassioned emails expressing love and hope were curtly and routinely dismissed. After a lifetime of hugs, games, helping in his classroom, bedtime stories, silly times, illness, homework, family trips, nights in the backyard tent, hikes, piano recitals, swim meets, Lego, Minecraft, shared books, movie watching, favorite breakfasts, and general family love, I was relegated in his mind to lowlife alcoholic. And a big part of me felt like *I deserved it*, because I was an embarrassment to him, and he was ashamed of me. He was stuck with an ex-boozer for a father.

Yet it was only a few months later, this staggering, breathtaking reversal in my son's attitude. My little boy, whom I had not hugged, laughed with, or spent any real time with in forever, seemed to be struggling free of his self-destructive anger-fear cycle and finally reaching out. His independent spirit was breaking ranks in the household, crossing the picket line, conjuring every ounce of courage to send me that glowing, fantastic email:

There's a thing happening soon that mom can't help me with, but you might be able to.

Even the title of the email, a simple "Hi Dad," was astonishing; it was the first time since I was banished from the house that he had referred to me as Dad. I took a screenshot of the paragraph and sent the picture out as a text to those closest to me—Cassie, Emily, Wally, and Tom. If I learned anything in AA, it was to reach out to my closest circle in recovery in moments of emotional extremes. The alcoholic lurking in my racing mind was still bent on self-destruction, waiting for the opportunity to seize me in a moment of weakness. The danger of relapse would hang over my head forever. I opened my recovery toolbox and was reaching in with both hands.

It felt as if life was about to flash-change. The years of innumerable lonely moments, the desperate longing for fatherly needs unmet, were about to end. All those tears in the dark bedroom, the mornings where I awoke disappointed that I woke up at all . . . that was all about to change. There was a breakthrough, a point of light in the void. *God is doing for me what I cannot do for myself.*

There had been a brief moment over the previous summer when I had had enough, and I became enraged; I initiated proceedings to drag my ex-wife back into court to demand visitation with the children. I ran the idea by my usual people and received mixed responses. After much prayer and meditation, I ultimately withdrew the idea. Now, with this email message from Robert out of nowhere, I thanked my Higher Power for my nonaction. Had I proceeded with filing a motion, as Emily eloquently pointed out to me, his message would never have been written.

Don't get too high on this, JD. Just as quickly as this opportunity came, it can disappear. You know it can.

For the rest of that morning and afternoon, it seemed as if the gravity on planet Earth had been turned down. I floated through my errands in town. The king crabs that had taken up permanent residence in my gut moved out. The jubilant text replies I received from my sober network through the day only added to my joy.

I reflected on the proper response to Robert. It had to be timed properly and the content receptive, yet not overwhelming. I had a tendency to overreact to the point of being overbearing. This had to be done properly, smartly. A frightened baby lamb had wandered over to me as I sat still, and I didn't want to make any sudden moves that would scare him off (or piss him off). Consensus was that waiting until the next day would be too long. I decided to respond to him when I knew he would be finishing his school day. The words were written, then revised, rewritten, put away, taken out, modified, and finally sent:

Anything, son. Whatever is happening that you need help with, I will do whatever I can to help you.

I am ready to work on a relationship with you at your pace. I agree we should take it slow.

Maybe we can go to a restaurant before services on Yom Kippur eve. Maybe the Indian place. We could just meet there or I can come pick you up.

If you want to meet sooner to talk about what you need help with, I am free all day tomorrow (Wednesday). Tomorrow night late I go in for night shift in Charlottesville, and then Thursday I fly to Chicago until Sunday night.

Just let me know.

Love, Dad

I went to bed that night, for the first time I could remember, without my chest aching.

▲▲▲▲▲

The next morning, I received the response:

For now, I think I'm only okay with emailing, anything else would be too much. I don't need help with the thing anymore, but we can email

Boom.

Sadly, Robert's response came as little surprise. Second thoughts, cold feet, some backpedaling. I desperately wanted to be grateful that whatever "thing" he needed my help with had been resolved over the ensuing twenty-four hours. But I wasn't.

Be honest with yourself, Joe. You are thinking what everyone is telling you. He caved in to them, reversing course under heavy influence.

As the weeks passed and my Sunday emails once again went unanswered, I questioned myself—perhaps I should have been less assertive, or more assertive? Should I try to call or text him? The phone was not a good option since I didn't have his cell number, and even if I did, my number was likely blocked, as it was on his sister's phone.

It wasn't until a small situation involving Hannah that the full picture came into view. She had been in a minor fender bender with Tom's daughter, and since the car she drove was technically mine, her mother emailed me. I deluded myself into thinking there might actually be an opportunity for co-parenting, and offered a solution. Tom and I would keep things out of the insurance company's hands; he was able to repair the dent in his daughter's car for $21.05. I wrote Hannah, asking her to be a responsible driver and daughter, and cover the cost of her minor blunder. I received no response from her, but did get one from Robert:

Leave Hannah alone

Evidently something was being miscommunicated, mischaracterized, or intentionally twisted in his mind. Whether or not it was under the influence of others was irrelevant. I emailed Robert back, asking my son for clarification. A few days later, as I was finishing up a shift at the Rock, this came in:

bye then you've not changed

I shuddered. *Please God let this not mean what I think it does, we can't go back, we came so close.*

In the span of three weeks, my son had reached out, then backed off, then completely withdrawn. What had I done? To say I felt distressed is an understatement. The crabs moved back into my gut. Again I scrambled for my recovery toolbox, as I so desperately wanted a drink.

That night, as I buried myself in bed, the meeting in my head commenced with the usual attendees:

Alcoholic Voice: You just got mind-slapped, and by your own son no less. It's OK to feel sorry for yourself. Is all this recovery shit even worth it? There are only two ways out of your undeserved, endless suffering, and one involves a bottle.

Higher Power: Things happen for a reason. Keep being honest with yourself, figure out what you did wrong. Do a tenth step on it.

Alcoholic Voice: Screw the Steps. You know what happened, face the bullshit. Someone got to him, influenced him, manipulated him—but not overtly; subtly and craftily, so that the chief influencer queen bitch can still claim plausible deniability. Listen to all those around you who warned you of this. He, like his brother and sister, are kept permanent emotional hostages. She will never release her death grip on them. Someone wants you to eternally suffer. Now he hurts, blames you, and you hurt. After all you have freely provided, above and beyond your legal obligations—the gifts, summer camps, extra money! You asshole, can't you see that they are blindly trying to kill the goose that lays the golden eggs and either don't realize it or don't care?

Higher Power: Whether any of that is true or not is none of your concern. His so-called about-face is nothing you can control. What others think of you—even your own children—is none of your business. Keep working the program, and in time you will learn to let this matter go. Discuss it in group therapy, in the rooms of AA, and with your sponsor. Accept the situation as exactly how it has to be, keep making daily living amends, and you will achieve a degree of serenity. Go to sleep now, and in the morning, wake up, go for your run, and go to work . . . and be grateful that you are sober and Robert is healthy and generally doing well. Be grateful they are all doing well, even their mother, despite your misgivings. Be grateful you can send her huge financial support every month because of the professional progress you've made these last three years. They will thrive, in part because you have taken the high road, as you have since the beginning of all of this. You have stayed righteous even through your abandonment, divorce, and parental alienation. Trust in me. Keep up the great work! We are all so proud!

Game, set, and match.

I prayed for Robert, and for all of those in the house in which he lived. Then I fell asleep. There were no reverse nightmares that night.

CHAPTER 13

BOO-BOO PICKLE

The lawyers had arranged a time for me to come to the house to retrieve a few personal items. I would not be going alone; I had been forewarned. A neighborhood couple I had known for years—she, an ER nurse I worked with, he, the sheriff's deputy who saved my life—agreed to accompany me. As we turned up the long driveway, I wondered what, just up ahead, awaited me.

A dozen cardboard boxes, give or take, were piled up outside on the front lawn. They overflowed with clothing, books, toiletries, photo albums, high school trophies, pictures in frames, personalized knickknacks, race medals, hairbrushes, desk files, athletic equipment, medical supplies, karate accessories, and seemingly any other item that could possibly serve as a reminder that I had ever been a member of the family. It was a thorough emotional house cleaning to be sure, wiping away any evidence of my previous existence there.

There was a box apparently too heavy to be dragged outside. She stood in the doorway like a Roman sentinel as we entered to retrieve it. Hannah and Robert were nowhere to be seen. Toby stood in the foyer, staring, and I froze. He cautiously approached me. Under her watchful eye, he wouldn't attempt to embrace me, but instead handed me a sealed envelope.

▲▲▲▲▲

Dear Daddy:
I made up this language because I like codes. My friends Lana and Charlie came over on Saturday. I really want to talk on the phone. In art class, I drew a cat. Do you want to be pen pals?
Thank you for the letter.
I want to take small steps to going face to face. Like, first letters, then calls, then face to face.
Love, Toby

The entire message had been written not in common words but in symbols he'd invented, and looked like a hieroglyphic code. With his note he'd included a code key so that, when I got back to my house, I could sit on the sofa and carefully decipher his secret letter to me.

▲▲▲▲▲

"He has a small pneumothorax, and he's mildly tachypneic."

Finn's face was stone serious. "For now, I think we can just watch it."

A pneumothorax. That was what our son had. Toby, who was not even a day old, had already had more chest X-rays in his life than I ever had. Apparently his tachypnea—continuously rapid breathing rate—had concerned Finn enough to look into it. My wife had spent almost three days in labor, spiking a fever of 101.7 on day two but pushing through it all—pushing, working, getting Toby's head to crown so all present in the birthing suite could see a scalp of red fuzz. Our baby was a redhead. Exhausted to the depth of her being, she continued to push, determined as ever to deliver her child the "old-fashioned way."

The obstetricians used the term VBAC, vaginal birth after Cesarean, to describe the process, since labor with his older brother two years earlier had culminated in a C-section. With a higher risk of uterine rupture, some in the obstetrical community felt a VBAC was too risky, that the chance of death from uterine hemorrhage was unacceptably high. For months, my insides had squirmed at her decision. Even more worrisome, and what truly gave me dyspepsia, was that she wanted to have a home birth with a nurse midwife and doula. I was uncomfortably familiar with the medical statistics on this and had voiced my concerns of unnecessary risk to her in one single conversation early in the pregnancy . . . and then shut up. There was going to be no changing her mind; she was dug in. It was her body, her physiology, and ultimately her decision, and the rest of the family would defer to her, as we kept our fears to ourselves.

Goddamn, I am married to an amazingly strong, brave, and stubborn woman.

She was absolutely obsessed with having a successful natural childbirth at home. In that lone conversation the previous summer, I had laid out what I felt was a sound argument for proceeding "the safe and reasonable way." I pointed out that despite the complications with Robert's birth, which were completely beyond our control, he turned out to be a happy, healthy almost-two-year-old, and the method by which he entered this world was far less important than the fact that he was in it. My pleas fell on deaf ears; she would have none of it. Who was I to deny what was, in her mind, an absolution?

We were fortunate with her pregnancy with Toby from the beginning. After we had attempted for two years to get pregnant, Robert turned out to be a "miracle" pregnancy (now in retrospect, I realize that all we did was eventually relax, get out of the way, and let God handle things). The relative ease with which conception occurred the second time around was a happy surprise for both of us. However, she developed some concerning symptoms in those first weeks while I was away visiting family, and so she went to see her obstetrician without me.

Hannah, then four years old, and I had made a trip to the New Jersey shore to see my dad; stepmom, Celia; and brother, Alex, twenty-two years my junior. I received a call from my wife indicating there might be problems and that an immediate ultrasound was scheduled; miscarriage was a distinct possibility. I offered to return home immediately, but she said no, that she would handle what was going on and call me with updates.

We were sitting at a restaurant with an outdoor dining area overlooking the Atlantic Ocean when she called me back. My brother had taken Hannah onto the beach so she could collect shells as the three adults watched from our patio table. My phone showed her caller ID, and I stepped away for privacy, my heart racing, to engage in what was going to possibly be a difficult conversation. What it turned out to be was something different altogether, as she gave me news of a healthy intrauterine pregnancy—an embryo with a heartbeat had been detected. A small subchorionic hemorrhage—blood at the site where the placenta takes root in the endometrial bed—was seen. This was not serious, but nevertheless, they had recommended some bed rest and close monitoring. My heart steadied and filled with relief and joy. We hadn't told anyone yet about the pregnancy and would likely keep it secret for another month or so, even though her doctor gave her a 95 percent chance of making it to the ninth month successfully. I returned to the dinner table in time to see a gleeful Hannah skipping along, hands full of seashells, back up the beach toward us.

▲▲▲▲▲

Fate smiled on baby Toby. He made it through the in-utero challenges without further complications but was stubborn, choosing to come out by Cesarean. By his second day of life he was stabilized in the newborn nursery, having completely recovered from his perinatal complications. Mama was not quite as fortunate. Between her febrile amnionitis (infected amniotic fluid during labor), subsequent C. *diff* intestinal infection, and C-section pain, she was beyond uncomfortable for a few weeks. In addition, she was doing her best to care for a two-year-old and a four-year-old. I was pitching in, doing what I could, trying to share equally in the responsibilities of the household, mainly by occupying Hannah and Robert so my wife could attend to our newborn and heal herself. It was not an unusual occurrence to return from the playground or park to find her in the bathroom, shedding her infection, a squirming Toby attached to her breast.

Months passed, incisions healed, and infections went away, but my drinking accelerated.

I justified moving out of the master bedroom and into the basement to allow mother and baby to rest while I worked a hectic ER schedule, which had me coming and going at all hours of the day and night. Settling into the lower-level guest room seemed to make perfect sense at the time. It was also the ideal place to stash my vodka bottles, which I would reach for immediately after returning home late at night from work. That instantaneous sensation of release after a stressful shift seemed to make all my efforts of the day worthwhile. It became so easy and habitual. The house was always fast asleep, and I could stay mouse quiet and content in my sublevel man cave with my trundle bed, TV, and cheap liquid therapy.

▲▲▲▲▲

Toby's preoccupation with and love of animals were apparent very early on. When he was unhappy in his bouncy seat and nothing else stopped his wailing ("the shriek of the Nazgul," as we Tolkien fans in the house liked to say), a walk-by from one of the house cats would not only quiet him, but elicit an approving coo; his change in demeanor when in the presence of the furry critters was so dramatic that we attempted all kinds of elaborate ways to keep our pets in front of him. Nothing soothed his tiny soul like a happy feline. TV shows with animals were a distant second.

The interpersonal dynamic between all three children established itself in those early years and became a wonderful phenomenon to watch. With two years separating them, Toby and Robert entered into a classic pattern of simultaneous sibling rivals and allies. They fought over toys and colluded in capers, always demonstrating affection toward each other as brothers. Robert often explained the underlying plot in a cartoon or instructed Toby in a video game tactic. One time we witnessed both of them in the backyard with their pants down, squatting, competing to see which one could produce the larger bowel movement. During the wedding ceremony of their aunt and uncle, Robert held the rings with his right hand and two-year-old Toby with his left as the pair of tuxedoed toddlers forayed their way down the church center aisle.

With a four-year difference in age with Toby, Hannah willingly acclimated to the role of mother's little helper. She enjoyed feeding her baby brother, pushing him on the swings, making up dances to get him giggling, and carrying him around the backyard when he didn't care to walk. During their years together in grade school, she would assist him, and during a school talent show one year, helped him prepare for his piano debut of "One Gray Mouse," a Toby original.

It was with an actual mouse that Toby revealed how closely attuned to the animal world he was. One afternoon, while playing outside, he discovered a wounded mouse, apparently attacked by a larger animal. He brought it inside, and we placed the injured animal, wriggling and kicking, into a shoebox with some straw and a lettuce leaf. Toby, then about eight, was overjoyed the moment he realized we would let him keep it in his room to tend to it. He carried the box around, keeping his cat, Serafina, away, intensely preoccupied with every movement his new pet made. Over dinner he kept it on a nearby counter and chatted continuously about where he might set up a home for it once it was better. He slept that night with the box on the shelf by his bed.

By morning, the mouse had died. Toby was overwhelmed at the reality that such an innocent "baby" creature could lose its life so quickly. His sobs of grief at times became wails, going on for hours. Later that afternoon we sat with him, stroking his head and talking with him about nature and the life cycle; he settled down. I dug a grave and we had a small but very touching memorial service in the backyard.

His pet for one single day had a major emotional impact on him. It was through this experience I reaffirmed my appreciation for the depth and breadth of our youngest child's sensitive side. As Toby grew older, his compassion for the animal world remained strong. He routinely donated part of his weekly allowance to animal-friendly causes, and on more than one birthday, asked his friends to make donations to the local SPCA instead of giving him presents.

While his older brother was partial to yellow, Toby's favorite color was green. Given a choice of crayons, clothes, or candy, he would inevitably take the green option. He took an interest in reptiles and amphibians, particularly frogs. We began to call him our little pickle. This nickname merged with the name of a character on *Mickey Mouse Clubhouse*, Boo-Boo Chicken, into Boo-Boo Pickle. He identified with and enjoyed the nickname, and we called him by it for years, eventually shortening it to just Boo-Boo.

Boo-Boo was a little boy with two gears—idle and fifth. For his size he could sprint surprisingly fast, and he and I would take many father-son walks around our expansive property year round. He would enjoy racing ahead to investigate, stopping, turning around, and running right back. Sometimes we would don backpacks filled with flashlights, multitools, potato chips, juice boxes, and other "survival gear," pretending we were on a recon mission to protect our home against intruders, an exercise we termed "walkabout squad." Robert also joined us for the more "dangerous" outings. We developed our own set of special hand signals to communicate "in the field" without speaking, special forces–style. The treehouse in the grove was the staging area where we would hold our pre-mission strategy sessions, and which would serve as our final rally point for our debriefing and snack break.

For as much as we enjoyed our outdoor activities, nothing bested the nightly evening ritual. For me and Toby, bedtime had its own special routine. After he was coaxed into pajamas, we would have some end-of-day chasing around, a snack prepared by Mom, and finally tuck-in time. This usually meant a bedtime story, or three. In his toddler days, I would be the reader; as Toby progressed through the years, he took over. *Magic Tree House*, *Diary of a Wimpy Kid*, and *The Adventures of Captain Underpants* were just a few of our favorites. As he got older, tuck-in time became increasingly involved and complex. After reading, I would attempt to leave but before I got too far from his bed, he would take a flying leap onto my back, and I would collapse back onto his mattress. "Dooon't do that again," I would mockingly scold him, and with an excited gleam in his eye, he would of course, like all silly boys, do it again. This would repeat half a dozen times, always ending in hysterical laughter. Finally, when it was time for lights out, he would give me an "I love you," demanding an immediate response in kind. My work was complete when he was satisfied that I had provided enough attention and "I love yous."

Toby and I became partners in karate. He was the second-to-last member of the family to join up, and I was the final; his two older siblings and mother were far more advanced than either of us, attending a different class entirely. Right around the time Toby graduated from Little Dragons (karate kinder-garten), I was donning a white belt. Family trips to the dojo became a twice-a-week regular occurrence. We would get into the studio before class, and I would begin my warm-ups. While he did the same, he also made sure to add the extra routine of leaping on my back at a full sprint, cutting me down at the knees with his compact body, or simply bear-hugging my feet so I couldn't move. I never, ever minded. Being on a soft mat, barefoot with my son, where we were encouraged to run, kick, and spar was another delightful opportunity and a chance to put our horseplay to good purpose.

As the years passed, father-son bonding also included trips to the cabin. Just after Toby was born, during Robert's third summer, I purchased a parcel of land in a remote backwoods corner of the county and constructed a small log cabin. It was tucked into the heavily wooded slopes of the Blue Ridge, standing just above an open field. A clear, shallow creek, with one spot deep enough to swim in, cut through the property. The boys and I made good use of our slice of wilderness, while my wife and daughter chose to stay home. Our day trips and overnights involved the great stuff of outdoor camping mem-ories—hiking, campfires, collecting small wildlife in buck-ets, and storytelling. The discovery on the property of an old, long-forgotten cemetery, complete with tombstones dating back to the Civil War, added to the excitement and intrigue. With each passing summer, our trips to the cabin became more frequent and lasted longer. Eventually we found ourselves hosting entire father-son camping weekends, inviting other boys and their dads.

▲▲▲▲▲

That afternoon, as I walked into the house for the very last time to collect my belongings, the camping, the karate, the walkabouts, the tuck-ins, WatchDOG school visits—every last trace of evidence of me—had vanished from the home as if these memories were just hallucinations, having never happened at all.

▲▲▲▲▲

About two and a half years into my recovery, around the time I was celebrating nine hundred days sober and mourning nine hundred days since I had tucked in my children, I received a rare email. Boo-Boo Pickle was requesting a kayak.

As with his brother and sister, Toby and I were incommunicado, with the exception of a rare word-or-two response to one of my messages. One April day I wrote him, asking him what he wanted for summer, and he responded:

I would like to have the kayaks from the house in New York. Can you get them please and bring them here while I'm at school?

He wanted a kayak from me but did not want to see me bring it.

Toby had always been a proficient kayaker, even as young as age four. During the period we briefly owned a summer house on a lake in the Catskill Mountains of New York, he would drag the hard plastic shell into the water and grab the paddle, and fearlessly off he went. He would spend hours on and off the kayak, paddling around within our sight, peeking over the side at tadpoles and minnows, and feeling generally content with being outside and on the water. I would feel his sense of accomplishment as he independently navigated his way around the shoreline.

Five years later, he wanted his own kayak, and *by golly*, I was going to get him one. The lake house kayaks were long gone, having been sold with the property, so I purchased a new one online—a tandem version so that his brother, sister, or a friend could be in the boat with him on outings. He asked for a green one (naturally) and I obliged. The very act of him asking me, even though we had spent no time together in years, had my heart singing. I deluded myself that I was making inroads. Around the time sixth grade was letting out for summer break, the kayak was delivered to my house. I remember on the afternoon of its arrival, removing it from its plastic packaging and painting Toby's name on the side as my neighbors watched. I heaved it atop my truck, secured it with bungee cords, and drove off, making the five-mile trek to deliver it to him firsthand.

I envisioned some happy scene, but it did not play out in reality. I turned the corner into the driveway for the second time post-recovery and didn't make it twenty feet. The barriers came into full view. Orange cones had been set across my path; behind them a wheelbarrow. The message was clear: *Stop. You are not welcome here. Put the kayak down, slowly back off, and drive away.* The smack to my gut was less intense than if it had been completely unexpected.

Alcoholic Voice: You are a glutton for punishment, JD. When are you going to stop torturing yourself?

I halted my advance well before the cones, put the truck in neutral, and stepped out. It took me less than ten minutes to untie the kayak and slide it to the middle of the field to allow full view of it from the house's front windows. Inside, I saw lights on. Near the top of the driveway by the garage sat Hannah's electric-blue Toyota.

They are home, probably watching. I completed the task, which included setting the paddle across the gunwale and securing the sign I had created with poster board and colored markers. ENJOY YOUR KAYAK, TOBY! LOVE, DAD was inscribed in big green block letters. Then I did exactly as the implicit message of the barriers suggested. I got back in my truck, put it in reverse to the main road, shifted into forward, and drove home.

Kayaks, summer camps, school wardrobes, video game consoles . . . this was the extent of my relationship with my son, with all the kids. *Stuff—lots of stuff, well above and beyond the child support checks.* Beyond gifts, they had no apparent interest in me, even after two-plus years of recovery and healthy living. Couldn't Toby . . . *couldn't all three of them* . . . see that I was trying, giving them what they wanted by staying away, all the while making sure I attended to every last economic need?

Recovery Voice: You cannot buy a child's love.

I found that my trusty old character defects, entitlement and expectation, reappeared at these moments. Shortly after dropping off the kayak, I mentally grasped for my recovery toolbox, pulling out what I most needed—gratitude and acceptance. Again.

Gratitude: I was sober to drive and had a driver's license. I was back in my chosen profession and was able to afford a beautiful, high-quality green kayak for my son that he requested and was willing to receive, even if not in person. That night in an email he thanked me for his gift. I felt gratitude that I was mature enough in my emotional development to give it unconditionally and did not attach any selfish, ego-driven preconditions to the kayak, just as with Hannah's car and Robert's bar mitzvah. Still, in all three cases I felt somewhat manipulated.

Acceptance: They were not ready for my physical presence. My relationship with my children was going to be glacier-like in its forward progress, at times seemingly stagnant. I accepted that I would work my ass off to continue to provide for their monthly living and future expenses with at most a cursory thank-you in return. My internal gratification would have to come in the form of the recognition that I was capable of making living amends, one day at a time. My children could live in their beautiful, mortgage-free home with their bellies full at night as they slept in peace and comfort. They would be kayaking and playing piano and swimming and driving to meet their friends for coffee and pursuing their dreams, while I was, for the foreseeable future, going to be observing from afar—doing what I could to be Daddy from a distance.

The remedy for resentment and entitlement, I am taught in my program, is gratitude and acceptance. The remnants of my relationships with my children are, in my mind, the ultimate litmus test of that theory.

CHAPTER 14

INKED

Vivid animations surrounded me. Busty, bikini-clad biker babes slayed fierce dragons while Jesus looked on approvingly. Flying monkeys with bejeweled crosses dangling from their necks circled a fiery mountaintop. A kaleidoscope of patterns and designs were interspersed between gremlins, cherubs, and satyrs. And everywhere, there were skeletons. I stood opposite images of skulls and rib cages, spines and femurs—some creating a whole, others standing alone. In a far corner was a full-size cloaked figure, hooded, with scythe. He was Death, or maybe a dementor. Staring at the walls that surrounded me, I saw that not a square inch of the place was bare.

The people moving about the room easily camouflaged into their surroundings. Their exposed epidermis was no more than the fleshy version of what was on display everywhere else. Sleeved and fully pierced, black leathered and chained in full battle array, they moved around in character, never rushing, communicating with each other through a series of f-bombs and slurs, ignoring the patrons on the waiting room sofa or at the counter. I couldn't say I blamed them; virtually every other customer around me seemed to be a fresh-faced college coed, impatiently waiting her turn, face affixed to a phone screen while fingers furiously texted away, probably overexcited at the impending transformation of her chest, back, or ass.

Is that burnt flesh I smell? I thought the process involved needles.

I don't belong here.

Or do I? Nothing, absolutely nothing, happens in God's world by mistake. Is that what this is, some perverted version of God's world?

Does God's world include a satellite office in hell? I guess it must. So yes, I do belong. My Higher Power brought me this far, so I must venture forth.

Permanence.

Statuesque with jet-black hair, the receptionist seated behind the glass countertop could have been a superhero-ine who'd leaped right out of the pages of some dark graphic novel. Her black leather vest was unbuttoned, revealing an overstretched black satin camisole underneath. Her breasts were impossibly large for her thin torso, nipples aiming at me like tiny daggers. In my judgment she didn't seem the type for implants. I found myself playing the always-popular real-or-fake game in my male mind. Tight black yoga pants and spiked heels completed the ensemble. She had enough ear jewelry dangling to serve as a human wind chime. Facial piercings, black lipstick, and a nose hoop accentuated her sharp facial features. When she looked up from her book at us clientele, there was no smile, only a chilly, pissed-off, sexy glare. I found myself simultaneously intimidated and aroused. I imagined her suddenly and without warning leaping over the counter, claws out, and ripping me to pieces. It would be a gruesomely fun way to go.

So there I stood, in the front room of the Rabid Fox Tattoo Parlor, intermittently studying the surroundings and conjuring sick erotic fantasies as I waited my turn.

My decision to get a tattoo was neither instantaneous nor impulsive. I wondered how many over-the-hill professionals walked in to get their bodies inked; it made absolutely no sense on paper. After all, I had hit a stage of life where many of my contemporaries were welcoming the arrivals of their first grandchildren. I had a retirement account and sang in my congregation's choir, had undergone my first colonoscopy and spent evenings watching Hallmark Channel Christmas movies with my professor girlfriend. But the real argument against this harebrained idea was that I had not been drinking. Who the fuck got a tattoo at noon on a Tuesday, sober? Two hours prior, I was folding my underwear and watching CNBC; later on I'd be in the CVS Pharmacy buying my preferred antifungal cream (it was on my to-do list). Yet there I stood, on that hot August day, among the party girls and demon worshippers. . . . *Really?!*

Palmer emerged from his side studio and approached me, holding the latest sketched version of my imagination. We had originally met two months earlier to discuss the design to be etched into my chest for eternity. He had come highly recommended by a friend in AA, and the two-month wait for an appointment was, I suppose, affirmation that this guy's mad skills were of acceptable quality. Like the others in the studio, he most certainly looked the part. Portly, goateed, and dressed in what seemed to be the standard parlor uniform of jeans, leather, and neck tattoos, he maintained a friendly demeanor. If I was going to have to look in the mirror every day at his permanent work, I wanted to make sure I had the best, someone I could trust with my virgin body canvas. More important, I needed someone who understood exactly what I wanted and whose artistic muse was able to reach into my thoughts and translate that image perfectly onto my skin. The original consultation that spring had been more than a discussion of a picture; I did my best to describe to him the image in my brain, my vision of the graphic that was already affixed to my soul, and what I needed for it to represent.

His first version had lacked detail, so I conveyed what I was after more descriptively. He retreated back into his studio, and I waited another hour while he redid the markup. I didn't mind hanging out in the front of the parlor, observing the goings-on in a place I had never set foot in and might never again. Biker Barbies in leather came in for touch-ups. College girls were ushered into a side chamber for their nipple piercings. Various tattooists conversed with each other from cubby rooms as they worked, remarking to each other about some ink convention they had attended, a random *bad fucking* situation, or what lunch stop in town made the best burrito. The front-counter vixen remained idle as she sat on her stool, reading her novel and tapping her black pointy fingernails on the surface glass, her (fake or real) tits pushing through thin material.

After a few more revisions, it appeared Palmer had come up with exactly what I wanted, or close. The outline seemed nearly perfect on the sheet of tracing paper. The extra wait was necessary. After fifty-two years of empty skin, what was another ninety minutes? It was finally time to rock and roll. I followed him into his studio, which was more of an open alcove off the main parlor. The decor of his walls was themed similarly to what I had seen in the foyer, with image after image of glowing skulls, centaurs, and near-naked nymphs riding bareback on battle horses. Off to the side was his workbench, covered with his inkwells and shiny, metallic, pointy implements of torture that would, very shortly, be utilized on my tender outer layer. He asked me to remove my shirt, and quickly I realized that I would be bare chested and in full view of the rest of the establishment for any customer, artist, or inked Elvira to see. I guessed modesty was not a consideration in this place. I wondered if I would have been covered up had I been getting an ass tattoo or a clitoral piercing. Maybe, maybe not. I didn't think the federal privacy standards implemented in hospitals applied here; this was not a credentialed surgical suite, as I was apparently slow to discover.

I stood before him, shirtless, as he shaved my left chest wall with his disposable razor and then used a cold, damp washrag to wipe the area down. *Shit, this is getting very real, very fast.* The well-worn padded bench beside us, where I was to lie supine for the next several hours, vaguely resembled a patient examination table. Palmer began drawing on me with his marking pen. *Not so bad,* I thought. When his sketch was complete, he had me take a look with a handheld mirror.

"Looks good, but make the eyes less fierce."

He erased, retraced. Voilà.

"Can you have her hug it as if protecting it?"

Erase . . . scribble . . . done.

It was go time, zero hour. I lay down on the table and there was a moment of quiet resignation as he set up. I couldn't help but notice that he never asked if I was comfortable. He never asked if I was ready.

Stop that kind of thinking, Joe. This is not a doctor's office and you are not his patient.

"Lie still and keep breathing. This is going to hurt."

This is going to hurt.

Finally, he said what I had known. It was the way in which he said it—in a monotone voice, as emotionless and cold as if he were an intake cop at the precinct taking my statement— that confirmed he was not my doctor, he was not my friend. There were no warm fuzzies here. He was a skin artist and I was paying him to literally stab me over my heart three thousand times per minute over several hours.

Physical distress at this stage of my life was less of a factor for me, or so I thought, and from talking to others, I felt confident of my tolerance for this "procedure." Word on the street was that Palmer was "heavy handed." I had envisioned some stinging and burning akin to a skin exfoliant or maybe infiltration with a local anesthetic—annoying but very tolerable. Given the emotional agony I had endured these last years, what was an afternoon of annoying irritation?

Ha!

By this point in my recovery, almost one thousand days in, I had really begun to pride myself on my ability to tolerate pain. Having sustained the emotional equivalent of a Spanish Inquisition torture chamber these last few years, physical pain was comparatively minor league, a footnote, something that could be joked about, laughed off. I felt that my degree of "spiritual fitness" could easily handle what was about to be delivered upon me.

The first pass of the rapid-firing needles of his vibrating instrument seared into my left pec like a surgeon's scalpel. I felt my breath stop involuntarily and my toes tense up in flexion. All the mind-over-matter crap flew out the window during the first few minutes he worked on me.

They say Palmer is heavy handed. I now understood what they meant.

No more heavy handed than you have been on yourself, you fucking pansy.

My hands grabbed the edges of the table in a death grip to control my shaking. Palmer ordered me to relax and control my breathing. I did control it—holding my breath for the thirty seconds he stabbed me, taking a few deep ones when he paused to reach over to dip into an inkwell. A switch went off in my head, and I reflected on the wonderfully distracting nature of physical pain.

Wasn't it just two years earlier that you were doing this to yourself? You were home, mowing the lawn shirtless, and brushed against that thorny shrub in the backyard, sustaining a deep scratch in your right shoulder. You jolted in surprise but quickly welcomed the pain as distracting, a welcome diversion from the real pain—the agony in your head, that ever-present emotional kind, worse than any bullshit skin wound by a magnitude of one thousand. It was technically a superficial cut that would have run its usual course of healing, disappearing within a week. But instead of tending to it the way an emergency physician or normal human being would, you chose instead to go inside and retrieve one of those scalpels stored away in your medical supplies.

You relished the ice-cold pain as you dug deep into the subcutaneous tissues of your right deltoid, alone in front of your bathroom mirror, and it hurt like hell and bled like hell into the sink but was so refreshingly distracting from the other *pain, the true pain, the intolerable kind that never leaves you, always haunts you, and you welcomed it.*

You let the tears flow and thanked your Higher Power for the discovery, finally understanding why those teenagers in the psych rooms of the ER do this, the act of self-mutilation becoming crystal clear. So that you wouldn't bleed all over your clothes, you cauterized the exposed raw tissues with a silver nitrate–tipped applicator.

Then, every few days, just to keep things fresh, or maybe just to prevent proper healing, you reopened the gash with your trusty scalpel all over again.

▲▲▲▲▲

We were just getting started and I was already second-guessing myself. *No—buyer's remorse be damned.* I had come this far, and Palmer was already well into the outline of the sketch. There was no turning back. *Accept it. Accept the pain, stay in the moment, and practice gratitude during those ten-second reprieves when he is dipping his tool in ink and those one-minute breaks when he is switching instruments.* Palmer's job did not require being delicate. I was laying out $300 for him to do the best possible job he could, not to be sensitive and nurturing. I thought about all those dislocated shoulders, elbows, and fingers I snapped into place without anesthesia, all those painful invasive procedures I performed on patients without it impacting me in the slightest. What comes around, goes around, payback is hell, and all those other clichés.

Accept that it hurts, and it is going to keep hurting for a while. Stop fighting and make friends, or at least frenemies, with the pain. Breathe it in, make it part of your essence, your moment. Experience it, just as you experience the rush of an exciting case in the ER, or a song on your guitar, or a wonderful dinner date and evening of intimacy with your love, Cassie. Relish the potency of the moment, its power strong enough to shove your pain over losing your children into the background, even over the horizon. That pain will always come back, but that does not matter now, because in this *moment, it is gone, and when it returns, you will be stronger, tougher, and more accepting.*

Something small was dangling over my left foot, something I could not see. It was hanging off a shelf at the end of the table, intermittently touching me. Something at the end of a small string. I began to tap at it with my great toe like a mini tetherball. Maybe it was a little plastic skull on a rope, or a quartz crystal, or maybe a token Baby Jesus for all I cared; all I knew was when I batted it around, I was effectively distracted from the searing fire burning at my left sternal border. Focusing my attention dropped my "pain score," to use clinical terms, from a nine to about a six, and that was quite tolerable. I had been given something to occupy my mind away from the immediate goings-on. Like guitars, medical cases, or Bubble Shooter, I was provided an alternative focus of attention. Something as trivial as a hard plastic charm on a string, if I concentrated on batting at it with my toe, reduced my distress significantly.

Cassie appeared, as promised. *My biker-babe angel of mercy has arrived. No leather, extensive piercings, or attitude, but she does sport a really cool tree of life tattoo on the underside of her right wrist.* The initial sweet smile on her face disappeared when she saw me trembling. Palmer never looked up, choosing to stay on the task at hand. He had obviously done this a thousand times and remained concentrated on his fleshy canvas.

I made a brief introduction during an equipment-switch break, and Palmer became as personable and pleasant as any office receptionist or kindergarten teacher as he said hello to Cassie. She pulled up a stool and sat beside me, holding my sweaty hand. Her palms were soft. Her fingers stroked my knuckles and it felt wonderful. While we spoke, my eyes remained shut as I continued to toe-bat Baby Jesus. When I did gaze up at her, I noticed the corner of her mouth quivering. A classic Cassieism; she's an empath, and by simply seeing and touching me, she was shunting away some of my pain, absorbing it into her own body. Just like the times I cried about my children.

The broad outline of the tattoo was complete, and Palmer gave me a break to get up, have a restroom break, walk around, vomit, breathe, or do whatever I needed to. He asked me to hydrate to reduce my chances of passing out. I walked outside, arm in arm with Cassie, into the humid summer day, shirtless but not caring, feeling a bit lightheaded. *You are such a wimp. Suck it up.* The building happened to sit at a very busy intersection in town, with cars and pedestrians constantly passing in all directions.

When I returned to his room, my painmaster engaged me with some of his preferred strategies if his clients passed out.

I listened, politely and with arrogant amusement. The emergency physician was receiving his tattoo artist's dissertation on "The Nonclinical Approach to Syncope in the Underworld Population." I paused, recognizing a character defect bubbling to the surface. A misguided sense of intellectual superiority began to well up in me. This was a prime opportunity for me to do a tenth step ego check. *When wrong, promptly admit it.* Palmer was proficient at his craft, and I was proficient at mine, and they stood separately, apples and oranges.

The flesh cutting resumed. I bid Cassie adieu, as she had to go back to her office. Palmer had moved on to the fill-in phase, adding in all the color. It occurred to me that I had not even so much as glanced at his work. The sharpness of his initial instruments gave way to the comparatively milder scratchy sensation of the fill-in pen. Lying passively as he hovered over me felt not dissimilar to my dentist working on a bad tooth, but that was where the similarities ended. Instead of the smell of antiseptic, an aromatic mix of incense and tobacco breath infused my nasal passages. Instead of boring old office-ceiling drop tile, psychedelic and demonic images flooded my field of vision. There were no requests to an assistant for fluoride; rather, commentary about some club scene or ex-girlfriend was intermittently flung around the room. Occasionally another artist would wander over, stare down at me, and exclaim, "Cool man! Fucking awesome work!" I was encouraged.

At one point, Palmer asked if I would like him to apply some topical anesthetic over the skin to lessen my discomfort. *Now you ask? Fucking ninety minutes into this torture fest, the worst of it clearly behind me, and* now *you offer me relief?* I thought about it briefly and declined. The pain of receiving my first tattoo seemed like some twisted rite of passage for me, and I needed to experience it all. It was my initiation. I had anesthetized myself far too much in my life already. Besides, he was almost done.

The harsh pressing of his sharp tools into my torso gradually gave way to more delicate touches and quick wisps, akin to a painter applying the final dabs of color to accent his creation. Either the pain had disappeared or my body was so flooded with endorphins, my femur could have been sawed off and I would have barely noticed. More ink dudes wandered in to compliment the master *arteeest*. I had stopped toe thrashing Baby Jesus.

"Get up and have a look." I rose from the bench the way I would have asked a drunken college student in the ER to at the end of his visit. I sat up slowly, waited a few seconds, then swung myself around, feet touching the ground, waited a bit more to make sure my legs could support my body, then slowly rose, holding balance with one hand on the table. It appeared as if I was in pretty good shape, physiologically speaking, so I got up and went into the bathroom to have a peek.

▲▲▲▲▲

The moment I looked in the mirror, it jumped out and grabbed me by my retinas. Etched into my inflamed and swollen left chest wall was my new tattoo, about the size of a grown man's palm. The visuals hit me at once, similar to rounding a hallway corridor and bumping into a familiar face. My initial happy surprise was followed by an assessment of its features.

The entirety of the final product dominated and mesmerized me, in a good way. Complete and final, it was now incorporated into my being for as long as I would exist on this planet. It was simultaneously awesome, shocking, and full of meaning, and I was beginning to experience its immediate physical, spiritual, and emotional implications.

I have no idea how long I stood in front of that mirror. I was existing in the *now*; all extraneous thoughts were not even a blip on my radar. Eventually I broke my gaze and made my way back to Palmer's work area. I was feeling a sense of awe, and relief that the discomfort was now behind me. I was exhausted in every way, feeling "floaty" as my brain was flooded with those great pain-control hormones. I must have felt much like the patient with the dislocated shoulder who still had all the happy drugs circulating after the joint was put back in place.

I received my aftercare instructions from Palmer both verbally and in pamphlet form, and he covered the area with gauze and tape, instructing me to leave it covered for three hours and to pick up some good moisturizer on the way home. For a moment I wondered if I could drive, thinking my endorphins might be so elevated that I could fail a DUI test if pulled over.

I crossed the street to the CVS and purchased my skin lotion and an apple juice (as well as my preferred antifungal). Leaving the pharmacy, I drove the few miles to Cassie's place. She wouldn't be home from work for a few hours, so I stretched out on her sofa. My head was warm and whooshing like a Caribbean beach tide. I felt relaxed and exhausted, similar to the feeling I would get after a hard run or difficult ER shift. Her cat, Bella, curled up on my belly. I became one with the couch cushions, and my mind and body went completely limp. The last sensation to flicker and fade was the waning burn of my chest area, which fizzled out just before my consciousness.

▲▲▲▲▲

For the second time that afternoon, I opened my eyes to see Cassie standing over me. She had on her trademark sweet smile.

"How are you feeling?"

How am I feeling? Exhausted. Exhilarated. Relieved. I wanted to walk to her bathroom mirror, remove the bandage, and stare at my forever stamp. "Awesome."

Still feeling wiped out, I rose slowly, traversed the kitchen to the bathroom and flicked on the light, and gently eased off the bandage.

There it was—his creation, my creation. Freshly seared into me, a blue-green outline of a heart glistened. Overlying its valentine shape, equidistant from one another, were three smaller drawings, each representing a child. Embedded within each drawing was a letter.

Near the base, at the lower point of the heart, was a green letter *T*, hugged by a lounging panther. This represented Toby, my animal-loving child, the boy who adored all creatures four-legged before he could walk. The kid who, despite all our house pets, had insisted on his own personal cat. The son who will someday grow from a spirited child into a spirited man, from a kitten into a lion. He will fiercely defend all he loves and all that is righteous while never losing the capacity to curl up in your lap or life. His love will be an earned love. If you give him a hug, his inner panther will hug back.

Black cat boy with a big green T
Strong, fierce when needed
Protective,
But warm and playful
Daddy huggy daddy squeezy
G'night I love you
Boo-Boo Pickle
Forever over my heart

The upper right corner of the heart featured the letter *R* in gold, inscribed on the page of a large open book. Robert, my Golden Boy, the deep thinker whose theories about the world are always well processed yet stored safely within the protective confines of his ample mind. He who figures things out, whose intellectual capacity is matched only by his compassion for, and loyalty to, those he loves. His passion for books, and academics in general, is for him a reward in itself. His book is not just any book, but an enormous, handsomely bound volume, beset by warm candlelight, full of mystique and character. A book one might see resting on a grand mahogany table in the Gryffindor common room.

Absorbing the soft, permanent light of knowledge
Pursuing the noble chalice of wisdom
Gently glowing brilliant
The boy in a corner, quietly diligent
Knows more, speaks less
Golden forever in my heart

In the upper left was a purple rose, its green shoots entwining a lavender letter *H*. Hannah, my Sweet Pea, whose compassion for humanity reflects a mere glimpse of her inner beauty. Full of animation and vigor, her delicate flower brightens the days of all those blessed to be near her. She has always been of help to others, reaching out to those in need. As she grows stronger by the day, roots firm and where they belong, her pristine face looks to the cloud kingdom.

Sweet Pea into lavender rose
Face to the sky
Roots in hardy soil
Beautifying the world
Planted forever in my soul

No matter how my story ended, my children were now etched over my heart, forever.

CHAPTER 15

IMPLOSION DAY

It was a crisp, sunny autumn morning outside, yet my darkness was absolute; I was enshrouded in the kind of pitch black a windowless basement room could provide. Not a glimmer of light, not an outline of a shadow, nothing. I was lying supine with my head on the pillow, trembling and sweating on my bed of nails in the downstairs playroom. I was desperate, begging for any escape from my subterranean alcoholic prison cell, any hope of a breakout. My cellmate, a near-empty plastic jug of vodka, owned me. I was its bitch. Valium, the other dude who shared me, was just one cell over. For years they took turns on me, occasionally double-teaming me. Even my daily runs at this point were nothing more than brief respites inside the prison yard's high walls and razor wire. It was a life sentence; there was no escape.

We had created the beautiful downstairs space for the kids to safely play. Years before, when they were younglings, after we had completed the family room addition off the kitchen to accommodate our growing clan, we took a dank, unused cellar and converted it into a bright, colorful playroom with all the feel of a kindergartner's dream. It was a place where Robert diligently constructed his Lego creations—cubes and pyramids with repeating color patterns—a place where Hannah assembled her Barbies for reenactments of *High School Musical*. Toby, when he wasn't launching himself off the bed and onto my back, joined in with whatever his brother and sister were engaged in. The flat-screen TV mounted to the wall was ideal for our video games—*Feeding Frenzy* and *Just Dance* to name two. Sometimes we would simply chill in front of (yet another) *Star Wars* episode. In a far corner was the treadmill, where I forced myself to put in some cardio time on snowier mornings.

If the kids got sick overnight with a fever or vomiting, they would wander down and ask to sleep next to me on the pullout of the room's trundle bed (I was long out of the master bedroom by this point in the marriage). I would get out the spare linens and cover it for them as they settled in; on the nightstand between us, I placed Tylenol, juice, a vomit pail, or whatever might be called for. This was my nighttime basement daddyhood commitment.

One weekend every February the room was converted from playroom into a workshop where the children and I filled cardboard boxes with supplies, food, and medicine for my Haiti medical missions. They would carefully select from their ample collection of toys which ones to donate to the far less privileged children of *Eglise de L'Arrière Saison & Orphelinat*. Every year, I found myself moved by their overtures of generosity.

But that fateful November day, all those memories were way beyond the event horizon of my mind. The room *that* day was nothing more than a cold, empty, childless place, dark as a starless winter night, and I was entombed there inside my chemical prison. Earlier that morning, I went on what would be my final run as a resident there, ending my presence in our dream home of fifteen years and the place where we raised our three babies.

I had shuffled out a single mile, arriving at the 7-Eleven, which was on the corner of the main road. I chose my destination carefully, fully realizing that Virginia law permitted the resumption of customer alcohol purchases daily at six o'clock in the morning. I had timed my run to get there right on schedule. I used the leash to tie up Tiberius, my trusty running companion, to a guard rail, uncomfortably close to the morning road traffic. He must have been thinking, *What the hell?* or the German shepherd equivalent, as I made my way into the store to buy three mini Bootleggers. I stood there in the checkout line, in full cold-weather running attire, attempting to hide my purchase from the morning work crowd with their coffees and breakfast sandwiches. How pathetic I must have appeared.

I emerged with my booty, untied Tiberius, and began the shuffle back home, dog leash in one hand, clinking bag of bottles in the other, trying to put some distance between us and the busy intersection before unscrewing the first cap. I raised the bottle to my lips and guzzled all eight ounces of green liquid, tossing the empty into a ditch.

It was still dark, and after making sure the coast was clear of all headlights, I pulled out the second, unscrewed the cap, and drained it as well. The apple flavor was sweet to the point of sickening. I flung bottle number two into the darkness, hearing it land off in some dried leaves. We resumed our trip back home, walking so that I could take an occasional gulp from the third bottle in between passing cars. I nursed the final bottle, finishing up just before we arrived at the driveway entrance. Empty bottle number three was chucked across the road without a second thought. On an empty stomach, the buzz would get me through breakfast and the school bus send-off. Then I would grab my reserve—the partial fifth hidden in my truck's toolbox, my emergency rations. After that, I was tapped out; I had no plan.

She was done with me, and deep down I couldn't blame her. After the kids were off to school, she confronted me about the bottles of wine she kept on hand for company in the garage. During the days I swore off vodka, I was routinely nipping from them, replacing what I had consumed in the bottles with tap water from the garage sink's faucet. I would never permit any bottle's fluid level to noticeably dip, but that mattered not; apparently my secret was out. In reality, who was I kidding? Even the most novice wine drinker would be able to notice the difference between a bold, earthy cabernet and the diluted purple mixture in those bottles. I fooled nobody but myself; I literally was turning wine into water. *Does that make me the Antichrist?*

I was deep down the badger hole, well past the point of no return, and knew it. So did my wife, who used that morning as an opportunity to inform me we were finished as a married couple. "At this point I am only around for the children." She told me this in the harshest of tones as I slumped, head down and cross-legged, on the hardwood in the foyer, sulking and wallowing in my own pathetic self-pity.

As a child, she had been the victim of an alcoholic, drug-abusing monster of a father; her pent-up rage finally exploded and she hit me with everything she had. It was pointless to respond, and I chose instead to affix my gaze on the floor as I took my beating. The words came at me forcefully and emphatically, eventually tapering. Her definitive closing statement was all that I really needed to remember. "We are finished." Drinking was my problem, and she told me to go get help, to get treatment for my own good and maybe the good of the children, but she had washed her hands of me. Upon completing her proclamation, she put on her coat and left the house. That was the last time I was ever alone with her.

▲▲▲▲▲

As I tossed uncomfortably in bed, gripping my last cheap plastic vodka bottle, my hand hit something smooth and glassy, suddenly illuminating the space near my head. My cell phone was next to me. Sitting up, I grabbed it, holding it up in front of my face. I could no longer tolerate being alone in this frigid abyss; I suspected these might become my final hours on this planet. I scrolled phone numbers, picked one, and called, not knowing who, but it didn't matter. I left a voicemail. "Please. Help me." I scrolled more. I saw the names of friends and family. More drunk dials. I saw my doctor's office number and tapped it. After ringing twice I heard a female voice recording offering me options, followed by the universal suggestion: "If this is a medical emergency, please hang up and dial 911."

Fuck.

I saw my brother-in-law's name; he had recently lost his father as well. I tapped his number and blurted a voicemail. Who knows what I said. I saw my sister's name. I called. More voicemail.

Please Sooz, pick up, please. It is so dark Sooz, please I need to talk . . . so cold and dark . . . Dad is dead, underground and alone in a coffin, and I barely remember.

▲▲▲▲▲

The day I got the call about my father's death, they sent me home early. By the grace of God, Tom happened to be working alongside me that afternoon and volunteered to cover my patients. The call had come in from my brother, Alex. I had been expecting it for weeks. I'd made many trips north, usually by train so I could drink on the way up, to meet my brother and stepmom at the hospital. Only six months earlier, Dad was still commuting into Manhattan from New Jersey for work. But his illness, held in check for years thanks to great specialists and cutting-edge pharmaceuticals, began to rapidly accelerate over that summer. His myelodysplasia had plagued him for years, but he soldiered on. "I'll retire when I'm dead," he had always confided to me.

My dad, who had been self-sufficient on the streets of New York from the time he was a young boy and who had created a thriving business from nothing, was in his final throes of life. I found it bitterly ironic that, for a long stretch of years, he lived as a vegetarian and marathon runner. He believed in neither religion nor a spiritual afterlife, choosing instead to practice a wholesome lifestyle to reduce his chances of premature heart disease, cancer, and death. The common pathologies of modern living he managed to avoid, only to find himself succumbing in the end to a very rare bone marrow condition.

I sat with Dad in his hospital room as he wasted away, no longer able to walk and barely able to speak. My once robust father was now an anemic shadow of his former self, and during those last days, I remained at his bedside, helping him sip juice or fetching his bedpan. I took on the role of medical liaison to the family when the doctors made rounds, helping to translate and interpret what they were conveying for my stepmother, Celia, and anyone else around. My runs to New York were usually a single night, sometimes two, after which I would take the train back home and sober up in time for work. The last time I saw him, he was a sunken and unmoving skeleton in the hospital bed, profoundly cachectic and in extremis, a hint of the man he had been even a month prior. His eyes beckoned me to come near; I put my ear against his lips, and he said to me, "I have nothing." I responded, "You have your wife and children, and we all love you." With effort he whispered back, "I love you too." A week later my brother called me in between patients in the ER. Our father had died.

The funeral was to be a few days later, in keeping with the Jewish tradition of burial as soon as possible after death. I would make the trip from Virginia to New Jersey alone; my wife and children would not be in attendance, because, as it was explained to me, school was in session. I didn't complain or resist when informed this would be a solo trip; on the contrary, the alcoholic in me welcomed the opportunity to go alone and drink the way I wanted to, the way I felt I *needed* to, safely away from my children and wife.

During the 350-mile drive I drained my first pint of vodka. There was no way I would be handling this event sober for even a single minute. While in attendance, I remained intoxicated, finding a steady state of emotional anesthesia comforting as I ministered my dad's graveside eulogy. I have no recollection of what I said. Was I fooling anybody? Did anyone notice or care? Did I care? I vaguely recall shaking hands afterward with an old high school pal, Scott, who was kind enough to make it to the funeral and pay his respects. It was about the only solid memory I could clearly recall that day.

During my stay in New Jersey, I threw empty bottles from the windows of moving cars, hurled them into the Shrewsbury River from the back deck of my stepmother's house, and even shoved one into well-manicured shrubbery. I have no memory of getting home to Virginia, yet somehow, miraculously, I did so without killing myself or anyone else on the road. Never once did I even consider the thousands of families on the interstate whose lives I could have destroyed in a millisecond. I was operating in full-blown egoic, fuck-the-world mode.

▲▲▲▲▲

I was empty, spent, finished, tapped out. Stick a fork in me, I was done. This was the end; I had arrived at my proverbial jumping-off point.

After the funeral I somehow managed to stagger another two weeks or so in the outside world, but my death spiral, accelerated by my father's death and sealed that morning by my wife's end-of-marriage proclamation, had finally become an unstoppable freefall. By a quirk of fate, my work schedule had been light, and I managed in those last days to sober up just enough for the shifts I did work to make it through the shift. Coffee, showers, and maximum avoidance of people sustained me. I managed to miss both Hannah's and Robert's birthdays, remaining sublevel, claiming "illness." When the house was empty, I snuck away to the ABC store and loaded up with as much vodka as I could, staying in the dark basement and blackout drinking, desperately trying to numb a deep, agonizing, bottomless pain. It was never that I stopped caring; that would, in a sense, have been a blessing. I cared so much about my family, just not about myself. My self-created alcoholic lockup progressed from low-security county jail to federal penitentiary, and finally to supermax solitary confinement in the bowels of *Shawshank Redemption* hell. For days on end I gulped room-temperature vodka from the plastic bottles in my black basement of oblivion. Drinking enough lessened the agony . . .

. . . until it didn't.

I hit a point where alcohol no longer did what it was supposed to do. When I was getting no relief from the bottle, yet couldn't conceivably stop drinking, I was out of options. I hit a dead end. There was only one way out.

That final day, the last bottle was emptied, and although still drunk, I wasn't nearly drunk *enough*. I was already experiencing the shakes and racing heart, sweats, and panic of a declining blood alcohol level. I prayed for the end. My brother-in-law had called me back.

"Soldier on," was his advice to me.

Did I respond? Did I cry? Probably, although I have no recollection. Memories and hallucinations ebbed and flowed, morphing together into unreality; people and situations from my past and present whipped through my brain like a violent thunderstorm, never sticking around long enough to keep me company.

I rolled out of my sarcophagus and onto the Berber carpet. I recall being on all fours, covered in gooseflesh, and crawling into the bathroom. The linoleum was cold. I stopped in front of the sink, kneeling, eye level with the undercabinet— that storage area where people keep cleaning supplies, random bathroom needs, and other forgettable items. I opened up the door and through the hazy vision of my half reality, spotted the rubbing alcohol.

▲▲▲▲▲

I grew up in a multicultural home, and remember being present, as a young boy, for many festive evenings where my family threw dinner parties with European flair. My mother and stepdad enjoyed entertaining, and their hearty gatherings were so much more than polite table chat over pot roast and Bundt cake. The evenings were complete fiestas, with food, nostalgic stories, and group singing from the moment the doorbell rang until deep into the night. As a twelve-year-old afraid of his own shadow, I found comfort in the jubilant atmosphere. Guests were often lifelong friends of my stepfather, whom my sister and I called Pop, to distinguish him from our father, who was Dad. He was born in Greece but immigrated to America at age fourteen as a refugee of war. He worked hard, spent two years in the army, operated his own delicatessen, and became a naturalized U.S. citizen. Many of our houseguests, unsurprisingly, had last names ending with "opoulos" or "idis." Mom prepared ample old-country cuisine, and the laughing, drinking, and singing lasted well into the wee hours of the morning.

The men drank beer and slammed shots of ouzo; the ladies sipped homemade sangria. In the European style, alcoholic beverages were available to us children not as some special treat but simply as part of the culture. I regarded beer as "soda for grownups," occasionally sampling, but usually opting for a nice cold Coke. I tasted the ouzo but was not a big fan of licorice, so I generally stayed away.

In this regard, adult beverages never seemed in the least bit taboo. I was routinely offered a beer at family dinner, but I rarely accepted, and even when I did, I never finished an entire glass, never experienced the alcohol's effects. I found the taste agreeable enough, and as a preadolescent, it made me feel like part of the adult world. It made me feel accepted, something I never felt outside the house.

The sangria, which was served on nights of entertainment, was different. Rather than a boring yellow or brown, it was eye-catching red or pink. It was served in a decorative bowl, ladled into a fancy crystal cup. Sometimes it was more punch-like, with pink foam, strawberries, or sherbet floating on its surface. It was so sweet and tasty; it felt like I was drinking liquid unicorn. In later years, when I was in college, I would reproduce the recipe for our fraternity cocktail parties, enticing coeds to overindulge; my college girlfriend Kim referred to it as the "fruity, punchy drink lure."

Unbeknownst to Mom and Pop, I drank the concoction heartily, and since everyone else was preoccupied in the dining room or around the piano, no one seemed to notice my degree of consumption. I remember the warm, spinny, happy sensation it provided, and how it transformed my tiny, insignificant, fearful self into somebody bigger, stronger, and braver. I was sure my mother had stumbled upon a recipe from a secret government science lab. I wished the school bullies were around so I could inflict upon them a sangria-powered smackdown.

Sangria was my childhood happy juice and power potion all in one, liberating me from an otherwise anxious and terrifying existence.

▲▲▲▲▲

There was no sangria in the bathroom cabinet under the sink on Implosion Day, only the gray plastic bottle of antiseptic with the skull and crossbones on the label, sitting unceremoniously among the toilet bowl cleaner, bleach, and empty bottles of Listerine (which I had long ago guzzled down). At that moment, I realized rubbing alcohol *was* sangria, finally unmasked to reveal its true identity and intent, much like the handsome, well-dressed, charismatic devil in a horror movie, whose hideous physical form is only revealed at the end. By this point in my life, alcohol was alcohol, and the only thing that mattered was that the bottle was full and in front of me.

I needed to sleep; I was due to report for a shift in a few hours. I laughed to myself at the absurdity of that thought as I kneeled there, sweaty and unwashed, in my collapsing netherworld. I reached for the bottle and unscrewed the top. The vapors reminded me of the pediatrician's office when I was a kid and about to get a shot—old men with white coats and stern, wrinkled faces. Now I was the one with the white coat, but instead of wiping clean a child's arm with a cotton ball soaked in it, I would be swallowing it. I tricked myself into believing that the shaking would end, that I could simply close my eyes and rest and in an hour or two, wake up feeling refreshed and head on in to the hospital to play the good doctor for those in need. After, I'd come home and be a good dad.

I put the open top against my lips and as I did so many times with my cheap vodka, upended the bottle. It came so easy. The smell was powerful and initially noxious, but I managed several large gulps.

Just sangria from my childhood in an alternate form.

My esophagus spontaneously combusted as if I had downed molten lava. My gut was long accustomed to hard liquor on an empty stomach, so it did not rebel. I found myself pleased, in a twisted way, at keeping down what would become, to this day, the last alcoholic beverage I would ever drink.

The bathroom swooned around me; I felt my body and mind relax and go limp, all the evils in my thoughts flowing out of my toes. Now I could rest; there was that fuzzy bathmat, placed under my knees just for me, a nice spot where I could lay my head down and sleep. When I woke up, all the pain would be gone and I would be refreshed and alive atop my winged unicorn, swooping in to assume my rightful place in the cloud kingdom as the perfect doctor, husband, and dad. For all eternity.

The black fog descended.

▲▲▲▲▲

A dog is barking. Is it outside? No, probably closer, it just sounds so . . . distant, like in some neighbor's backyard. Except the bark sounds too familiar. It's Molly, our other family dog. She's here, sniffing me, licking my face. It stopped. I never saw her. Was she truly here? It must have been my dream. I hear screaming, muffled. Maybe it is me screaming, but it sounds female, from the throat of a woman I know.

I feel hands on me, large hands, a big man's hands, holding me, shifting me. A deep southern voice telling me to calm down. My eyes open. I know his face. He looks like my neighbor, Deputy Swoops, the one married to nurse Belinda.

"Settle down," he orders. *Am I screaming? Is everyone? Just who is everyone?*

It is a foggy, crowded room, my bathroom, uniformed men everywhere, moving in and out of my echo tunnel's view. An orange backboard appears in the doorway, just like the ones EMS uses for traumas in the field. I loved being medical director of the county's EMS, teaching the medics or bringing them to the kids' school for ambulance demonstrations. Maybe I'm on a ride-along now. I loved taking my children to the rescue squad building, where they would volunteer as mock victims for trainees to learn proper pediatric spinal immobilization. *Am I teaching EMS?* Probably not, because I'm on my back and my armpits and balls are soaked. I hear even more men, different men, again telling me to calm down. *I'm not calm?* I am fading and the fog is once again getting heavy.

▲▲▲▲▲

"Room twelve."

Fucking room twelve.

I scream something. I am in perpetual motion, rolling, squirming, the Velcro spider straps holding me supine. There is more clarity in my vision now. I recognize this ceiling as no longer my bathroom. These walls, the beeping and buzzing, the lights. I am at work.

Holy shit. I am at work, but I don't think I drove here, because I am strapped to a fucking backboard like some goddamn lowlife—the 3 a.m. kind I would usually scoff at. I recognize faces I am passing—the charge nurse. *Are they going to keep me in four-point restraints? Intubate me? Defibrillate me after bilateral tube thoracostomy? Or even worse . . . place a Foley catheter?! Holy shit!*

I scream and struggle as they roll me into room twelve. I look up and see good ol' nurse Eileen. Her face displays a combination of shock, pity, and disgust. It is the perfect reflection of *This is what you have come to, Dr. Joseph David Remy.*

My mind flashes back.

▲▲▲▲▲

It was twenty years earlier, a Sunday morning, and I was relaxing with my wife in our new home, lounging on the sofa; the place was way too big for just the two of us, but we had negotiated a great deal on the price from desperate sellers. With no kids and few responsibilities, we could spend my whole day off just lying around, reading, and planning our next vacation, maybe a cruise. The *Washington Post* was spread out; I had the sports section; she, the food section. The corner TV displayed the usual array of talking heads on *Meet the Press*, volume turned down. We were in a cocoon of comfort, not a care in the moment, still aglow in our post-honeymoon bliss.

"Who is Eileen?"

The question startled me, like a wasp sting on the back of my scalp. I looked up from the NFL scores. "She's one of the nurses I work with in the emergency department. Why?" Just as the response left my lips, I had a flash, and it immediately occurred to me exactly why she'd asked.

"Because you shouted her name out last night in your sleep. A couple of times."

The dream, which had begun to fade, rushed back into my head, in all its horrid detail.

I was brought into the department by rescue squad, wheeled into the resuscitation room, supine on a backboard. The hard plastic endotracheal tube stretched my vocal cords, keeping them apart, making any attempt at sound futile. Its tip was tickling my carina—that spot where the trachea branches into the two mainstem bronchi serving to carry air to each lung. Although I was "fully awake" and could feel everything,

I couldn't move, not an eyelash. The medics must have intubated me in the field using a paralytic without pairing it with a sedative—a very cruel no-no in the world of emergency medicine. I could feel every blast of the bag-valve device as a pair of meaty hands squeezed far too much oxygen into my chest.

I taught them better than that in skills drill, to squeeze the bag gently, evenly, slowly. Have they learned nothing?

At the peak, each forced breath overstretched my lungs like a party balloon about to burst.

Good ol' nurse Eileen was assigned to the room to run the code blue. Her face displays a combination of shock, pity, and disgust. *This is what you have come to, Dr. Joseph David Remy.* She sported an emaciated frame; the two defibrillation paddles she held made her look like she had Mickey Mouse hands. She planted them on my exposed torso, one just to the right of my sternum, the other just under my left rib cage, exactly as I had instructed her back in ACLS class. The stainless steel felt icy cold on my skin. I braced and waited for the lightning bolt to sear my brain, and my body convulsed.

Please, stop, I am awake. I have a pulse, I am awake, I feel this.

The well-secured plastic breathing tube violated my airway, making my scream impossible. Eileen looked down on me with fleeting concern. In the periphery of my vision I could see a hive of nurses, techs, and EMS personnel buzzing about; some were stone faced, some smirking, some just pointing and whispering. There was no doctor in the room because it was me scheduled for that particular shift, and well, here I was.

"Charge to 360, again." *Damn, she doesn't even have the courtesy to use the new biphasic Zoll machine?* She again dug the paddles firmly into my chest. This time they were searing hot, like a couple of irons. I was being branded like a steer on a ranch, about to get the next electric punch in the heart.

Please, not again, I thought at her.

This time she looked me straight in the eyes, grinned sadistically, and in a relaxed, almost patronizing voice, recited the emergency provider's universal motto: "I'm clear, you're clear, everybody's clear." *Pow!* Lightning blew apart my head; my back arched involuntarily and then collapsed onto the board.

The pain stopped. Suddenly I was calm, almost peaceful. I felt the lights in the room dim. Eileen was the team leader in my own extra-special code blue, and her expression now morphed into one of compassion, almost love. Her face transformed into my wife's. My gut went hollow; I knew what was coming next. Her statement was calm and monotone, as if in a trance.

"No pulse . . . asystole . . . discontinue efforts. Time of death: 15:35."

But, but . . . I felt alive, awake. I was still thinking, still feeling, still trying to move as the staff slowly filed out of the room as if departing a wake. A plastic sheet was being pulled up over me, briefly stopping at my chin.

Please, I'm still alive! Don't give up on me!

My wife-nurse stood momentarily in the trauma bay's doorway. Then she slowly turned away, reached to the wall, flipped off the light switch, and walked out, shutting the door behind her. The sheet went over my face, and all was black and forgotten, save for a long-dormant twenty-year-old dream, resurrected on Implosion Day.

▲▲▲▲▲

I was a patient in my own ER, my senses fading in and out, writhing uncomfortably in my own vomit and urine on a stretcher in room twelve, intermittently looking at Eileen, babbling, and shouting at anyone passing the door. Was I a Glasgow Coma Scale of fourteen? Thirteen? Less? Although I was aware of my location, I was completely detached from the implications of the situation, as no rational cohesive thoughts had any hope of coalescing in my churning, spinning brain. A fat, ugly head floated above me, obscuring my view of the ceiling, and I tensed when I recognized the face of my attending ER physician. *Lovely*, I thought. *It had to be this jerk.* The biggest asshole on the medical staff, and he was going to be the one in charge of my care for all the world to see. I thought I was going to lose my very last marble.

"JD, we're gawna git a CT scan of yawr heyd." His Forrest Gump drawl grated on me. I nodded OK to him while thinking, *Fuck you, you arrogant, narcissistic prick. My life is officially shit, it's game over. So fuck you.* Then, thankfully, he was gone.

▲▲▲▲▲

I was taken to the computerized tomography suite, received my scan, and was wheeled back to room twelve. Nurses and techs came and went. The next doctor in the admission process, one of the hospitalists (physicians who take all hospital admissions), came in to take my history. *(My history?! Ha!)* It was Dr. Black. I liked and respected him enormously as a practitioner and as a colleague. He was always professional to me when I called him for a patient requiring admission. Intelligent, efficient, and meticulous, he possessed a gentle, caring bedside manner. As we spoke, I felt a drop of warmth in my otherwise cold, swampy blood. He entered my admission orders into the bedside computer, and a short time later an orderly whisked me out of the emergency department and upstairs.

None of this life-saving crap mattered, because my life was completely fucked. My health, marriage, family life, and career—everything I held sacred—was destroyed, and it was me who destroyed them. Gone forever.

Dr. Remy, your bottom called; it said thanks for landing on it so squarely.

▲▲▲▲▲

I was brought upstairs to a floor bed and placed on IV medication drips, mainly tranquilizers. Nurses checked on me; techs took my vital signs. I asked them what pharmaceutical regimen I was receiving, but nobody gave me a straight answer. I had been assigned "sitters"—people who stayed in the room with me, sitting in a corner chair to monitor my behavior, lest I try to elope or kill myself. These were usually young women, and I remember engaging in pointless conversation with them during my rare lucid moments.

The next morning, as my medical condition stabilized, the on-call psychiatrist, Dr. Mohammad, arrived for consultation. I had known him only peripherally from staff meetings and casual interactions in the physicians' lounge. He was a calm man with a relaxed face and had a solid reputation among his colleagues. He sat and interviewed me; I have absolutely zero recollection of our conversation. What I do remember is that he recommended intensive therapy and treatment for my alcoholism and chemical dependency in an environment my hometown hospital could not provide. He departed my room, tasked with finding such a place for me. One thing had been made crystal clear: there was going to be no discharge to home. Home for me had vanished, and I'd left forever, never to return, in the most dramatic and deplorable possible way: unconscious, in the back of an ambulance.

▲▲▲▲▲

She entered the room unceremoniously that next morning, carrying only a small tote of overnight needs and her trademark stony expression. She didn't need to speak a word; all conversations had since ended. In twenty-three years of being together, our marriage had survived the scorn of parents who opposed our engagement, a medical residency in inner-city Baltimore, a near-failed adoption, difficult pregnancies, and her stint at a trauma center after being hit by a truck while bike riding. It would not survive this. November 4, 2016, my sobriety date, was also the last *real* day of our marriage, consisting of her brief appearance in my hospital room to drop off a toothbrush, socks, and underwear. Then she was gone.

Other visitors came. Pastor Janice, with whom I made many Haiti mission trips, sat with me and imparted her soothing prayers and love upon my raw, tender soul. As long as I had known her, she had served as a wonderful spiritual presence for me. Two days after Kidney Stone Lady died her septic death, I remember phoning Janice. I called drunk, from an Atlantic City hotel room, a bottle of Grey Goose barely making a dent in my anguish. Her words had settled me, allowing me to sober up just long enough to make the drive back home. In Haiti, she, along with her pastor husband, Harry, and the other missionaries would gather nightly with the orphaned children for play, song, and laughter. If there is a heaven, she is the embodiment of it. Her mere presence at my hospital bed raised me up oh-so-slightly off my bottom. She was my elven charm as I lay wasted in Mordor.

Tom also came, along with Marcus, another ER colleague and friend. Although the details of the conversation still elude me, I remember breaking down and bawling uncontrollably before the two of them, no longer caring about holding back. It might have been the hardest I have ever cried in my entire life, and Tom, normally not the emotional type, gave me a giant bear hug, which only caused me to sob harder. They were my dear friends (and still are to this day), and I was blessed to have them in my life. Tom, Marcus, Finn, Pastor Janice, Darryl, and so many others from my "before" life sustained and supported me in my "after" life. They, along with my friends in recovery, represent the core group of my recovery mosh pit.

▲▲▲▲▲

The transport crew arrived to take me away, looking very official in their neatly pressed company uniforms and matching caps. I recognized them from my EMS medical director days—many of the volunteers in rescue squads parlayed their years of experience running EMS calls into careers in medical transport. Although I had worked with them regularly in training, I had always paid them little mind, usually forgetting faces and names quickly after a practice drill or lecture.

The pair that appeared that fateful day—the day I was to leave my hometown hospital and be admitted into a psychiatric detox unit on the other side of the Commonwealth—I recognized, and I was pleased I did. They were young, fresh faced, and very pleasant. Somehow I absorbed that momentary nice feeling for what it was. Unknown to me, that day was my "white chip" day: day number one of my sobriety and long-term recovery. These two young folks (I could think of them that way, since they were twentysomethings and I was on the cusp of turning fifty) were assigned by their dispatcher—and God—the task of shuttling me out of my old life and into my new one. They shifted me onto their transport stretcher, gently secured the harness, and off we went.

That night I would be locked up in a psych ward for several days, followed by almost three months in an unknown city living among strangers in residential recovery, followed by several more months in yet another city with more strangers at a halfway house. I would have virtually zero contact with my children. I would work for near minimum wage, stocking supermarket shelves, get my dinner from church charities and food pantries, fraternize with society's downtrodden, and listen to fellow alcoholics' accounts of pain, misery, and anguish on a daily basis.

I learned to distinguish between pain and suffering, and to live my life as a single man, unmarried, functionally childless. I diligently worked the Twelve Steps of AA with four different sponsors, studied the *Big Book*, and cultivated a wonderful sober network of friends. I lived one day at a time and learned how to better handle irrational, ego-driven fear. I accepted that I must abandon the illusion of control and let God do the job I never could. I learned to ask for help—and help was provided in many ways, including from a dear friend who gave me a room in his house. I played my guitar, learned how to date, jumped out of airplanes, and braved a return to the medical specialty I so love.

In divorce, I remained true to my fourth step, looking for defects in myself rather than assigning blame to my ex-spouse. When she moved beyond simply divorcing me and attempted to destroy me, I prayed for her, asking my Higher Power what I could do to ease her burden. I remained true to myself by being a complete provider to her and the kids, yet stood up for myself when it was called for.

I continue to recognize that I absolutely cannot do any of this alone, that without my program and my network, surviving what I endured while staying sober would have been impossible. With assistance from them and my Higher Power to guide me, I have received three sobriety anniversary chips, have been invited to speak at AA meetings as well as my treatment center, and wrote this book.

I do not know what the future holds and will not waste energy predicting it; doing so is a futile, quasi-insane, ego-driven exercise that takes me out of the present. I have already lived in a resentful past and a fearful future. Regardless of my route, here I am, in the *now*, exactly where I am supposed to be.

Thy will, not my will. The future will take care of itself. I will see the fruits of my effort when I make good, sound decisions today—in the moment—divinely inspired and unrushed. My life's event horizon extends out only as far as bedtime tonight.

After much effort, patience, and twenty-four-hour sober cycles, when I have achieved a certain degree of spiritual maturity, I will commit myself to living Step Twelve and helping other alcoholics and addicts.

After we put in our work, practice the Steps, and attend daily meetings, "we rise"—as my old sponsor Doug put it—"to become servants of our fellow humans." This is the place where true peace of mind exists, the greatest gift. Living outside the prison cell of my own cranium and offering myself to the service of others is a blessing beyond blessings. This is where the ego is defeated and love and compassion can be unleashed on the world. Eternal acceptance, eternal gratitude.

CHAPTER 16

BIG HITTER, THE LAMA

I graduated from medical school deep in debt, with zero in savings and a credit score in the toilet; over the years, I had spent and charged myself to a financial bottom. It took decades of hard work and self-discipline to save what I could and square up with my creditors, until I was finally able to create some net worth and become loan worthy to banks. Financial trust took time. The transition happened slowly and almost imperceptibly, glacier-like. During the comeback I opted for peanut butter sandwiches over dinner out, Folgers drip instead of fancy lattes.

My spiritual growth appeared to follow the same basic formula. By the autumn of 2016, I was morally bankrupt, deep in spiritual debt, and completely unworthy of humanity's trust. A cold, sharp bottom and near-death experience was the only life event capable of shocking me to my core, propelling me into turning my life around. Although my comeback has been a measured success so far, I am nowhere close to attaining the level of emotional sobriety I aspire to or believe I am capable of. My life is a one-day-at-a-time program, a series of single-serving mini-lives I call days. I am guided by a set of self-evident truths I must follow, a hard-learned set of principles I adhere to as I trudge the road of happy destiny. Far-off goals make for an entertaining fantasy, but too much preoccupation with future thinking takes me out of my moment, clouding my vision and stillness in the *now*. If I stick to a few simple ideas on a repeating twenty-four-hour loop, I find I get to relish the *now* while simultaneously building spiritual wealth for a joyous and free future:

1. Accept everything, expect nothing. The *Big Book of Alcoholics Anonymous* states that acceptance is the answer to all our problems. When I first read that, I thought, *You've got to be kidding me. I'm supposed to just roll over and take without question the idea that the world can shit on me, and I should not respond?* I now recognize how flawed that initial reaction was. I assumed I was one hundred percent in control and that external events created my emotional disturbances.

I held the position that the world had dumped on me, and I shouldered little or no responsibility for the end-result events.

When I am disturbed, it is because I find some person, place, or situation unacceptable. Destructive thoughts, like a parasite, will crawl into my ear canal and take up residence inside my brain—space that could otherwise be used for more productive thinking, selfless ideas, or just a plain relaxed existence. It is very difficult for anyone who feels wronged to simply accept it—whether they are the alcoholic divorcé, harassed employee, or odd man out. How can I simply accept these injustices without question? It is so much easier for me to act out in self-pity or righteous indignation, to mentally run my own show. If only the world did as it *should*, according to *my* plan.

Nobody ever said that acceptance feels pleasant, or that when immersed in a dark moment, we even have the clarity to understand. Acceptance does not necessarily equate with *agreement* or *resignation*. Nor does acceptance mean we need to sit still and wait around for some magic moment to come along and fix things. Far from it. Sometimes, acceptance means recognizing an opportunity to take action and make a situation better. In other words, in our awakening, we take the chance to move forward.

I live in a universe exponentially bigger than myself, and I must remember this at all times. Centuries ago, the persecution and blood of American patriots gave way to the greatest democracy in the history of the planet; several generations ago, the Holocaust birthed the State of Israel. On an infinitesimally smaller scale, my alcoholic bottom and subsequent series of negative events led me into a solid recovery, a healthier lifestyle, a profession I fell back in love with, and more robust relationships.

My children, although not in my life at the time of this writing, appear to be content and successful, and I am blessed with the opportunity to support them through their adolescence and into adulthood. Whether they choose to continue to exclude me or decide at some point to reach out is their decision and well beyond my control. As much as it still aches to this day, I must let go, accept my reality as it stands, and feel grateful if I am to move toward inner stillness, serenity, and true sobriety.

2. Stick a pin in the ego. We humans take ourselves way too seriously. Our egos are astounding and drive much of our behaviors through the majority of our days. At its core, a strong ego pushed our human survival mechanism, driving us eons ago to act in our own self-interest to acquire food and shelter to ensure our survival, and to attract mates to ultimately

propagate our genetic lineage. This was pretty huge in cave-
man days, but as societies formed, ego took on a life of its own,
extending beyond its intended programming.

Fear is self-centered and ego-based. *I am too important to
die; I need to thrive and procreate, but that can't possibly happen if I am the slowest in the clan fleeing the angry bear. I need
to please my king so I am promoted to officer and don't become
cannon fodder on the battlefield. I need to secure that promotion because I deserve it more than the guy in the opposite cubi-
cle, and I'm behind on my mortgage.*

With the alcoholic and addict (and most of the rest of the
world, I suspect), our modern-day living has enabled our egos
to expand well beyond their original utility of survival to literally take over our lives. We believe life is completely ours to
run, and that anyone or anything that detracts from our version of the way the world *should* be is an impediment and needs
to be dismissed or discarded. *If only my boss/family/committee
saw things my way and acted accordingly, things would go much
smoother!* Really? As an ego-driven alcoholic, my "best" thinking won me a trip to the hospital, rehab center, and divorce
court. This is because when the world didn't behave according
to my master plan (which was daily), I would immerse myself
in my character defects (self-pity, self-righteous indignation,
passive-aggressive behavior), which would inevitably lead to
a sense of imagined entitlement, followed by "well-deserved"
liquid therapy.

We need to get honest with ourselves. Ego-driven pleasure and self-seeking are not the paths to serenity. Feeding the
ego—even under the pretense of humanitarian causes, such as
running a charity—temporarily activates our pleasure centers
by creating a contrived sense of overimportance. Like a drink
or drug, the temporary high achieved inevitably leads to lower
lows, prompting us to seek out even larger ego-boosters. In the
end, we sacrifice enduring serenity for the fleeting euphoria of

temporary gratification. We sell ourselves short for personal gain and pleasure; developing a habit of true selflessness falls by the wayside.

Behaviors seen by the outside world as charitable can be, at their core, narcissistic endeavors dressed up as altruism. I have traveled many times to Haiti in the name of charity— ostensibly for a noble cause: the welfare of an impoverished rural orphanage and the surrounding village. While the service to humanity was a motivation, even my primary reason for going, it eventually morphed into an ego-driven exercise. *Dr. Remy's famous merry medical mission band.* At what point the primary purpose shifted from selfless charity work to feeding my ego is hard to say, but it happened, and although the recipients did still benefit, it really did become less about Haitian children and more about *me.*

Look, Facebook people! Look, world! I'm cool as shit!

Living for praise is empty and self-destructive. I needed to be relieved of the bondage of self. What I ultimately learned and have come to practice is to first pause and do a motivational gut check before acting. What are the true motivations behind my actions? The welfare of others or my own aggrandizement? The gut-check exercise comes in very handy when practiced daily and is an often-used tool in my recovery toolbox. I use it routinely before opening my mouth or acting. It takes effort, but in the end, it is far more satisfying in a deeper way, an honest way.

3. Embrace the suck. Life can suck. Sometimes it sucks a little; sometimes, massively. Whether our car won't start in cold weather before an important meeting, or we wake up one morning in a lockup psychiatric ward listening to schizophrenics reading Bible passages, life suckage seems only to ebb and flow but never completely cease. Of course, we humans overdramatize this. When a squirrel in the forest faces a sucky situation, its fight-or-flight response is triggered and it proceeds unimpeded to some end result: momentary safety or death. *Coyote alert, where's the nearest tree? Snow is falling, find the buried nuts.* The whole reaction is reflexive and pure, uncontaminated by excessive human-like thinking.

Because of our overdeveloped, overly survivalist, ego-driven brains, upon facing an adverse or frightening situation, we alcoholics and addicts usually:

1. Panic
2. Engage in self-pity
3. Portray self as victim
4. Blame
5. Drink (or use)

After the initial shock, tremor, and palpitations, we package the problem as unfair, that it somehow "shouldn't be this way." Portraying ourselves as the victim of a situation, we attempt to recruit the sympathies of those around us. *Poor me, poor me . . . pour me a drink.* We lash out, get reactive, cave to our emotions: *Fucking car! Fucking mechanic! Fucking weather app said it would be warmer!* Our overinflated sense of self-importance could have it no other way.

Well, guess what? The universe pays little mind whether we arrive on time to an "important" meeting; it's too busy expanding galaxies and forming black holes. Fourteen billion years after the Big Bang, it doesn't bat an eye at some ER doc pacing the hallways of a mental ward. We humans need to face up to the fact that we are not nearly as integral to the universe as we think we are. Whether we choose to call it the universe, our Higher Power, or God, we just cannot, and should not, attempt to overinflate our importance.

Embracing the suck, experiencing it, and learning to grow from it can be a powerful tool for spiritual enhancement. We can use it to handle difficult situations that might have previously caused us to fold up our tent or just lie in a fetal position, rocking back and forth. Out of our pain, we can transcend the totally unnecessary suffering component, gain confidence in ourselves, and in time, become less fearful.

There couldn't have been a more emotionally devastating event for me than enduring the loss of my children. Given my new, healthier relationship with pain, I am slowly learning to not let the *suck* dominate and own me. Rather, by experiencing and processing, letting go of the fight, I can allow the pain to mature into a force that makes all other nuisances in my life quite insignificant. This is what those in the program refer to as the gift of desperation. It is the gateway through which we find the strength to ask ourselves, *OK, so how can I be better?*

Never in my life did I think I could play guitar in front of others, jump out of a plane, return to my old emergency department, or write a book. Paradoxically, I have newfound gratitude for pain; as my drill instructor and professor, it pushes me to heights I could have never otherwise achieved. I have developed a level of respect for pain so that it does not morph into energy-zapping *suffering*. I cannot cocoon myself from pain inside my blissful little alcoholic comfort zone. Spiritual growth is happening whenever we step outside our self-declared happy spaces. Whether this means finally confronting that domineering coworker, overcoming the fear of vulnerability in a new relationship, or simply stepping onto a roller coaster, spending time in and processing uncomfortable, painful moments expands us, expands our comfort zones, and makes the foreboding landscape outside less scary.

4. Take the plane up in altitude, and expand range. Pushing out the boundaries of our comfort zones through diligent processing of pain and erosion of fear is an incremental process. When I was learning to be a pilot, my instructor told me the most impactful flight training occurs when pushing the envelope, maneuvering the airplane on or beyond the edge of my skill set. Beginning with simple straight-and-level flying, we proceeded to turning, setting up for a landing, and actually landing. After a dozen hours or so, I was ready to solo, flying one lap around the airport alone in the aircraft. We moved on to emergency situations, stalls, off-field emergency landings (aka controlled crashes), and then flying in darkness and clouds. From there we traveled outside our known area to distant airports, then, finally, I was routinely traveling by myself.

In proceeding this way, I pushed out the border of my comfort zone, then stepped just outside it, intentionally making myself uncomfortable as I expanded my technical skills envelope. When I began to feel too far out of my depth, I momentarily retreated back to what I was already confident in doing. Each push-out led to an expanded comfort zone. Had I merely soloed and spent my fly time doing laps around my home airfield on cloudless, no-wind days, there would have been no broadening of my flying world, only stagnation. No flights to visit Mom on Mother's Day or overnight air getaway weekends with the wife to Atlantic City. My symbolic "twenty square feet" of comfort space, at least as far as flying was concerned, became twenty-five, then thirty, then fifty, then one hundred.

There were times when I was flying around the Shenandoah Valley and temporarily lost my way. Needing to recover my bearings and position over the landscape, I learned to simply climb in altitude. Views from the cockpit that seemed foreign or unrecognizable at three thousand feet made more sense when put in perspective from seven thousand; the broader topography allowed me to see exactly where I was and how to proceed. This metaphor applies well to most life situations. Temporary household budget squeezes, petty arguments with loved ones, or project deadlines become immensely less stressful when we mentally ascend to obtain a higher vantage point.

Doing this seems so basic and simple, yet we forget this when immersed, constantly losing the forest for the trees. We fail to put our momentary challenges into a bigger life perspective. Increasing altitude and having a look around make all matters of concern that much less foreboding.

5. Stay in the moment. This takes practice and concentration and more practice, and even as I become proficient at it, I find I can still easily fall back into the past's old resentments, or project myself ahead into a fearful future. One is an old, tired movie; the other, a sick fantasy.

Ruminating over past events, whether from way back in childhood or the previous day, seems to be an American pastime. We routinely use our mental time machines to teleport ourselves back to reflect on happier times in our lives or to relive the painful ones. In doing so, we reexperience some critical moment in our history, subconsciously hoping we can step on a blade of grass, figuratively speaking, to create a more acceptable present outcome. All this does is heap additional unnecessary pain or remorse on the present moment.

While we should never shut the door on the past, we need to accept that it cannot be redone, and that our lives consist of numerous but finite sequences of individual moments, each one decisive, bringing us to exactly where and who we are presently. It can be no other way. If we believe that everything that has happened thus far in our lives is exactly as intended—as was predetermined at the moment of the Big Bang or as was created by God Almighty—then our frustrations dissolve. Living in the past is very different from reflecting on it. Stewing over an agonizing memory is staying trapped in an old movie; the present slips away, never to return—another wasted moment.

In the same way that resentment lives in the past, fear hides in the future. The time machines in our heads are just as effective at transporting our present-day situation into some imagined future as we pile on the what-ifs and create useless and unnecessary worry. This once again steals our moment, drains our *now energy*, and detracts from the only true reality—the present. Our overused time machine can trap us in a contrived, illusionary future that does not truly exist. Projecting about some upcoming family gathering, job interview, or medical exam is nothing more than an exercise in creating mental fiction. In doing so, we permit our fears to dominate our thinking and thus control us. Negative emotions influence our mind-author to write the most frightening scenarios possible, causing us to suffer inside our own dark fables as if they were real. *A coward dies a thousand deaths.*

Newsflash: the future is not what it used to be.

If we view the moments of our lives as individual stand-alone components that cannot be tampered with, like the pieces of some giant, four-dimensional jigsaw puzzle, precut and fitting together perfectly, then we can more easily *stay in the present* and mentally assemble the pieces into a coherent life story, accepting each individual piece as a necessary part of the whole. For me, this opens the door to some semblance of logic in my reality, giving me internal serenity over the whole ball of wax.

6. You can't do this alone. It was not until I completely surrendered and made myself vulnerable before the collective that I reached my emotional bottom and *truly* began my recovery. While it may have been true that I had not had a drink in over a year, my behavior and actions on sobriety day number 365 were still controlled by my old thought patterns, dominated by my character defects—ego, self-pity, blame, justifying, defending, intellectualizing. It was through practicing Step Three, turning over my will and my life to a Higher Power, that I could begin to develop new patterns of thinking and behavior.

This step awakens us to the futility of going it alone, trying to run our own shows. We surrender ourselves to something greater, in whatever form that takes. This transformative decision changes our whole approach to how we live our lives and hence our consuming addictions, whether alcohol, drugs, gambling, shopping, dependency in relationships, power, overeating, pornography, habitual lying, or passive-aggressive behavior. All our egoic thinking over the years landed us in a self-created universe of agony and despair. Our best attempts at exerting willpower over our vices yielded temporary success at most, after which the inevitable relapse occurred. The destructive habit would return, only this time we would be that much more emotionally tapped out and lacking the stamina to try again *alone*.

For ego-driven souls who like to control the world, this gigantic mind shift cannot be understated. It is said the first step is the only one we addicts need to perform perfectly every time in order to experience and maintain true recovery. Admitting "I can't do this alone" and flinging ourselves into the mosh pit of the support crowd can be intimidating for independent minds like ours. But when everything else has failed, is throwing "caution" to the wind really the case? Is it entirely possible that ceding all control, untensing our protective muscles, and collapsing will allow our mosh pit to hold us high and strong, that the relief of no longer having to struggle will paradoxically create a new strength within us? Can we believe in victory through surrender? Letting go to acquire? Eventually those supportive arms might just ease us to the ground so we can be part of them, available to hold up the next desperate mosh-pit jumper in the freedom and safety of the crowd. It takes a village.

7. Not everyone is with you. There will be many people in life who will not be standing below with waiting arms; many won't give a shit; others will be downright hostile. Over time they will reveal themselves. Simply confessing to the world, "I am an alcoholic and in long-term recovery," does not magically convert all to your cause. That is reflective of self-centered, narcissistic thinking, driven by ego.

Many in my local community—piano teachers, summer swim team directors, hospital colleagues, religious leaders, co-parenting counselors, and others—were ambivalent or even resistant in my attempts to reconnect with my children, choosing to see alcoholism as less of a disease and more of a moral failing. They were neither fans nor believers in my spiritual conversion, and it would have been presumptuous and self-centered of me to think so or react. The sooner I let go of trying to convert them to my own higher purpose, the sooner I was able to make peace with them and move on in my recovery, as the fourth step teaches.

I am not on this planet to proselytize. This is a program of attraction, not promotion. I am here to get well and assist others who are ready to do so. The naysayers and detractors, regardless of their own personal demons and addictions, must find their own paths to salvation. Some will and some won't, and my only business with them is to pray for them, as I change myself. If they reach their hand out to me for help, I will respond.

8. Step out of God's way. There are times we are divinely inspired to take action, and there are other times we, well, just stand there and wait. If we can relax our minds, clear the frenetic thoughts, and connect with our spiritual guide, then we soon recognize when to do which. This requires us to improve our conscious contact with our Higher Power. My entire life I found myself running in fifth gear, abandoning my present reality so I could race ahead to make hasty decisions based on an imagined future, one which, as discussed previously, only really existed in my head. I was constantly leapfrogging the *now* in favor of the *what might be*, and found the resultant decisions were bad, made not on immediate, sound facts but on projected, nonexistent, emotional fiction, on ego and fear. I was deaf to the divine message. Once I let go and lived in the present, making only the decisions required *in the present*, then my result was sound. In this way, I felt inspired to make a choice with a mind free of background noise, with an open heart. No decision *needs* to be made, save the one that is two feet in front of me.

9. Be just another bozo on the bus. It feels good to melt into the crowd on the Island of Misfit Toys that saved my life, be one of the collective, relieved of the constant stress of trying to stand out as somehow special or unique. In the end, we are all far more alike than we are different, and dismissing self-importance is a cornerstone of ego destruction, and thus, my recovery. Ego is the archenemy of true sobriety, chemical or emotional. Once we realize we are just not all that fucking special, life gets much easier. As much as our culture encourages us to celebrate our differences, let us not forget to rejoice in our similarities.

▲▲▲▲▲

I have heard it said that when the student is ready, the teacher will appear. When we slow down, stay in the *now*, reduce ego, and calmly float forward into the immediate decisions, inspiration materializes into our field of vision and we gain new understanding, and our days seem to flow more smoothly. Bad, impulsive, emotional decisions based on future projecting will still happen. We are, of course, human. This is a process of spiritual progress, and we will never be perfect. Opportunities for learning and growth will always appear and must be accepted as part of ongoing self-actualization. Growth will always be a "two steps forward, one step back" pattern.

▲▲▲▲▲

The restoration to sanity is an uneven, rocky, unmarked dirt path winding through a thick forest, which must be navigated carefully by those in recovery. We move along like barefoot, vulnerable, but excited children in twilight; the trail is fraught with stones, sharp briars, poisonous berries, and murky mud puddles. Terrifying noises from unseen creatures echo near and far. Images, both imagined and real, flash before our eyes. We trudge this towpath because the spell of the dark magic of addiction has been broken within us, and with every step, we feel our sanity returning, our diseased spirit healing. We move cautiously forward at a pace that suits us, knowing that nothing—absolutely nothing—is as frightening as where we came from. We grow stronger and braver with every passing moment. We have escaped the gates of insanity and death. Hand in hand, we are never alone.

Yea, though I walk through the valley of the shadow of death, I will fear no evil: for thou art with me; thy rod and thy staff they comfort me.

A slip, loss of faith, or return of self-will can be a frustrating setback, and we know we can afford only so many of those, because a return to addiction means almost certain death— and the end of our (improving) lives as we know them. So we right ourselves and march on, noticing a progressive illumination of our surroundings. Yet we understand we will never be completely out of the woods. We so desire immediate glorious sunshine on day one—our impatience demands it—but we come to understand that *time takes time.* Our journey is a thousand miles of single steps. Slowly, the sunshine of the spirit breaks through the thick overhead canopy, and we learn how to be happy, joyous, and free, regardless of external factors, the world of the "not me." Acceptance and gratitude support us on either side; pain pushes gently from the rear to keep us moving. Ego grows weaker, falling behind, and fear and resentment fade into the thicket. Our disease becomes less noisy, and eventually goes dormant. We keep on keeping on, as the flames of our baby souls grow hotter and stronger.

EPILOGUE

I am on my knees, literally.

The frigid, unrelenting January wind bites my face. There are no trees to block it, no screen of any sort to protect the open field as I kneel here, motionless in the deceptively cold afternoon sunshine. The golf bag lies on its side in front of me. I have not dumped out its contents—yet.

It is day 1,173 since my last drink, since Implosion Day. I chose this day because it feels right; the decision floated down from above: today, now. Still, I pause. *Just breathe,* someone once texted me, so I do.

Move through your fears, isolate them, make space around them. They will exhaust their fuel supply and self-extinguish.

My sponsors instructed me to feel the pain—experience it, process it, and then move along, leaving it dormant and power-less in a past that no longer exists. Only I can revive it by pull-ing it back into the present, this pain-monster. I imagine this is much like how Frodo Baggins, his shoulder still aching four years after having been stabbed by a Ringwraith's blade, must have felt. *Observe it, then let it go.* I reach for the bag, pull it toward me, and stand it vertically, as if in direct confrontation.

It had been stored just a few paces away at Finn's place all this time, even though for two full years I have been settled in my own house. I had delayed retrieving it—somewhat out of laziness, but mainly because of what it represented. Years ago, I purchased the secondhand set of clubs at a community yard sale with every intention of taking up golf (because that's what doctors do, right?). I played a few times with friends, but never really caught the bug. The old blue leathery bag, with its worn wood drivers and rusty irons, ended up sitting for years, unused, in a far corner of the basement closet, collecting dust.

That's not all it collected though, is it?

Long before the proverbial wheels came off, when I was still in the shallower stages of my hell-bound spiral, I had switched my vodka of choice from the high-quality stuff to the low-shelf variety that came in a plastic bottle. Plastic bottles were great. They didn't make any noisy clinking sounds when being snuck into the house, but even more important, they would not break if dropped. They had become my daily standard, and I bought them in bulk from each of the three local ABC stores, carefully rotating among sites so as not to be recognized at any one as a regular customer.

I would come home with them, stealthily hurry them down the stairs and into the basement closet, where I would perform the next task—removing their annoying pour tops. The smaller bottles didn't have them, but I almost always purchased the larger ones. Those grayish plastic caps, used by bartenders to control the pour rate into the glasses when mixing drinks, were nothing but a nuisance to me since I never bothered using a glass. My method was to go bottoms up, straight from the jug. I did this daily—usually while spending time alone downstairs, but also while sneaking down during upstairs activities, or even while spending time in the playroom with the children. (I had a locking mechanism on the closet's inside doorknob so I could quickly take a few gulps without an accidental intrusion by an unsuspecting child.)

The trick was dispensing with the tops in my immediate surroundings and hiding them in a place nobody would accidentally stumble upon them. The most logical place, it seemed, was down the old golf bag. I considered just putting them in my pocket and carrying them out, as their diameter was no bigger than a nickel, but that created the very real risk I would forget about them when I put my pants in the laundry—and that *could not* happen. The bag, ignored by all, was a simple, fail-safe solution. On a much deeper level, I was measuring my history of alcoholism not in days or benders, but literally in pour tops.

So I chucked them down the bag with every liquor purchase, usually two or three at a time, every few days, week after week, month after month, for a long, long time.

We are only as sick as our secrets.

Years later, the bag found itself alongside my other belongings in that front yard pile on the day I was definitively sent away from my home forever—the day Toby slipped me his encoded letter. It found a new resting place in a storage space underneath the stairs in Finn's garage, where I chose to once again forget about it for a long time. While my little alcoholic time capsule sat alone in the dark, I achieved long-term sobriety, rediscovered my profession, and returned to society. But I have been thinking about it, and today is judgment day.

My fingertips hurt in the cold. My gloves remain in my jacket pockets because the need to soon feel the handfuls of tops in my bare hands takes priority over my physical comfort. Next to where I kneel sits the beach pail I brought along just for this occasion. It is lavender; it's the one Hannah used at the lake house and on family vacations to the shore. She liked to fill it with the shells she collected. I will be filling it with the pour tops and bringing it home as a visual reminder of the sheer volume of alcohol I put through my body over the years. At moments of weakness, despair, or emotional crisis, I can look at what I have overcome. It will be my own personal hunting trophy.

I can also view my child's sand pail as a reminder of what all that alcohol cost me: my marriage, my children, my profession, and almost my life. It ravaged my body, my brain, and my soul. The chemical may be gone, but its long-term effects will always remain. Scar tissue and emotional phantom pains declare their presence alongside me, waxing and waning in their severity. I keep ever-present tinnitus. I have accepted this and must surrender to it.

The chilling wind blasts continue to cut through me. The field is well manicured and rectangular, placed in the center of the neighborhood by the development planners to serve as a place for children to play, for dogs to run, for couples to picnic. It is lined on all sides by fresh new townhouses. One of them is Finn's; another, just a few doors down, is Cassie's. Cassie, whom I loved. Our relationship collapsed under the weight of our collective pain. Pain I unfairly unloaded on her, while not being nearly attentive enough to her own. My self-absorbed woe-is-me ego damaged us badly. I see that she's home; her car is in the driveway. I miss her. Perhaps someday when we are both more emotionally whole, we can be friends. Maybe.

I lay the beat-up, ratty bag on its side and pull out the big driver, the woods, and the irons, neatly stacking them to the side. Then I take a deep sigh, begin to flip the bag over—but stop. Instead of dumping out the contents I gently lay the bag back down on the ground *and let go*.

Right up until this moment, I was confused about what to do. Only an hour earlier I spoke to my sponsor and friends at the noon AA meeting, and they reminded me that I am already aware that I am an alcoholic and do not need to beat myself up by looking at a bunch of old pour tops from the past.

What I had planned on to bring me closure, I recognize, in this instant, is only going to reopen unnecessary wounds, create unnecessary pain. So instead of dumping out the golf bag, I close my eyes and recite a prayer of gratitude.

I remain kneeling, staring at the frozen grass; I half grin in amusement, my decision final. Turns out I will have no mementos of my drinking career in a child's toy bucket after all, no tokens of my self-destruction to look at reflectively from time to time on some shelf in my bedroom.

My toes are completely numb now and I can't feel my hands. The weather is exactly what one would predict on this Martin Luther King Jr. Day holiday. It is time to go, but I hold still, on my knees, for just one more moment. I glance to my right; in the distance I can see the Rock, where I worked for decades, burned out, became a patient, and eventually returned. I have been professionally resurrected, prepared to help take on a pandemic that began in some farmers market in a Chinese city and will soon grow to biblical proportions. To the left of me I see Finn's place, where my good friend, for whom I can be nothing but eternally grateful, helped pull me out of the muck. Only a short walk beyond, Cassie, so beautiful on the inside and out, is at this moment probably sitting on her living room sofa and working on her laptop while an old *Friends* rerun plays on her TV.

I put the clubs back in the bag, sling it all over my shoulder, get up, and begin to walk. In front of me is my truck, which I will use to drive to the Goodwill thrift store, where I will make the donation. Beyond that is whatever is and whatever may be.

Free at last, free at last, free at last.

ACKNOWLEDGMENTS

Without the people and institutions listed below, there would be no book because, quite possibly, there would be no me. For the gifts you have given me, my gratitude is endless.

To my sponsors: Doug, who took a trembling, fearful shadow of a man, adrift and rudderless in Williamsburg, and pulled him out of the muck. You taught me the basics of Step One and beyond, how to *turn it over* and accept. Michael, you received me in Charlottesville with open arms and proceeded to pound the Steps into my head, forcing me to do the work I so desperately needed to do. Brent, you got me to stop feeling so damn sorry for myself and to take ownership of my sins. Most of all, to Walter, my happy "garden gnome" sponsor, who guides me through the peaks and valleys of daily sober living to this very moment.

To my sober network of friends spanning Virginia—Laura, Forrest, David, John, Bob, Bawb, Herc, Dennis, Joan, Cowboy Charles, David, Rick, and countless others who comprise my *recovery mosh pit*, for holding me up in the times I was utterly lifeless, strengthening me, then easing my feet to the ground so I could join you in holding up others taking the same leap.

To nurse "Celine," who years ago took me by the hand and reminded me to *first just breathe.*

To Barbara, who taught me that being sensitive and emotional *is manly.*

To my friend Victoria, who talked me off the ledge on more than one Father's Day.

To "Finn," who took me in when I had nowhere to go, assisted me through those difficult early months, and helped me recognize there is a pretty good life out there in the world for guys like us.

To every nineties grunge band that ever existed.

To my friends at open mic—Brian, Robbie, Chris, and Cheryl—who tolerated my awkward attempts to play said nineties band covers. To Tom the Poet. And to my dear friend Corie, wise beyond her years and the very definition of openness and warmth, a friend with whom I seemed to bond at amazing speed.

To my family: my sister, Susanna, who did everything she could for me; Laura, my cousin in long-term recovery and my sobriety mentor, who picked me up over and over again; my aunt Marcia, with whom I shared and exchanged seemingly endless pain; my mom and pop for their endless support and kind words.

To the Farley Center, which helped me get sober and provided me with the mental tools and framework to go out into the world.

For Kroger supermarkets, which provided me a recovery job, for teaching me humility and making me one of the team.

To the crew at the "Med-O-Matic": Laura, Kim, Jen, Wanda, and Liz, and especially Jennifer in Winchester.

To Tamlyn and the gang at the wound care center, thank you for teaching this ER doc something new.

For Dr. Steve in Roanoke, who took a chance and returned me to emergency medicine. To all my friends at the

Cave—Mike H., Julie and Julee, Molly, Mark, Melanie, Kayla, Tanner, John, and others. To Kay from the lab, who befriended me and helped me secure drug testing. Special gratitude to Jen from housekeeping, who always took the time at the end of her difficult shifts to give out hugs to all.

For everyone at the Charlottesville freestanding emergency department: especially Jenn, Kevin, Gabe, Ambrosia, and Hummingbird Kelsey. To Dr. Dan and Stacey, who knew my history and hired me anyway.

To "Dr. Steinberg," who facilitated my return to the Rock. To all in the department who knew me before, advocated for me, kept an open mind, and accepted me.

To Rachel at LabCorp, who drug tested gallons of my urine over the years.

To Kevin Doyle and the Charlottesville professionals' recovery group, where I got to spew all over the room, emotionally speaking, twice a month, and listen as my peers did the same.

To "Emily," for her love and enduring friendship in sobriety, and our many heart-to-hearts in rehab and at Bodo's.

To Dave, Bruce, and Evan, my old medical school buddies who supported me the way only lifelong friends could.

To Bill W. and Dr. Bob, for obvious reasons.

To my Haiti family: Pastors Janet and Henry, Renel Marilien, Gladys Amizard, and my dear friend Pastor Geordany Joseph—who knows how to keep faith, love, and acceptance in perfect balance.

To my friend Jonathan, for his multidecade friendship and therapeutic Sunday runs.

To my friend Tomer, who saw me at my absolute worst and was there for me before, during, and since, and who reminded me of my successes and the good in me.

And to Cassie, whose light warmed my struggling heart and whose gentle blue eyes could make it speed up, slow down, and occasionally stop. You showed me how to love again; you taught me to laugh at *The Big Bang Theory* and *The Office* and tardigrades; you kissed me in a moment of absolute perfect bliss atop the Eiffel Tower; you sustained me and protected me again and again from myself. You showed me how to live, unencumbered, on my own two feet. First, kindness. ☺

ABOUT THE AUTHOR

Dr. J.D. Remy has been a practicing emergency physician since 1995. Born in New York City, he and his sister were raised in the suburbs of New Jersey by their mother and stepfather. After graduating medical school in Washington DC, he completed an emergency medicine residency in Baltimore and has since worked full-time in several emergency departments throughout the Shenandoah Valley of Virginia. During his career he has served as medical director for local EMS agencies, president of his hospital's medical staff, and has led five medical missions to Haiti from 2010 to 2015. In his spare time, he enjoys running and playing acoustic guitar. He is father to a daughter and two sons, whom he loves dearly.

Made in the USA
Monee, IL
05 July 2021